MARCHING *Through* SUFFERING

CONTEMPORARY ASIA IN THE WORLD

SANDRA FAHY

MARCHING *Through* SUFFERING

LOSS AND SURVIVAL IN NORTH KOREA

COLUMBIA UNIVERSITY PRESS ◣◢ NEW YORK

This book was published with the assistance of
Sophia University Support Program for Academic Book Publication.

COLUMBIA UNIVERSITY PRESS
Publishers Since 1893
New York   Chichester, West Sussex
cup.columbia.edu

Library of Congress Cataloging-in-Publication Data
Fahy, Sandra.
Marching through suffering : loss and survival in North Korea / Sandra Fahy.
pages   cm. — (Contemporary Asia in the world)
Includes bibliographical references and index.
ISBN 978-0-231-17134-2 (cloth) —
ISBN 978-0-231-17135-9 (pbk.) —
ISBN 978-0-231-53894-7 (e-book)
1. Refugees—Korea (North)—Biography.   2. Refugees—Korea (North)—
Attitudes.   3. Victims of famine—Korea (North)   4. Famines—
Korea (North)   5. Human rights—Korea (North)   6. Korea
(North)—Social conditions.   I.   Title.
HV640.5.K67.F35   2015
951.93050922—dc23
2014020106

Cover image: © Seung Woo Back, Blow up #042, 2006
Cover Design: Chang Jae Lee

To the North Koreans who shared their stories with me,
to those who may in the future,
and to those who never will.

CONTENTS

NOTE ON TRANSLATION, CONFIDENTIALITY, TERMS, AND ROMANIZATION

Translations of Korean language texts and the transcribed oral accounts are mine except where indicated. The name, age, and hometown of interviewees are altered slightly and pseudonyms used to adhere to requests for confidentiality. Throughout the text the transcriptions of oral accounts are followed by pseudonyms and the age of the speaker at the time of recording. Familiar names and places appear as they are conventionally written in English (for instance, "Seoul," "Pyongyang," and Kim Jong-Il); otherwise the McCune-Reischauer System of Romanization has been used. "North Korea" and "the Democratic People's Republic of Korea" (or DPRK) are used throughout, and no political implication is intended with either. Former North Koreans in Seoul and Tokyo variously use the terms *Chosun, buk-Chosun,* or *buk-han* to refer to their home country—each containing a political tone. Those terms are not used except where they appear in the oral accounts. The word "defector" is used, but I prefer "North Korean" or "former North Korean" to avoid overt dissident associations, particularly strong in the Korean word *t'alpukcha* (one who escaped the North). In contemporary South Korean scholarship and government documents the term *saeteomin,* meaning "new settler," is increasingly used. I tend to avoid the anthropological word "informant" because in relation to North Korea this word takes on an unfortunate hue; in such cases I opt for the more neutral "interviewee."

ACKNOWLEDGMENTS

Many people contributed to the creation of this book. I thank the North Koreans who worked with me in Seoul and Tokyo. Without their generosity and strength of spirit, this work would not exist. Thank you for sharing your homes, offices, and inner worlds with me. Two academic institutions gave this book a home. I am indebted to the Korean Studies Institute (KSI) at the University of Southern California (USC)—in particular, David C. Kang for his excellent guidance to young scholars—for granting me a postdoctoral fellowship during which I wrote this book. The generous support of the Sejong Society provided additional time to focus on revising the writing. Thank you, Peter Y. S. Kim and Chul Lee. I also wish to thank Elaine Kim, Linda Kim, and Timothy Lee for their warm encouragement throughout those years and for making the Ahn House an intellectual home.

My book's first reviewers, Stephan Haggard and Suk-Young Kim, identified crucial areas for improvement during the manuscript review, again hosted and supported by the KSI at USC. For their time reading and critiquing the early drafts of the book, I am honored and grateful. Prior to my stay in Los Angeles, Valérie Gelézeau at the Centre de recherches sur la Corée (EHESS) in Paris provided much needed encouragement as I began the earliest writing of this book from its roots as a dissertation, supported by the Korea Foundation Post-Doctoral Fellowship. My dissertation research, which formed the earliest beginnings of this book, was supported by the Korea Foundation and supervised by the two best advisors a doctoral student could ask for, Johan Pottier and Keith Howard at the Department of Sociology and Anthropology at The School of Oriental and African Studies. I thank them for believing in the original questions that drove this work.

I am also indebted to my family—my mother and father for always encouraging my education and my sisters for putting up with me—and friends who helped with research and personal support: Hyunsoo Kim, Soohyun Kim, Eunyoung Lee; thanks also for the kindness, encouragement, and help of Lucia Melito, Sangbum Kim, and June Lee, and a special thank you to Carol Dussere. Thanks also to Pastor Kim, Elizabeth Batha, the team of North Koreans at the Democracy Network Against the North Korean Gulag in Seoul, and Kato Hiroshi at Life Funds for North Korean Refugees in Tokyo. To my two first Korean teachers, many years ago, Mr. Ham and Mrs. Oh, I am grateful for your endurance!

I also extend a personal thank you to the following people: Aleesa Cohene, Noreen O'Sullivan, Bill McCarthy, Radha Upadhyaya, Atef Alshaer, Amaia Sanchez Cacicedo, Hildi Kang, Danielle L. Chubb, and Peer and Geraldine Fiss. To those at the very start of all this—Daniel Zanth, Tony Banks, Gerald Bullock, Richard Teleky, Rinaldo Walcott, and the late Bob Casto—deepest thanks.

The final touches on this manuscript were completed as I joined Sophia University in 2013, a collegial and supportive environment for my continuing research. I am thankful to my colleagues for their warmth, humor, and smarts. My thanks also go to Columbia University Press for encouraging this publication, in particular Anne Routon, and to the copyediting staff for polishing and improving this book. I am grateful to the anonymous reviewers who read an earlier manifestation of this manuscript, providing valuable feedback. While so many people contributed to this book, any shortcomings are of course my own.

MARCHING *Through* SUFFERING

INTRODUCTION

LOSS AND SURVIVAL

As the late 1980s turned into the 1990s, the Democratic People's Republic of Korea (hereafter, North Korea) began to struggle in the absence of former Soviet trade partners. Debts to China were due. Once-strong infrastructure ossified beyond repair. Into this dismal mix the leader of the country, Kim Il-Sung (1912–1994), died. Agriculture practices driven by blind trust in scientific advances struggled to bear fruit in nutrient-depleted soils. Crops farmed on mountainous slopes, to maximize arable land, grew tenuous in the heavy floods of the mid-1990s. The distribution of food according to an existing system of entitlement that measured and delivered caloric intake according to age, occupation, gender, and geographic location became increasingly unreliable. Good nutrition, already a modest affair throughout the North, dwindled to concerning levels. The North Korean government turned to the international community with its first request for aid, identifying the floods as the root cause of trouble. By this time it was too little, too late. The famine of the 1990s was well under way. When international nutritionists finally gained access, they identified protracted malnutrition in the North that predated the floods. North Korea sought food and medicine as well as the sovereign allocation of these as they saw fit to remedy its perennial problem with deficiency. This complex set of failures that produced the famine of the 1990s and subsequent problems is the backdrop of this book. The focus of the book is on the subjective experience of those years.

In the pages that follow, the typical paradigm of examining North Korea and North Koreans, or even famine itself, as characterized by lack is eschewed. Instead of focusing on what was absent in the lives of North Koreans, this book explores what took place in the lacuna: what kind of experiences took shape in the face of crises? What messages did the government communicate to explain the difficulty in accessing food? How did people speak to one another, directly or indirectly, about their frustrations and difficulties? How did people get by? When we examine North Korea as a country that lacks, and as a people who lack, the starkness of such reductionism distracts us from identifying how both individuals and the state make do, come to terms, and cope with difficulties. Crises do shock, but they do not extinguish the desire for local interpretation and meaning making.

What North Koreans did, how they understood things, how they made sense of difficulties—answers to these questions go a long way to explain how countries such as North Korea have survived as long as they have. Throughout the years this book covers, many in the international community assumed the collapse of the North Korean government was imminent. But the calculus that a reduction in trade partners, diplomatic networks, adequate food and medicine, and so on would equal deterioration of government legitimacy inside the country and thus propel hoped-for political change has not been borne out by reality. Among the North Koreans I spoke with, reflecting over those same years, few assumed as much. Consider: when Kim Jong-Il died in late December of 2011, the international media fixated on the question of whether the North's government would collapse, but in the North Korean defector community the question was considered with severe brevity. A detestable figure in their personal life history had died but, they acknowledged, the difficulties for North Koreans back home would continue.

The oral accounts I recorded in Seoul and Tokyo, with North Koreans who left the North after surviving and witnessing some of the worst years of its contemporary history, describe how individuals, community, and the nation at large got through the famine years and the subsequent economic shocks. The government triaged resources prior to the famine, but during the famine years the triage grew more severe. This produced a gap in the promissory government–governed relationship. What then filled this gap, this opening? The original research data drawn from transcriptions of the oral accounts explains how North Koreans made sense of this complex situation, how they coped on material, social, and emotional levels with the great difficulties that confronted them. What individuals and states do when confronted with difficulties reveals the durable features of a society and its national cohesion. The famine and co-emerging socioeconomic difficulties was not a bell tolling the necessity and opportunity to overthrow the government. Instead, the "busy years," as they were called colloquially, were a time to bind more tightly together against outside forces that were the source of the problem.

In this book I examine transcriptions of oral accounts I recorded from North Koreans who survived the famine and witnessed the years from the late 1980s to the late 2000s, individuals who crossed out of the North and settled in Seoul and Tokyo. By drawing on the oral accounts, I explore an approximation of both a subjective and collective experience of those years. Food is fundamental to life, and to identity. The practical and emotional aspects of food and eating both connect us to and can disconnect us from our wider world. Acquiring, preparing, and eating food is tied to social concerns. Famines do not famish equally. People are not hungry in equal measure because existing social inequalities grant increased ability to access, and alter access to, food entitlements.

How did people make sense of these years and in so doing make sense of the failure of state responsibilities? By shifting the paradigm from a focus on lack to an accounting of what came into being in the absence, this book shifts the focus from North Koreans as inactive objects of suffering to active agents making sense and negotiating the difficulties of their lives. Further, the book examines how they reflected on these experiences and North Korea more generally, on the lived experience of those difficult years, the breaking points that led many to cross out of the country, and the legacy of their experiences. How people thought about those incredibly disastrous events, how people thought about things as they lived through them, is largely unexplored both within the global literature on famine and the existing literature on North Korea. The notion of a famine survivor is conventionally understood as an oxymoron, but it shouldn't be. In North Korea the number of famine victims is estimated between 600,000 and 1.5 million. At a maximum, famines typically claim 5 percent of a population; far more are affected, and far more survive.[1] Yet, the world over, the process of famine is hardly explored from the perspective of survivors.

This book addresses two big issues as informed by the subjective experience of North Korean famine survivors. The first is the temporal sequence of events as articulated by North Koreans in their oral accounts. Famine theorists have long known that famine is a process, not an event. The oral accounts detail how people understood the earliest stages of the famine process as temporary hardship, putting their trust in the government's promises that things would soon turn around. As the temporary crisis became the norm, many acknowledged that they earnestly adopted the government's standard framing of the "downturn" as a result of imperialist sanctions. North Korean infrastructure and economy was weak because the United States, Japan, and other enemy nations were running North Korea into the ground. As the famine progressed, social relations began to strain. Changes in the direct social environment were attributed to failings of proper socialization rather than to structural failures of North Korea's political economy. Unlike before, doors were locked. Theft and the appearance of orphans and beggars were increasingly commonplace. This resulted from weak social character, I was told—something was wrong with the society. Responsibility for difficulties was attributed to the self; individuals, like the state, should be self-sufficient. Social, economic, and political apparatuses were imbricated in ways impenetrable to ordinary people; access to money could change this, but even this was precarious, tenuous.

Across the oral accounts consistent trends emerge in how the early period of the famine was interpreted and understood. It may be possible to deduce that these trends could be generalized to areas in the northern portion of the country badly affected by food triage. Famines do not impact locations equally but rather map preexisting inequalities. So, for instance, a few years' delay in the timeline of the famine is detected in the oral accounts of interviewees from Pyongyang, where resources were more plentiful. However, while it might be tempting to deduce that the severity of factors precipitating defection is what distinguishes the individuals whose oral accounts I recorded from those North Koreans who remained in the North, the accounts themselves caution against such an interpretation. The experiences of family and friends much more badly off who stayed inside the country identify a variety of factors that demonstrate what choices were conceivable and desirable. Because this book relies on the oral accounts of those who did defect, the temporal sequence identifies breaking points that led to defection but also attempts to furnish a picture of other types of "breaking points" that resulted in people staying put in North Korea. In some cases the breaking point of defection was almost accidental: being brought to China while sick and realizing it was too dangerous to return. In other cases the breaking point brought the contradiction of values sharply into focus: witnessing the military shoot a man dead for his act of stealing potatoes.

After the breaking points, the book continues to explore the temporal sequence of events but here acknowledges how North Korean acts of defection reawaken the division of the peninsula. In crossing over the Sino-Korean border, North Koreans become newly divided from family back home in a metanarrative that replicates the 1953 division of the country that still separates families to this day. This temporal sequence is one of two main issues addressed in this book.

The second issue addressed in this book is recursive. In a country that regulates and orders all print media, literature, art, and speech, how ordinary North Koreans communicated with each other, and how they communicate their experiences after the fact, is crucial. North Korean state discourse encouraged a perception and interpretation of the famine as well as any co-emerging difficulty as a temporary economic downturn brought about by the confluence of environmental factors and imperialism. The remedy for this downturn was to march through the suffering and, as Kim Il-Sung had done in 1938 Manchuria, not give in to enemy forces that would destroy you.

In North Korea, as access to food grew increasingly difficult with the government's repeated failures to deliver food as promised, social qualities associated with attaining, preparing, and eating food grew more complex. In a country that champions national self-sufficiency, the government's advice to use ersatz and foraged food was a customarily productive gesture in the face of deficiency. People's increased difficulty in accessing adequate amounts of food met with recurring state rhetoric that pacified doubts and deterred incisive questioning. When the state's provision is part of protecting filial identification between the people and the nation, a mental and emotional replacement for the absence of provisions becomes necessary. The oral accounts reveal that, as the famine worsened, the government increased discursive strategies aimed at ensuring a public response that adhered to and did not threaten internal national security.

Yet it was natural that as the situation grew worse people needed to communicate about medicine, food acquisition, black-market selling, and other coping mechanisms. Protracted hunger and illness are deeply frustrating, but to communicate these things directly was to criticize the government. The oral accounts reveal how proper methods of communicating were sometimes directly taught: a knock on the door by a local official reminding you that your father had died of high blood pressure, not hunger. Sometimes the consequences of speech were silently observed: the neighbor who vociferously complained about Kim Jong-Il yesterday is nowhere to be found today. The proper ways to communicate were reaffirmed in a social environment submerged in state-regulated media, weekly self-criticism sessions, and the standardized talk of local government officials. As then, so today physical violence or the threat of it plays no small part in regulating the spoken worlds of North Koreans. Nearly every oral account details witnessing a public execution, often a local affair with a gathered audience. While the criminal might have been sentenced to death for theft of livestock, the cause of the crime was the individual's thinking: to clearly identify this, the criminal's mouth is filled with stones and the head is shot completely off. Belief that thinking is inherited is part of the logic behind imprisoning in the North Korean penal complex all living generations of a family. Thought and speech were carefully self-monitored.

Speech operated on multiple registers that both revealed and withheld crucial information. The oral accounts show that parts of proscribed speech could be used among trusted company to carry more critically useful information. Slang and jokes used normative state terminology to refer to incongruous phenomena in ways that established momentary exchange networks, identified inequalities, and shared commiseration over the difficult expectations of the state. These were not overtly shared in the oral accounts, but rather they were interspersed among other recollections. For example, when discussing alternative foods, an interviewee explained that the government advised foraging substitute foods from the mountains; when exchanging greetings with friends, they would inquire, "Have you had the substitute today?" There was, he explained, such a similarity in the way people and machines in North Korea used substitutes to energize themselves— trucks and people using substitute fuel—that it was humorous.

The way people communicated was a product of the state but also a means for people to indirectly communicate. While recording the oral accounts, I asked interviewees to remark not only on their communication with others but also on their internal dialogue or self-talk while they were in North Korea. The accounts were analyzed for references to reported speech, such as when the speaker mentions that she heard someone say something, whether a rumor, an announcement by a local government official, or an overheard conversation. Combined in this way, I have tried to examine the spoken discourse of North Koreans to gather a sense of daily communication styles. In the regulated, ordered Panopticon of North Korea, the oral accounts indicate that people used indirect speech to hide meaning as if in prepackaged, state-sanctioned phrases. While the majority of this type of speech resulted in purely functional exchange, portions of the oral accounts reveal long-lasting recollections of humorous exchanges. These resultant quips, jokes, and "black humor" stories challenge the notion that North Koreans are brainwashed and instead identify a population that intelligently observes and critiques, managing speech like other resources to make ends meet.

The natural question is why people didn't rise up in the face of such deprivation and difficulty. The oral accounts reveal insights into this question. First, there were cases of small uprisings, but all were suppressed. None of the interviewees I spoke with had direct connections to these protests. A few of the interviewees had heard of an uprising here or there, but only in a vague manner and always with reference to its purge. Second, the lack of information about what caused the famine and co-emerging socioeconomic difficulties severely confused people and critically delayed individual coping strategies. Deluded into believing that the problem was temporary and that reprieve was around the corner, people waited it out while their bodily and material store of resources diminished. By this time some were too critically weakened to insist that the government provide better opportunities for people to live. Equally significant, the lack of information was further complicated by the fact that interviewees reported no single opportunity for people to discuss the famine or their hopes and fears without bringing great risk to themselves and their family.

This book is not so much an account of absences; such absences will be clear as the book unfolds. Instead this book explores what comes to life when certain fundamentals—a consistent source of food—ebb away. What social, emotional, and mental responses take the place of the missing fundamental? To begin, we set aside the simple binary that imagines loss as the inverse of gain, absence as the inverse of presence.

Over days, months, then years, loss is about the absence of something you once had and the presence of something different. To paraphrase from the accounts, loss is making do with substitutes, having sleep for lunch rather than food, noticing how quietly life leaves death behind in your neighbor's house. My first interviewee, Jae-young Yoon (45), wept as his narrative brought us to the point in his past when his son died. In the child's belly was hunger, and with it a gnawing, hot turning of the body's demands, demands that later spoke for the infant in the presence of a fever, a rash, and the limp limbs of his body. Now his father sat with arms open across the table, palms up, lifting an invisible weight. He was showing me the place his son died. "There was nothing I could give him," he said. Who would say this death was not a wailing, agonizing presence that bore the heaviest weight in his memory of North Korea? The promises of the state to deliver food had gone unfulfilled again. If it came now, what use? In that moment, having had enough of the expectation that man and child could live on air alone, Jae-young Yoon told me he made the decision (ma'um mogottda; lit., "heart-ate") to leave North Korea. Loss is generative. Loss is an unusual, bewildering character. Objectively, loss is due to the failure to have, the failure to get. It is about what went missing and long periods of deprivation. But the subjective experience warrants investigation because it sheds light on the mental, social, and emotional ways of responding, and it inductively reflects on how collective perseverance and social norms contribute to national survival at the expense of individual suffering.

The accounts describe the lives of North Koreans, how the familiar character of loss was an obstacle to overcome between them. Asking what it means to survive years of famine is a question that asks what gradually built itself into life, what filled the space left behind when the custom of receiving, sharing, and enjoying food disappeared. This book examines the experience that took place in the lives of North Koreans, from their earliest memories of the famine, from their gradual adaption and refiguring of material facts, up to their individual breaking points, through to the moments leading to departure and to their lives in Seoul and Tokyo, where the legacy of the famine and the loss of nation, place, and belonging awaken the division of the peninsula in a strange historical repetition.

What Makes a Famine?

The objective causes of famine are clear, and famine prevention is possible. In the last half of the twentieth century, developments in technology, infrastructure, and early-warning systems have meant that, where famines do occur, they could have been prevented. Surrounded on all sides by leading global economic nations, North Korea endured one of the worst famines in the last years of the twentieth century and continues to struggle with food sufficiency to this day. Arguably, North Korea suffered privately for well over five years before 1995, when a series of natural disasters devastated crops and the government requested international assistance. North Korea used the floods as an explanation for the food shortage. The flooding did cause extensive damage, but when aid agencies gained entry to the country, they saw medical evidence of severe malnutrition that predated the floods. Agencies confirmed malnutrition rates inside North Korea as within the top ten highest in the world.

North Korea's famine was caused by multiple factors. At the end of the 1980s, North Korea lost its Soviet bloc trade partners. The country owed many debts that came due. Agricultural decisions made during the Kim Il-Sung era left the country vulnerable to natural disasters. Bad agricultural reforms solidified the vulnerability further. Equipment was broken, outdated, and required great creative skill to achieve operation. Farming practices were not sustainable. When natural disasters struck by the mid-1990s, the country's agricultural sector was hypervulnerable, as were its people. The insistence on self-reliance and Juche socialist cropping strategies justified the triage of resources to the military and elite of society; so too the rationale to use international aid in a like fashion.[2] What probably led to more starvation deaths was the strict control of population coping methods through restrictions on such things as migration and through unsanctioned selling of goods, theft, and of course punishment for famine crimes. In addition, the lack of free information flows inside the country led to misinformation about what had caused the famine and how best to deal with it. This delayed a timely response to the famine.

The North Korean famine is anachronistic because it resembles famines before the twentieth century: it was set into disastrous momentum by natural disasters that left communities without enough food to survive.[3] But North Korea's famine took place at a time and in a region of the world where it easily could have been averted if only there had been the political will to do so. This is why Devereux referred to it as a "priority regime" famine.[4] In other words, the regime triaged resources according to a system that ensured security of the nation over securing the lives of the population. In contemporary times, technical and infrastructure advances eliminate environmental factors alone as a sufficient cause for famine, regardless of where it occurs. Increased capability of governments and international institutions can predict and respond to impending crisis, so when famines do occur nowadays, prevention was always a possibility.[5] The famine in North Korea was not inevitable. However, avoiding it would have necessitated restructuring existing government priorities of international isolation and civilian control, which could have led to changes to ordinary ways of life and possibly the end of North Korea as we know it today.

The North Korean famine did not lead to political unrest or structural changes in government, but it was the first time a threat to national sovereignty might have emerged inside the country.[6] In this respect, it was a worrisome time for the government. The escalation and height of the famine co-emerged with the death of Kim Il-Sung and the eventual leadership of Kim Jong-Il. The famine had the potential to create widespread dissatisfaction, and thus social unrest, resulting from how the government triaged resources and denied the right to free market activities. For the North Koreans I interviewed, the distribution of food according to political loyalty, gender, age, and geography were identified as ordinary practices. Keeping such practices in place secured the state and ways of life but not life itself. Indeed, these practices predated the famine and also mapped the lines of increased famine vulnerability that arose as resources dwindled.

However, the famine did compel people to live differently. Oral accounts identify how the reluctance of some to live in ways that indirectly challenged existing regime values resulted in death or suicide. Famines do compel people to live differently, though often with great cultural and social reluctance. Typically, one of the first responses to famine is migration. People are compelled to migrate in search of areas with increased access to food and other resources. Such movement within North Korea was, and remains, unlawful without government consent. Where possible, the development of private farms or secret gardens is another early famine response. This level of privatization and individualism signaled a new and uncomfortable way of life for many North Koreans; indeed, the illegality of it was also discomforting. The sale of personal and homemade items is another coping mechanism. The appearance of people selling in illegal markets in North Korea was an uncomfortable sight for many to adjust to in the early stages of severe food shortages. All of these coping mechanisms are characteristically nonsocialist in nature. In this respect, the famine threatened to bring about social behavior that was heretofore uncharacteristic of the North Korean way of life. However, changes did emerge and take hold. The oral accounts demonstrate how such changes were understood and responded to over time.

The absence of food is perhaps the first thought that comes to the public mind in defining famine. But famine is not so much about food as it is about the inability to access sufficient food for survival. Famines happen when an aggregate of individuals is unable to alter access and entitlement to sufficient food.[7] Who gets enough food is tied to how power is distributed among people in the home, community, nation, and world.[8] Beliefs about who is and is not entitled to what amount and type of food is informed by day-to-day, local practices. Without a fundamental awareness of this, famines can be profoundly misunderstood, and relief efforts can prove a hindrance more than a help.

For example, in the aid community, deducing food shortage from the fact of starvation will result in the perception that supplying food is the best remedy when in fact there may be the need to increase access equality or provide resources to generate self-sufficiency. The structural features that give rise to famine are often opaque and case specific.

Existing structural conditions give rise to where and who is worse affected by famine. Such conditions render questions of whether to send aid to countries such as North Korea increasingly complex. For example, whether the international community should give food aid to North Korea in the face of anecdotal reports that some or all of the aid is siphoned off to the military is not a simple yes-or-no question. The problem is not simply that the military take advantage of their privilege. Perhaps this is to be expected. The problem is that there are no legal avenues for ordinary people to alter their ability to access food in the same way that the military—certainly not everyone in the military, but arguably many—access privilege in society. The problem is not simply that the military or any other group takes an inordinate share. The problem is that access and the means to ameliorate deficits are not equally shared. Here we run aground, compelled to acknowledge that human rights violations are always plural phenomena, co-creating and cosustaining. If North Koreans had access to even the most basic of human rights—the freedom to speak their minds without threat of violence, the choice of where to live, the right to depart their country, the right to study for and select an occupation of their choosing, the opportunity for enterprise and personal development, for example—then the story would be entirely different.

So far in this introduction I have referred to the backdrop of failure in 1990s North Korea with uncritical use of the term "famine." By contemporary standards in famine theory, such a term applies, but on the ground a different discourse prevailed. Most likely influenced by state-sanctioned discourse, interviewees called that time the "March of Suffering."[9] When I used the words "famine" (*kikun*) or "starvation" (*kia*) in our discussions, many interviewees did not make a connection between their experience and those terms. "Famine is something that happens in Africa, or South Korea," it was explained to me; and, by another interviewee, "No one died of famine in North Korea." Though the latter individual was sharing in jest, the echo of the regime's insistence on its version of reality can be heard. As for the former interviewee's reference to Africa and South Korea, such a link is not totally amiss, but it is strikingly without context.

In the 1960s North Korea provided aid to West Africa, and although the timing for the North's agricultural promotion couldn't have been worse, in 1997 they taught Juche farming methods to farmers in Ghana. It is possible that information about these aid operations was taught in North Korean schools. As for famine in South Korea, particularly in the earliest stages after the division of the peninsula, the standard of life was not as good as in the North, and it is unlikely that the North would let this slip from required course readings in school. South Korea did fare worse than the North in terms of food and other resources—North Korea had inherited Japanese colonial-era infrastructure that the South had lost, and this contributed greatly to its comparative advancement.

People who live through famine typically do not identify their experience as famine but rather use locally situated terms to identify the experience.[10] Indeed, though for quite different reasons, states too have proved skillful at producing terminology that refers to these periods. China's Great Leap Famine, which claimed the lives of 45 million, was officially referred to as the Three Year Natural Calamity.[11] In North Korea, the famine was referred to as the "March of Suffering" and less directly as "the downturn." The point here is the enduring relationship between famine and language or, more broadly, power and discourse that reaches back in history for a panacea to today's ills. This is evidenced not only in how colonial or state governments have used language but also, as this book will show, in how language is used on the ground. The nuanced way that North Koreans communicated and how this links to relations of power is explored throughout.

The Accounts

Because this book uses oral accounts from North Korean defectors as the primary, though not the only, means of analysis, how these accounts were collected, treated, and examined and how they are applied throughout the book requires framing. The oral accounts were recorded over a two-year period from 2005–2006 during field research for my doctoral dissertation. I worked with an all–North Korean defector-run nongovernmental organization (NGO) on a volunteer basis, helping out with translations, grant applications, and international community outreach. Although none of the individuals I worked with have accounts in this book, the NGO helped me connect and network within the community to meet unseasoned arrivals to South Korea and Japan, and those not politically active or high profile in the South Korea and Japan defector community.

More than thirty individuals were interviewed, and interviews typically lasted between one and three hours, depending on the length of time interviewees wanted to share. Consent to record the material and use it in writing the dissertation and book was granted both orally and in written form. It was agreed that names and other identifying markers would be changed, and often at the point of the first recording false names were already in use. The interviews typically took place in my apartment or the homes of interviewees. The interviews were open and unstructured, but each interviewee knew that I was interested in the famine years. Though it did initially strike me as unusual, every North Korean I approached agreed without hesitation to share their experience, stating, "No one has ever asked me about the March of Suffering."

This book uses oral accounts, so the tendency to evoke the typical hypervisibility of famine is paradigmatically eschewed and attention is given to the inner and external worlds detailing subjective experience. The original spoken nuances are retained as much as possible. The sonorous qualities of resonance, pitch, rhythm, tone, hesitation, and the way that the voice exits the speaker and positions both speaker and lis-tener in its sonorous matrix cannot be rendered except in the form of narrating the effect of listening on myself. In this respect, some of the composition, the sense, the meaning, and the aspects of my experience of listening cannot be fully rendered. The voice is about participation, sharing, and even contagion; the sound of a voice has the capacity for "impact, a capacity to affect us, which is like nothing else, and is very different from what has to do with the visual and with touch. . . . It is a realm we still do not know."[12] There is almost the wish to write these accounts with symbols lifted from modern musical notation to capture this unknown aspect of the voice. I would insert breath marks and caesura, ties where two words played one on the edge of the other to indicate the unbroken glide where words became one word drawn out. I would insert a coda to show the abrupt end that closed some accounts. How do I write the long pause, the heavy quiet that settled in the room after an account of children, hunger, and crying? It is not possible to capture everything.

One of the most important parts of conducting the interviews was the point in personal experience at which the account began. I prompted all interviewees by asking them to recollect positive memo-ries of their hometown. I assumed this elicitation would prove less stressful than asking about the height of the famine years. I began each conversation the same way: Tell me about your hometown. What are some of your fond memories of it? This was essential because it estab-lished a point from which we entered and departed from the famine. The interviews were conducted in Korean and transcribed. The full body of accounts was read and reread to identify what new informa-tion the accounts contributed to existing research on famine, social suffering, political violence, and North Korea. The transcripts were then coded for use of metaphor, correlations, and associations be-tween antecedent and subsequent event in narration, reported speech, and inner speech, also known as self-talk. This was not a simple exer-cise. In a language that typically omits the subject, the "I" is contextual if not directly stated and, thus, "we" is also contextual. This seeming absence of subjectivity in spoken discourse, though it appears through the context of speech, reflects how the ownership of word and deed may have been used in the North.

I judge the oral accounts of North Koreans to evince the subjective experience of living in the North throughout these difficult years, but I also view the transcribed oral account as material for analysis in and of itself. Taken collectively but recorded individually, the narratives exist singularly and in chorus. Patterns of metaphor, word choice, humor, and phrasing are traceable across the accounts. With the benefit of context provided by secondary sources, thematic consistencies and asymmetries are identifiable. For example, interviewees used the word "pain" in place of the word "hunger"—on asking for elaboration I was told, "You couldn't say you were hungry." Through other interviews it was determined that speaking about hunger resulted or was perceived to result in disappearances. It was possible to imagine that someone could be disappeared for speaking about hunger. It is also possible to bring further interpretation to this evidence, exploring how articulating hunger as pain did not implicate the state but rather the body as the objective cause of suffering. Interviewees used the Korean word *chungkyok* (shock) to refer to certain scenes they witnessed in the North. The word might more rightly be translated as "to unsettle" or "to surprise" as it is used in context.

How the state managed discourse—words, semantics, and speech— was a way of inhabiting the internal universe of the social. We can turn to state-produced materials to find the operation of this, whether through newspaper articles, radio and TV broadcasts, operas, plays, songs, or documentaries made by the North Korean government. Oral accounts offer a delicate bridge to private subjective worlds where state ideology was inferred and personal agency negotiated.

The Structure of the Book

This book moves through a temporal, rather than explicit, chronology exploring the social, economic, and political shifts that took place in the subjective experiences and thought-life of North Koreans throughout the worst years of North Korea's recent history. The book is laid out according to stages of personal experience described by interviewees from their earliest recollections of the famine years, through the most difficult years in North Korea, up to the present, their decision to cross the border and their lives outside of North Korea.

The first chapter, "The Busy Years," shows how a confluence of factors led to confusion and delayed coping strategies during the early years of the famine. Preexisting familiarity with austerity along with the gradual emergence of the famine meant that perception of the problem was difficult to discern. Lack of accurate and timely information compounded by misinformation resulted in delayed coping strategies. Early perception of the famine adhered to narratives provided by the government.

The second chapter, "Cohesion and Disintegration," explores social relations between family and friends as well as between the government and the people as the famine years worsened. As the famine worsened, Kim Il-Sung died. For many people these events are interrelated in memory. Kim Jong-Il's rise to power is associated with the downturn in the economy and the food shortages. Early signs of doubt and dissatisfaction are discernible, but there is still opposition—or resistance to hunger—as the state would prescribe it in the form of resisting the enemy outsider. There is a growing awareness of the famine dead, but hard work is understood as a means out of suffering and as a way to give meaning to suffering.

The third chapter, "The Life of Words," identifies differing speech registers in the oral accounts of North Koreans. In particular indirect speech, humor, and sarcasm were used in North Korea as a way of negotiating the difficulties of life. This chapter explores terminology for the famine as well as the ordinary language used to refer to hunger, starvation, and death during the famine. This chapter also examines how "smart" language was learned and used. Nobody died from hunger but from pain, food poisoning, and high blood pressure. Language helped to convey the paradox of living in North Korea, both offering and withholding freedom.

Chapter 4, "Life Leaves Death Behind," explores the inevitable question of how the increased body count as the famine worsened raised alarm in society. This chapter identifies how the famine dead and dying were responded to and how communication about the famine dead was conducted. As the previous chapter explored the role of language and the voice, this chapter explores the body, the starvation dead, as subjects that incriminate the state. The impact of witnessing public executions for famine crimes, or coping strategies, is also explored here.

Chapter 5, "Breaking Points," highlights the exceptional nature of defection and the factors that led interviewees to leave the North. Through the oral accounts, factors that led people to stay put are also identified. Giving up, dying indoors and out of sight, and the seeming absence of revolt and revolution in North Korea is also critically addressed in this chapter. "The New Division," chapter 6, explores the experience of leaving North Korea and family behind. Perceptions of the Koreas and Japan are identified. This chapter also addresses the continuation of the past in memory and in worry over relatives through guilt and the ambiguity of leaving a place that you love but that also caused suffering. Finally, this chapter identifies North Korean defectors on the plain of geopolitical history as a new wave of separated families embodying the repetition of the traumatic event of peninsular division on an individual level. The conclusion of the book returns to the issue of communication within North Korea as one of the central concerns in the continuation of suffering and human rights violations in the country. The appendix provides a brief history of the famine.

1

THE BUSY YEARS

"Famine is something that happens in South Korea, or Africa, but not in a socialist country like North Korea," Hye-jin Lee (23) explains; it never occurred to her that what she was living through was, in the international arena, referred to as a famine that was both contemporary and anachronistic in its character. Precipitated by the floods of the mid-1990s, food insecurity was well under way because of political and economic stubbornness toward opening up in the wake of the Soviet bloc collapse, but for Hye-jin Lee (23), what was happening in North Korea was first understood by what it was not: it was not a famine.

North Koreans, cut off from the information flows of global media, still managed to learn the stereotypical representations of famine: a skeletal body, usually black, in a parched and sun-cracked landscape. Not well known in the wider world, least of all in North Korean school books, is the history of socialism's relationship to famine or the conspicuous way that censorship and famine occur together. In North Korea, famine is a feature of capitalist systems, which naturally run amok. In such descriptions, usually seen in the North Korean media organ KCNA, hunger in places like America is conflated with famine.

What North Koreans were experiencing was, officially, a March of Suffering. On the ground it was often referred to as "the busy time." Life got busy. People were swept up in the process of getting by. In the oral accounts, in the earliest years of the March of Suffering, people identified the starting point differently according to where they lived geographically and their occupations. Those farthest from Pyongyang and to the north, for instance, and those farthest in the employment network from government office, such as farmers and miners, identified the start of the busy years as the late 1980s into the early 1990s. Because of the gradual and insidious way famine occurs, and because famine is not general to a whole nation or area, this gradually developing archipelago muddles recognition of what is happening. For North Korea, too, preexisting undernutrition already predisposed people to going without and making do, and this blurred recognition of anything being amiss.

In the late 1980s the Soviet Union cut aid to North Korea, there was a 10 percent reduction in Public Distribution System (PDS) rations under the rationale of patriotism. The vast majority of people in North Korea obtained access to food through the PDS, which was tasked from its earliest history with distributing food, among other things, throughout the country. This food came from the surplus production of farmers, purchased at low cost by the central government. In exchange, farmers were given seed, fertilizer, insecticides, and farming equipment, and they were permitted to grow a small plot of vegetables for personal household consumption. Farmers were also given a food ration from the harvest. The central government transferred the purchased food into the PDS. Non-farmers received a ration twice monthly at a low, subsidized price.[1] Local warehouses were tasked with distributing the food rations.

Two key features of the PDS food ration system are worthy of note. First, the system ensured that mobility was discouraged. To receive their ration, individuals had to appear at their designated local warehouse. Second, the system of distribution was not equal, but differences in political rank, among other factors, determined the amount given to each recipient. At its earliest history, North Korea had sixty-four categories. The Kim family and Politburo were at the top, "below them Communist Party Cadres, internal security, military officers and at the bottom descendants of families who had been members of the old Korean nobility, business people and large land owners." Although this sixty-four-category system simplified its categories over time, the PDS was in operation from 1950 through the mid-1990s.[2]

> The food shortage got to the worst point during 1988 at Cheongjin. I lived in Cheongjin. But how did the food situation change since 1988? The distribution started to slow down bit by bit. Before in 1987, there was some sort of distribution. In society, when a woman gives birth, then she gets some benefits. It was good treatment. When she gives birth, they give 10 kg of rice to congratulate her. That was the happiest moment. For instance, if the mother would try to breast-feed her child, but there would be no milk, then there was a special powder for the baby to eat, a formula called *ahm*. They would give you that for six months. So the baby can eat even when it isn't being breast-fed. There were those benefits. That program was there during 1987, but it started to slow down in 1988. Because of the food shortage, the supplies that would be given twice a month changed to once a month. Then often the supply cart would just check in at the supply station and say that you would get food the next time the supply comes in, and leave. Then you just go back home. After a few days, when you hear from the department that the new cart had arrived, people would get in line to get the food. You were supposed to get 15 days' worth of food, but we only got 3 days' worth. So the people would start to complain on the way back home. Can't we get more? Why aren't the supplies coming in? We would start saying those kinds of things. (Mi-hee Kun, 53)

Seasonal variations in nutrition are reflected in the development and height of children born in autumn, who fare better than those born in the winter.[3] Son preference, a feature of both Koreas before the division, is largely absent in the North. This has been attributed to the resiliency observed in women and girls, particularly during the famine years.[4] North Koreans had adjusted to inadequate food resources since the partition of the peninsula. The society Jung-ok Choi (21) knew was described as hard-working and determined: "Whenever, whatever happens, people are quick on their feet, North Korean people. They always lived like that. They were ready to do whatever they had to do on their own." North Koreans were used to shortages of food and other resources such as fuel and electricity. Adapting to fluctuations in resources was a regular feature of life.

It was difficult for interviewees to recall a precise moment in time when the famine took hold in North Korea. This is certainly due to the fact that famine is not a sudden event, but it is also because North Koreans were familiar with undernutrition and shortage. North Korea has long triaged resources and food according to regional and occupational rationale. Whether or not the situation slipped into famine for certain individuals depended on their geographic location, social class, occupation, and some means by which they could increase their access to food. The emergence of famine was contingent on these variables. Therefore, a family in a northern remote town who earned their living through farming or mining fared far worse than someone in the same town who was a factory worker, a member of the labor party, or a local authority figure in charge of supervising the housing estate. Greater inconsistency for the starting point of the famine emerged in the oral accounts of those individuals coming from Pyongyang, for many of them didn't realize anything was amiss until the late 1990s. A family in Pyongyang may only have known about the famine as late as 1997, while others in Cheongjin noticed food shortages as early as 1988.

The year 1995 was suggested by many as the year it all began, perhaps because that was the year floods first destroyed enough crops to compel the government to seek international aid, setting a precedent. The floods were a convenient opportunity to request aid without losing face. Shortages of food had been an issue many years before this, but the shortages resulting from the floods brought a new point of comparison. The spectacle of famine is seen long after the contributing and precipitating factors have already done their damage. By the time people saw wandering, homeless children, beggars, and bodies of the dying and dead piled in train stations, the famine process had already been well under way for years. When the state provided an explanation for what was wrong—the flooding and cold snaps, sanctions from the outside, enemy forces, U.S. and Japanese imperialism—this seemed rational, and the solution for it, which was collective endurance, would ensure both individual and, more importantly, national survival.

Lack of information, misinformation, and extensive adaptation to undernutrition and shortages limited a critical interpretation of the earliest famine years. Reaction to shortages was dulled by previous familiarity with shortage, which had been met with ingenuity, adaptation, and endurance. Adept at getting by on little, interviewees explained that they put their hopes on the future, trusting that soon things would turn around. They prepared themselves by enduring as best they could and waiting. People continued to work hard; they knuckled down, endured the hunger without complaint, and reassured themselves that the postponed delivery of the public distribution was only temporary.[5] As this cycle between reprieves grew larger, the famine years created a new norm. It was only when coping strategies were more socially extreme—for example, theft, disappearances, and parents leaving children to search for food—that interviewees identified signs that the busy years had become something different, that the social life they had once known had begun to change. Jung-ok Choi (21) shared her earliest memories of North Korea, just before the onset of the famine.

A lot of people from my region, North Hamgyong Province, come out [from North Korea]. It's because the region is near the Chinese border. I was born in Cheongjin in 1984, my parents were laborers, average laborers. From when I was very small we had livestock. We raised pigs. With those pigs and our labor we were able to eat. We didn't eat well, but we had enough maize growing up. (Jung-ok Choi, 21)

There were others who were comparatively better off, deemed more politically loyal. They were in charge of keeping an eye on others. Young-mi Park (65), a grandmother, lived comfortably in North Korea, and although she lived in the same small city as Jong-Ok, she never had the experience of eating maize. She lived on a better diet that was the privilege of her class, but she also witnessed how differently those around her ate and lived. As an apartment "monitor," a position that involved keeping an eye on the activities of others and rounding up people for work units and other activities, she understood the circumstances of her surroundings better than most.

From the time I was born until I escaped North Korea, I never tried the so-called maize. My family never ate that. My kids had friends who ate it, but we didn't. We lived in an apartment, and I was positioned as the monitor of the entire apartment complex (inminbanjang). The office selects people who are better off for the position of monitor because you aren't working all the time and can keep an eye on things. In that job I got a close look at things. There were many occasions where people were so poor it was considered fortunate to have two meals of maize a day. Many people passed lunch and dinner hungry, leaving for work early the next morning. If they earn some money they can then buy some corn rice or corn flour to live on. Being monitor of the whole apartment, I knew the situation of all thirty families I was responsible for. You just know, once you are monitoring, what they are eating in that house, what is going on in this house or that house. There was a family of five that didn't even have proper clothes to wear. There was nothing for them to wear when the clothes were washed. And nothing to eat. They would head out each day to figure out what to sell to make some money to get food. On the days that they didn't get anything I would give them some of our leftover food, I would call them over during the holidays to give them a little bit of meat and some side dishes. The mother told me that her children always had diarrhea after visiting, but it was because they weren't used to eating foods with oil or fat. (Young-mi Park, 65)

The greatest number of defectors in South Korea left provinces such as North Hamgyong, South Hamgyong, Ryanggang, and North Pyongan. These regions, in addition to Namp'o, were some of the worst-affected areas during the famine years. Leading the way in numbers of defectors is North Hamgyong with over 65 percent. In terms of occupations, a great number of defectors are farmers, miners, or factory laborers, followed by office workers and professionals.

Each individual family experienced these earliest stages of the famine as shortage, but there were sometimes wide variations and contradictions among them. The North Korean government made decisions based on political classification, which meant that certain portions of the population were relocated to the northernmost provinces of North Hamgyong and Yanggang-do. In 1957–1960 North Korea engaged in purges similar to those under Stalin (1936–1938). Political classification determined not only employment but also geographic location. These classifications should not be understood as accurate for assessing genuine political loyalty as many individuals who were staunchly loyal to the state were classified as wavering and relegated to marginalized positions in society, both geographically and socially.

The northernmost provinces of North Hamgyong and Yanggang-do are where the largest number of defectors comes from. These are also the two provinces most harshly affected by the famine of the 1990s, and they continue to experience consistent food shortages. The preexisting inequalities in society mapped the greatest impact of the famine in terms of the decline of food availability and extreme difficulty in altering one's access to food. Some households did not belong to collectives, while others did. People were able to benefit if

their jobs provided an opportunity to do so. The type of work individuals did was determined according to their degree of reliability and
loyalty to the government. Those working in the mines, for instance,
were some of the least trusted classes in North Korea, and of course
the prison camps were full of so-called hostile class individuals and
their family members.[6]

There is evidence of regional variations in biological living standards in North Korea throughout the 1990s, revealing that children
living in triaged areas of reduced food distribution, the northeastern provinces, fared worse, and there is evidence that as early as the
1970s North Koreans were living with nutritional stress.[7] According
to Schwekendiek, children born in Pyongyang are healthier, providing
evidence that elites residing in the capital seemingly possess comparative advantages in food supply.[8] When controlling for further variables, Schwekendiek found that boys and older children suffered more
during the crisis, although cohorts born before the onset of the famine
were significantly better off.

Pyongyang, the capital of North Korea, is home to those deemed
most politically trustworthy. Entry into the capital is strictly controlled. Although movement within North Korea is tightly regulated,
Sung-hoon Kang (36) traveled from Pyongyang to his hometown during his military service.

We first knew of it when, for instance, we went to school and
people would fall asleep. You know, so hungry you fall asleep. Or
people had symptoms of illness, that kind of thing. When I was
in North Korea I was in my military service during the time of
the starvation deaths. I was working on a construction site in
Pyongyang. We were sent to our hometowns later and that's when
I knew all of North Korea was starving. In the military we were
hungry too. There was always very little. No side dishes, no rice, so
we couldn't eat. So how could things remain ordinary? What shall
I say? Was there no rice from early times? When I was little, we

got the food distribution and it was shared out. But from 1992, it collapsed. When I went into the military, I was very hungry.

People were hungry so they cut down the trees to grow corn in their place. There was corn, barley, millet, potato. Because the farmers couldn't farm—the farms couldn't be farmed in the condition they were in and so there was no food distribution given. So what was the connection with the trees? People couldn't cultivate, because there is no private land. It is all collective. The mountains were set on fire and the trees went up in flames. Some people just went up into the mountains and died of starvation. People went to plant corn. So at the very start the country tried to regulate it. They couldn't stop the famine. From the time it started the mountains were taken over for farming. The people who got there first had the lower parts and those who got there last were way up at the top. So for that reason, none of the mountains had trees. There were some regions that were given over to tobacco farming, but not all. They were called tobacco farms. There were tobacco farmers in Onsang, in the village. (Sung-hoon Kang, 36)

A government decision to allot large sections of northern land to tobacco production, when farm land was already scarce and depleted of nutrients, demonstrates a distinct lack of foresight for the needs of the population. Chi-hye Kim (25) left North Korea in 1999, but she recalled a time when the farms in her village, Dongkwon, with around three hundred families, were converted over to tobacco production. She correlated the agricultural conversion with the military. Preposterous as it may sound by contemporary global standards of health, interviewees told me that North Korean soldiers were encouraged to smoke, perhaps because tobacco is a stimulant and appetite suppressant. However, North Korea's illicit economic activities may indicate another explanation for the transition to tobacco production. In 1995, twenty forty-foot shipping containers were seized in Taiwan. The contents: counterfeit wrappers of a major Japanese cigarette brand, bound for North Korea.[9]

Up until 1989 we had farmed corn, but at the end of the 1980s that changed and we were instructed to plant tobacco. I can't recall the exact year, but there was some story about the change. Something related to how soldiers who lack tobacco did not fight as well. We were growing tobacco for the soldiers. Kim Il-Sung gave a directive that the entire area should farm tobacco for the soldiers. The entire area was changed over to farm that crop instead of corn. When people are in school, until they graduate, until they are 17–18 years old, they do not smoke, but when they join the army they are told to smoke. I remember from an early age, my mother was farming tobacco. Because the entire area, pretty much, was growing tobacco, it was very difficult to get food. If we were growing corn or rice, we could eat it. But you can't eat tobacco. (Chi-hye Kim, 25)

In the past, she said,

houses stood at the foot of the mountains, and just beyond the houses were fruit trees such as peaches, apricots, and pears. In the spring, the apricot trees would blossom and the peach trees would blossom in pink. In April, azaleas covered the hills. That is the way it was in the past, but around 1993 and 1994 all the trees were cut down for fuel. We had neither electricity nor oil. In the end you could not see a single tree. People had no more trees for firewood. The town was beautiful. Though political undesirables were sent to the region, the mountains acted as a natural means to fence them in. In addition to this, there was a training center for the secret police.

By 1994 there was complete collapse of the PDS in the northeast regions. That same year Kim Il-Sung died. The following year the country experienced unseasonal cold snaps in winter and floods that destroyed crops. The government then made official appeals for food aid. Hye-jin Lee's description illustrates the stratification of society.

We got the food downturn from around 1994. Up until that time, the miners got the food ration tickets from the country, didn't they, so we would get food. We would get a monthly wage too. They give a wage to those working in the mines. Then in July of 1994 Kim Il-Sung died, didn't he. Up until then we were okay. We had enough food to live, even if it was cornmeal. Even if it was only cornmeal, we still had three meals a day of it. Then after Kim Il-Sung died in 1994, in our house after that time we got the food downturn. The food ration was in short supply, and they didn't give any wages. The miners were not given any food rations or wages. There was no way to live like that. In that situation we ate two meals a day. My mom worked on a farm and the food rations came there for them, so by virtue of that we were able to live a bit. My family was in "level 2" of society. That meant that we were given dangerous work to do. Sometimes level 2 people were given outdoor work to do, carrying coal, that kind of work. If people have some sort of health problem they are in level 3 or 4, like disabled people, that's how it is. My father was in a higher up level, beneath him there were many levels, down to level 5. We were in level 2 so we got about 800 grams of food relief a day [prior to the death of Kim Il-Sung]. I do not know how much the level 5s got. That system was around before I was born. We had become used to that. (Hye-jin Lee, 23)

People had grown accustomed to the style of distribution, which was politically stratified according to social level. Now they grew to know it also as infrequent, delayed, and unreliable. Inside the country, low-grade fluctuations in access to food were in operation for several decades. When the floods came in 1995, there was little chance—short of a massive appeal for international aid and opening the country to help, direction, and investment from foreign and South Korean donors—for the country to have avoided the deaths and extreme hardships that were sure to come.

The system of food distribution in North Korea was an inbuilt system of social and political control that allotted food according to factors such as gender and age but also according to perceived political loyalty and occupation. You could only access your allotment of distribution by appearing at the distribution center in your housing area, which controlled the movement of people within the country. Persons deemed of questionable loyalty, along with those in lowly occupations such as mining, were given less distribution. This preexisting social inequality identified the groups that were first and worst affected by the famine. Kyung-hee Kim (45) grew up in a family of six, her mother a widow, in the northern town of Danchon.

We lived far from the coast, so it was really difficult for us to live. Everything has to be brought by train. Our village can only survive if things are carried on the train. If the trains came carrying food, we got it. Even though we were surrounded by mountains. Mountains all around. Women who came to our area used to say they look up and can only see three stars, the mountains were that high. Because it was in the mountains, even if you wanted to sell something you couldn't; if you wanted to sell, you had to come down into town and sell.

My father died when I was eleven, in 1971. My mother had a hard life, rearing five children. With no father, we had no choice. Unavoidably we congregated near the mines. No matter how capable we might have been, we had to work the mine. It was a wretched life. Even with no modern facilities or equipment useful for health and safety, we were told to work. We had to. If you see mines here in South Korea, people go when safety is guaranteed, but there is no such thing in the North. When they set dynamite they don't wait until all the risk is clear. One day dozens of people died that way in a rockslide weighing many tons. There were people underneath it. They had been smoking, taking a break. Those kinds of things happened, multiple times. (Kyung-hee Kim, 45)

Kyung-hee's friend, Sun-young Kim (43), also grew up in a mining family.

We could commute down into the mine by an elevator, down 800 meters. At first it was deafening, and then sweaty. We worked together pushing a two-ton tram car, after they set off the dynamite. We put the metal inside and pushed it with all our human strength.

It's different for everyone. Work is such that if they say, "Go to the mines," then you go. But if they say, "Go fish" then those people go fishing. If they say, "Go farm," then they farm. We absolutely had to do it. We absolutely had to say yes. No excuses. No justifications. Those mining natives, those whose family was there since before their parent's generation, they are used to the difficulty of the situation so they would use the land or the mountains to make a living. (Sun-young Kim, 43)

Those habituated to some of the most difficult work in North Korea, beyond that which takes place in the political prison camps, are the miners. Miners in North Korea often inherit their occupations through being born into a mining village and family. Such individuals were first relocated to these regions because their political loyalty was deemed questionable. While some miners might have secured small secret plots of land for themselves, the majority lacked access to land such as farmers had, so miners were in a more precarious position than others within the society during the famine years. Jung-ho Park (65) graduated from high school and, like her father, went to work in the mines near Najin. She shared the following insights about her employment and access to food in the years leading up to the famine.

After graduating from high school I worked in the coal mines. I was a charger. A charger goes into the coal mines and sets up lights made from the factory, attaching lights so you can see where you are going. Putting minus and plus together to charge the electricity. I did that until I was 22 years old. Then I married. After I married I worked for a year and then left that work. The Party in North Korea is the best organization for work, so I joined the publicity department. My husband had political dreams, and I reared the kids and worked a lot. I worked in the farms and then made snacks and candies in the night factory, I made bean paste. I did many things like that.

Back then they usually didn't give all 700 grams to the family, they gave roots in addition to the distribution [PDS]. Maybe they would add 300 grams of roots, and the distribution center decides that that makes it up to 700 grams.

Even though war broke out in the 1950s, by the 1960s North Korea lived pretty well. In the stores there was plenty of snacks and candies; there was lots of taffy, for instance. Back then they refined the corn, put in sugar and some other stuff, to see the taffy melting and dripping. There was plenty enough. There was honey, sea cucumbers, meat. All these things were on display. There was plenty, like South Korean markets today. And the 1970s were good too. The 1980s were okay, but from the late 80s things started to become tight. At that time, distribution for one person of 700 grams was expected to last about two days; each time you receive, say, 15 days' worth of distribution, there would actually be 13 days and so on. (Jung-ho Park, 65)

Hye-jin Lee (23) arrived in her mining village after her father was instructed to move there following his military duty.

I grew up in a small town in Hamgyong Province, which was mostly a coal-mining town for social outcasts. We grew tobacco, corn, soybeans, the usual agricultural products. What was unique about that place was that we were all outcasts there, people who were sent there for being undesirable. People who had some sort of political problem from Pyongyang or those kinds of places were sent there. Most of the people were sent to do mining. My father's home town was Sinuiju. My mother was from Kangwondo Onsan. My father was sent to live in the mining town after his military service. Most people do not want to go to the mines, so they are discharged there from the military. So the village where I grew up was a mining town. You don't have a choice about going there. You don't go alone, you are sent there in groups. People who were politically unfavorable were sent to what was called the Ahoje coal mine.

North Koreans had lived with rations and long-term undernutrition since the division of the Korean peninsula. People were often so habituated to this that only at times when rations dropped off completely did they feel the difficulty. Jung-ho Park provided further insights of the earliest onset.

It started getting worse gradually. Life got more difficult from how it was before. Distribution rations were not their full percentages. A person who is supposed to receive 700 grams would only get 576 grams, for instance. People who worked in the coal mines used to get 1 kilogram 300 grams, but they started reducing and reducing it until it was only 900 grams for those in the mines. Then the average office workers and laborers got their regular distribution taken away, and things got very complicated. In North Korea at that time there was no market at all, so even if you wanted to go somewhere and buy food, you couldn't. We wanted to eat and be satisfied with the distribution. Some went up the mountains to pluck up grasses and roots to supplement distribution. By 1993 we didn't even receive 1 kilogram, so what happened? From then on, North Koreans went to the mountains to dig herbs. (Jung-ho Park, 65)

Preexisting social and political factors predisposed geographic regions and occupations to have increased vulnerability to food shortages. These inequalities were more complex than we might imagine and didn't always fall along predictable lines. Soldiers released from military duty were often transferred to mining towns because there was too much work and too few hands.

Zinc is used a lot by the military. What was special about the zinc mine in Danchon is that there were not enough people to work the mines, so they brought soldiers who had been serving for eleven or twelve years from all over the country. Some kind of policy was set saying "you guys, just go to the mines." You might not want to go, but if it's a policy then you absolutely have to go. If I don't go then they capture me and send me; they will certainly catch you and ask why you would disobey the policy. They force you, politically. The soldiers are powerless. The soldiers would have lived apart from their parents for maybe twelve or thirteen years, from the age of seventeen. In North Korea, military service is long. So after they finish it would be nice if they could go back home to their parents, but they are not sent back. The government sets out policies to send them to mines, farm villages, and coal mines. If they wind up working there they have to stay through the generations. (Kyung-hee Kim, 45)

Life for those newly arrived soldier-miners was not easy during the earliest signs of famine, as Sun-young Kim (43) explained: "The soldiers who came after their military service came from all over the country. In the military they know only how to be soldiers, they don't know how to be in society. They didn't know how to live in society and couldn't adjust, so even more people died. So many people died. So many."

The oral accounts show a lengthy period of confusion and hope that things would turn around. Reliance on ritual, tradition, or custom is common to all peoples in times of crisis. It was so in North Korea too. Ritual increases at the beginning of the onset of famine.[10] In North Korea, there is an absence of open religious ritual, but there are certainly social and cultural rituals, such as self-criticism sessions and regular readings of literature on Kim Il-Sung and Kim Jong-Il as well as the daily ritual propagating Juche ideology, resilience, and resistance to Western imperialism through the media. Hwang Jang-Yop reported that the media strengthened ideological messages about solidarity and endurance during the famine.[11] The government maintained and enforced former lifestyles at the level of life and death by promoting certain types of farming and the foraging of certain alternative food items. If people engaged in activities deemed "capitalist" (buying, selling, or trading in black markets) or "treasonous" (defecting, stealing), the consequences were various: disappearance, imprisonment, and public execution. At the earliest stages, North Koreans did not want to act in ways that strongly differed from traditional ways of living.

At its earliest stage, interpretations of the famine followed existing social norms. Existing social narratives of problem-solution were relied upon to make sense and give meaning to the famine. It is useful to step back for a moment and consider what it was like to have the main source of food distribution in the country become gradually and then totally unreliable. While sharing their experience of the famine with me, many interviewees explained their conviction that the government would, surely and at some point, come to the relief of the people. By this they meant that the government would eventually uphold its promise of delivering food through the PDS. And yet the PDS had been unreliable for several years. In the face of an already proven unreliable system, even well into the 1990s, people continued to hope food would be delivered. For some this belief was rewarded, as the government did at some times and in some places deliver food, though never with consistency or dependability.

Outside of Pyongyang, the capital and privileged center of North Korea, in rural and urban areas alike, people went hungry as a result of food shortages. Their suffering was sometimes assuaged by food distribution from the government, however erratic or uncertain, along with mountain foraging. It may be that this dynamic worked to recreate or establish the North Korean government, paradoxically, as the guardian of suffering people. This is not inconceivable, as the government has been at pains to present this image—of Kim Il-Sung as savior of the Korean people and the Korean land—since its formation.[12] The dominant narrative North Korea created about itself and the outside world, with a simultaneous severing of access to knowledge, helped to further entrench the belief that the government knew best and should be trusted. Although Party members in good standing in Pyongyang have extensive knowledge about the outside world, only a few of my interviewees could be classified in this social group. The message of reciprocal loyalty between the population and the government is strong. Concomitant with this message is that no other government can be trusted. The on-again/off-again cycle of PDS delivery meant that the population could never be sure when the food would come. Whether or not they were loyal to the government in their hearts, this precarious position regarding food placed people in a state of uncertainty and confused dependence.

The PDS was the major source of food for most North Koreans, and with the famine this was disrupted even though the PDS was also the main conduit for food aid. The PDS was implicitly a "central pillar of political control."[13] Food shortages and famines frequently result in increased ritual, tradition, and adherence to former ways of life. Often preservation of self is not the aim but rather preservation of "ways of life." A controversial starvation experiment in the 1960s known as the Minnesota Starvation Experiment showed that victims of protracted hunger adhered more to authority and sought support from authority figures to punish those victims around them who broke the rules. Because so much social change occurs, as people witness these changes, they may long for former ways of living as a way to rebalance social behavior.

In North Korea, ritual as it is typically understood in the religious context must be expanded to encompass a nonreligious society that ritualizes loyalty to the government, self-criticism, and dominant narratives of national persecution. As for the cause of the famine, the United States and other foreign countries were said to be responsible. Therefore, preparing for conflict with enemy countries was seen as a necessary step. A focus on the future even while suffering through the present was the best approach.

They didn't tell us anything about the food situation. So we came to realize there was a problem when we went to pick up food at the supply station where they hand it out. They of course gave out the tickets to get the food, but not the food. You could go to the supply station, but you wouldn't get anything. Outside the supply station there was a big line of people waiting to get the food. That's how we knew there was something wrong. We naturally knew.

It was the day to collect the food from the supply station. On a particular day they give out the food, and then on that day you went, but they weren't giving out anything. They weren't giving out wages either then. It wasn't just us who didn't get it either, but everyone.

You couldn't get angry. You couldn't be angry, not in North Korean society. I thought there would be food next month. North Korea is a country that lives well, other countries don't eat as well as we do, that's the way I thought. There wasn't a lot of dissatisfaction. I thought we had nothing to be envious about with others, we even sang that song. That is truly how I thought. Truly, North Korean society will get better, it might take a long time but we would get there.

To see that, how people had given up . . . I too had thought of giving up; just the same as they had, but I didn't give up though things were very difficult. At that time I just thought I must have some foresight. Like it won't be like it's been. "In the future I won't live in this poverty absolutely by whichever means. Though I am in pain, in the future it will be better, it will be better . . ." I told myself. (Sung-ho Lee, 29)

When the food shortages turned into sustained famine, the social behavior of many North Koreans still adhered to these earlier responses to shortage. As in other countries where tradition, ritual, religion, or adherence to authority figures increases, so too in North Korea there was a phase of increased belief that the government would eventually provide. Interpretations of the famine, projections about

what the future would hold, even the way they spoke about the situation suggested this. Lack of accurate information, assured by the physical and intellectual isolation of the population, meant there were few
alternative interpretations. These oral accounts, and a report by Human Rights Watch, indicate that another characteristic of the North
Korean famine was endurance, trust, and loyalty to the government,
with the result that some people died waiting for food distribution.[14]

Significantly, the famine was called the March of Suffering [*Konanŭi
haenggun*] and the Red Banner Spirit, two historical periods that are
characterized by national usurpation of foreign powers, and the messages carried in the media were intended to bolster the economy.[15]
There were not just references to the famine as resistance to destruc-
tive outside forces, but often the language used to describe the famine
experience was what could be called the rhetoric of warlike struggle.
War was used as a point of comparison to establish the severity of
the effects of the famine on the people and community around them.
Interviewees metaphorically calculated that "more people died than in
the war" or that "many died as had in the war" and so on. Throughout the oral accounts of interviewees, the Korean War was cited as
a historical referent against which to measure the degree of suffering witnessed around them. This suggests that war stood as a proper
or comparable reference for the damage brought by the famine. The
blackened faces of starving people were likened to those during the
Korean War, but worse.[16] What is of concern is not the accuracy of
these statements but rather the links established between famine and
war and the influence of this relation on people's experience of famine.

Framing the crisis as the people's own March of Suffering—just as
Kim Il-Sung suffered, so too they suffered—unified the masses and
discouraged alternative coping strategies. It also provided an atmosphere of justification for the harsh treatment of those people who did
not manage their hunger according to acceptable means. It has been
said that "hunger poisons the well of human kindness, sets brother
against brother, and tears at the bounds between mother and child,
destroying the fiber of any society," but strategic framing can establish

an object of resistance that unites behavior.[17] Rhetoric is a mechanism well known to unite a nation; it can have a unifying effect on people. When rhetoric is part of a larger social complex, such as that found in military settings, it can prove even more effective. A study for the U.S. armed forces in the 1960s found that starving soldiers did not dissolve into chaos; rather, they maintained mutual respect and congeniality despite mounting difficulties with food.[18] This suggests that a higher ordering of power and shared ideology found in military settings may strengthen the expectation of mutual respect and honor that otherwise dissolves in stress situations. It may be possible to extrapolate from these findings to the collective militaristic mind-set of North Korea. Even though interviewees reported starvation deaths within the military, this does not necessarily imply dissolution of camaraderie, particularly since a soldier's death is always a service to the nation. In addition, a certain amount of unfortunate side effects can occur without disrupting the entire power structure. Jae-young Yoon, discharged from the military in the early 1990s, explained:

This is what they taught the people: "America and the international community, along with the puppet South Korea," that's the way they explained it. "America, the international community, and the puppet South Korea are ceaselessly preparing for war. We have to tighten our belts to build up the national defense, to build up the economy. So let's build up the economy." And for that, the citizens suffered through hell, not anticipating the rain and snow storms that came and destroyed the farms. "Let's tighten our belts and forward march!" That is the way they propagandized it. (Jae-young Yoon, 45)

A common reaction to major and painful life changes is to draw on cultural beliefs and create new mental worlds, perhaps in an effort to justify events and maintain a sense of security. Interpretations of suffering are contingent on collective and cultural ways of coping.[19] The causes of the famine were attributed to natural disasters as well as to nonsocialist enemy nations. Collective action and solidarity were called upon to resist the effects of the famine. Thus, the North Korean way of life was under attack by the enemy, and efforts needed to be taken to ensure its survival. The population was united against a common enemy even though it was objectively living in peacetime. In instances such as this, the very valid ideas regarding famine and the reaction of victims in famine times are reconstituted as something entirely different; opposition to hunger is mobilized and cast as support for the regime against a collective enemy that is the cause of the problem.

Put forward in the ideology as natural, war appears inevitable. This may have created the sense that the famine was also inevitable. War is often phrased impersonally, and by implication so is famine. The *Konanŭi haenggun* is done as a collective against a collective enemy, and none are alone in this struggle. It distances the subject from self-perception as being in charge of her own destiny, so she is part of a plurality where there is mutual responsibility, thereby furthering the notion that the March of Suffering is as necessary as war and that one is duty bound. Individual or counterhegemonic views of how to better engage the problem are preemptively squashed. Violence and, of course, war create difference, but they are also a means by which ideas of identity and belonging are reinforced.[20] Violence, then, is a mysterious creature because it divides as it unifies. In the metaphoric conversion established by the March of Suffering, and reinforced throughout Juche Ideology, outside countries are established as distinct and at war with North Korea while the population of North Korea is a unified collective working together to overcome. Jin-ho Moon (41) explained:

Kim Jong-Il promoted to the general population, to farmers, that America and other countries were to blame. The blockade started from the 1990s, after the collapse of Western [*sic*] Europe in the 1990s, America kept blocking to prevent economic trade. With such prevention, we could only trade with Russia and China. And Kim Jong-Il makes weapons thinking that the U.S. is going to attack his country. This is the only way for the country to survive. Because he uses the military as a method to attack America, rice and oil all go to the army. That's why it doesn't go to the people. So that's why the situation in the country is as it is and all the blame goes to America. That's what Kim Jong-Il emphasizes, because the country is in conflict with South Korea and the U.S. army in the South, so they need to keep investing in military forces. A country can improve through the military, that's what Kim Jong-Il emphasized.

Famine theorist Alex de Waal observed that the "concept of a right to be free from famine can be a mobilizing principle."[21] In the case of North Korea, the local interpretation of the food shortage was that it was caused by a national enemy, so mobilization to be free from famine takes the expression not of individual or even collective freedom from hunger but of national defense. Alliances will be necessary, de Waal continues, in order for leadership to flourish and for there to be cohesion among those vulnerable to famine. In the case of North Korea, the government gave cohesion to the population, managed and mobilized the population, encouraged them to overcome difficulties, and promised a better life to come. However, the object of resistance was not the state but the international community.

Some of the earliest responses can be categorized as denial and doubt combined with patient endurance, faith, hope, and trust that things would pull together eventually. The accounts show that some individuals struggled to adapt to the makeshift food options, holding on until the bitter end, revealing that they thought the food supply would turn around in time and that they could avoid eating things they detested. Those who were young children at the start of the famine recollected how school life began to change. A young man named Sung-min Noh (19), who was ten years old when the famine appeared, told me: "You just did what you had to do." This echoes what David Turton was told by the Mursi of Southwest Ethiopia, a people long accustomed to undernutrition, "Hunger is something you just have to put up with: one just binds one's stomach tightly and waits till it passes."[22] Loyalty to the government manifested itself in repeated deferral of one's needs:

> I went to this guy's funeral. I went, and I asked them what he died of, and they said he had starved. He died in his house. "Why did he die of starvation? Wasn't there anything he could find to eat? Even if he had managed by eating weeds?" But then, was it as easy as that? That man was a loyal follower of Kim Jong-Il, that's the kind of character he was. He did his military service for thirteen years then he joined the Party, was a secretary there and then [died]. (Chun-ho Choi, 43)

This notion of deferral, the hope for reprieve, has arisen in other contexts. Suffering has the sometimes unexpected result of entrenching in one who suffers even more loyalty or dependence on the source of suffering. Klaus Mühlhahn has written about the use of postponement or "states of deferral" as a prominent feature in the People's Republic of China in the period 1949–1979.[23] This idea is similar to an idea put forward by the psychologist and Holocaust survivor Viktor Frankl, who calls it the delusion of reprieve. He explains: "The condemned man, immediately before his execution, gets the illusion that he might be reprieved at the very last moment. We, too, clung to shreds of hope and believed to the last moment that it would not be so bad."[24] Judith Herman, writing on the near-death trauma and recovery of oppressed subjects, explains: "After several cycles of reprieve from certain death, the victim may come to perceive the perpetrator, paradoxically, as her saviour."[25] These characteristics of suffering are somewhat similar to a syndrome that arises under hostile duress called Stockholm syndrome, the condition in which prisoners become bound to their captors, trust them, and protect them, or at least recognize that mercy is determined by them.[26] Additionally, it is not without possibility that some chose death, a sacrifice for the next generation, rather than devious behavior.

Which people starve to death is really ironic. Who do you think would die first? People who worked the hardest in North Korea and who were devoted to the Worker's Party. The workers were the ones with good hearts and were diligent, but they died of hunger. Why? Because the Worker's Party didn't distribute food. These good people who trusted the government still went to work hungry thinking, "Eventually the Worker's Party will distribute." We can say that they are ignorant in some sense. They are brainwashed and almost became slaves of the ministry. They had lost their independent and creative thoughts under the control of the Worker's Party propaganda. I guess they can be considered as religious fanatics. . . . Some reckless and blinded people would say, "We still follow the Worker's Party and Kim Il-Sung and Kim Jong-Il," when they are not getting distribution. Do you know what they say starving to death? They say, "We don't care if we starve to death! Just take care of the great dear Kim Il-Sung and general Kim Jong-Il." I was one of the main officers in the Worker's Party. I saw it happen with my own eyes. (Chun-ho Choi, 43)

Of course, in this instance it is worth noting that many North Koreans do not view the government as oppressive but rather as their protector. The paternalistic nature is typical for classical socialism, as János Kornai observed, where the "bureaucracy stands *in loco parentis*: all other strata, groups or individuals in society are children, wards whose minds must be made up for them by their adult guardians. . . . So long as the citizens do as they are told they will not have a care in the world; because the party and state will see to everything."[27] Perhaps more than for other subjects in near-death situations, the degree of trust within this group must have been great. In this context, it is not surprising that there were increased numbers of famine deaths in that part of the population characterized as more loyal to the regime.

"After calling it the March of Suffering, when it got harder, they referred to the famine as the Rigorous March of Suffering. They'd say it's temporary, so if we endured this period and survive, it'd be only temporary" (Jung-ok Choi, 21). But as the food shortages progressed into famine, increased difficulties led people to feel that the food situation was no longer *ilshichŏk* (ordinary), and there were other indications that in some areas there was a growing awareness that the promised miracle would not arrive. "In the town where I used to live, they are starting to say it looks like a day of good living will not come," Chun-ho Choi (43) told me. "People began to think it wasn't temporary. They said they had gone too far, reached the end. It is hard to get back on your feet on your own. It was too difficult to get back on our feet from there" (Jung-ok Choi, 21). Rather than subvert the ideological apparatus, as some might presume, knowledge of these registers of reality kept North Koreans operating in ways that kept them alive and, inadvertently, kept the system that delivered their suffering in place. With highly limited options for coping strategies available to North Koreans and with famine stresses growing more complicated and complicating their legitimate loyalty to the country, many were deeply conflicted.

> Well, whether we liked the government or not, if you were to live in North Korea, you just had to always think about what others had on their minds. There were terrible people who worked for Kim Jong-Il, but there were also good people. Some gave people good jobs that would feed them. There were people who trusted each other extremely well. In a small town you see certain relationships can form, especially after being there for thirty years. So a kind of club forms, for those who are established, and it became easier for them to live. (Jin-ho Moon, 41)

In the 1960s there were virtually no markets in North Korea. Even in Pyongyang in the late 1980s, markets were incongruous with representations of the capital as a socialist paradise.[28] After ten years of military service, Jae-young Yoon was discharged. It was October 1989. He shared what it was like when he returned to his hometown:

At that time I kept hearing about how my younger brother and my older sister weren't receiving the rations. Then I went to work on a farm, and I had exactly the same experience. So because of this the people went to the black markets or the farmer's markets, and they would be selling the clothes they wore, selling liquor they made, selling tofu they made, noodles, I witnessed all kinds of things being sold in the markets. I was a member of the Korean Worker's Party and had learned that we weren't meant to do this. So why were these people doing what the Party and the government were telling us not to do and selling like capitalists in the market? I thought that, but then after working on the farm I realized there was no other way for the people to live. (Jae-young Yoon, 45)

"As damage came from the cold and storms, we were able to get by a bit from selling the household items. In 1994 we had a TV, which we sold. We did needlework after that" (Hye-jin Lee, 23). Hye-jin Lee's father worked in the mines. She explained the means by which her father, though exhausted, tried to secure enough for them to eat. Her father's social rank, or class, was two, she explained, and those who were ranked "class two" were given the hard labor of working in the mines. As the food problem progressed, her father planted his own field, an act forbidden for miners. She explains,

In North Korea, if you plant your own field they'll stop you. My father worked in the mines, but there was some flat land nearby and my father planted some beans and some tomato plants for the family. But it was illegal for my father to do that for the family. Before we escaped, when I was in high school, at some point all the plants were pulled up from the field, the country [military] pulled them all out. So those kinds of farms were not allowed. We went to the mountains and tried to find an empty spot. We pulled out the trees and planted some corn plants and we were deprived of those, as we had been the others.

So you cannot use your own energy. Look at my father's situation. He was working in the mines and heading out at the break of dawn to plant in the fields. In the morning, at lunchtime, dinnertime, that's when he worked on it. Without fail, every morning my father worked on the field he had cultivated, and in the evening he would go out again. Seriously, my father worked so hard. He didn't even have any fertilizer. In North Korea they use human waste for that. My father worked really hard. The beans he planted came up well. I saw them. There were big differences between the fields that people were planting personally, and those they were planting for the government. The individual fields were worked on with such earnestness, and the corn grew tall and strong, and their numbers were high (Hye-jin Lee, 23).

Private plots of land were also extremely rare. Up until the late 1980s the government only permitted small kitchen gardens where farmers could cultivate between twenty to thirty square meters.[29] The size of the gardens meant that farmers could not subsist on them alone; this ensured that their farming efforts would not be divided between state and personal farms. The labor of the farmer could be entirely given over to the state farms and the wages and rations earned accordingly. It is unclear how much of the harvest farmers were permitted to keep.

There were instructions given in some areas as to what alternative foods, such as items in a botany textbook, were available during the famine and how to procure them. Because the "food shortfall" had already been attributed to foreign countries, perseverance and sacrifice (ch'amŭlsŏng) were championed as the moral characteristics needed to survive. The population was educated about how to get by through official lectures delivered in the villages.

They didn't tell us about it on television, or in the newspapers; rather, it was the material of a lecture they gave called taeyong shingnyop'um [substitute food product]. The idea was that instead of food, we ate weeds and the leaves of trees, the bark of trees and so on. This was explained officially through a lecture as "*taeyong shingnyop'um.*" (Jae-young Yoon, 56).

The government supplied the population with alternative methods of survival and managed how people understood their coping strategies as a vital act of national preservation. These new foods were substitutes, necessary for a short period of time, and were fully endorsed by the government. But government-directed coping strategies failed to work: there were not enough of these substitute items, and they could not supply all the nutrition people needed. Strict social control ensured those loyal to the government and those fearing persecution were overly dependent on these meager resources. Also, as with other famines in history, some people did not want to eat what was so unfamiliar and tasteless, or they had grown so sick and tired of eating tasteless nonfood items that they gave up. Sun-ja Om (67) said, "I was starving. I hadn't had anything in three days, and because of that I had no energy, no pulse even. So I went out and caught three pockmarked frogs and ate them. I didn't want to have to eat like that." Jung-ok Choi (21) explained,

> There was certainly less for us to eat. So when the food downturn came we were eating lots of what would usually be garbage, weeds and things. That I wouldn't eat. No matter how many meals I missed, I wouldn't eat them. Well, if they were mixed with porridge then. . . . I really tested my mother. Now I am very sorry for that, for what I put on her. Really. I had five siblings. There were seven of us in total. Having to take care of that many.

Perception of the food crisis influenced the way people responded. Because Jung-ok Choi believed the famine would end soon, her willingness to avoid foods she didn't like was strong. Some came to know about the famine in their area because people started getting sick. One interviewee's mother was sick. She was brought to the hospital, and there they saw many people who were dying.

I asked Sung-min Noh (19) what the first sign was that something was wrong. "My friends stopped attending school," he explained. "Or if they came, we'd all be so starved we'd sleep at our desks."

Even if you just went to school to sleep, you had to attend. If you didn't your friends would get the punishment. If you didn't go, your friends would suffer. So we would push each other to go. The teacher would hit the students. You'd be called up to the board and hit until you were red. Girls or boys, no difference. Well, you went because you didn't want your friends to suffer, even if it was just to sleep at the desk, you went. Well, and during class time the teachers too. Because of the economic difficulties the teachers were also affected. The teachers would read books and fall asleep. They had no strength. If you want to study you have to eat. During school hours we slept a lot. I too was so hungry that I would just go to school to sleep. You didn't go to study, you went to sleep. Of course, still once a week we would do the self-criticism. So during those times, people who hadn't attended school would explain during the self-criticism why they hadn't attended and that they would remedy that in the future.

Sung-min Noh's parents were civil servants. He had an older brother and sister. They wanted to do market selling together after graduating from high school. After the famine began, independent trade started, although the town worked in steel. Kim Jong-Il visited the area and declared it a great spot. So other people began looking at the area as a place where they could be successful. The town is located on the coast, so there is a lot of fishing and boat making. His friends and school mates were involved with that kind of labor. Because it was a port town, there were lots of things coming in from China, Russia, and Japan, as he remembers it. He lived in an apartment. The majority of apartment houses were six or seven stories tall, with no heat. There were no trees on the mountains, he said, because they had been cut down for firewood. There was mandatory agricultural service in the spring planting season, and they all had to take part.

His home was all right at first, he told me. As civil servants, his parents were better off than many others. His mother passed away before the famine, and his father stopped working during the famine and started selling on the black market because there was nothing to eat. The people were told by their bosses not to come to work but to go and trade in the markets. There was a period of a few days where no one in the family had food to eat. They went to other houses to see about something to eat. His family sold their furniture; his brother and sister worked in the market to sell the furniture. They did well at this, he reported, especially in relation to avoiding having to pay bribes. I asked another young North Korean, Chul-su Kim (23), how the famine was made public in his area. He explained:

It was not reported. It didn't need to be, you could go onto the street and you could see; wherever you went you could see the *kkotchaebi* [lit., flower-swallows, a term used to signify orphan children]. Their hair and skin was the color of dirt. There was talk, too, rumors, talk, among the people in the towns: they are just eating vegetables in that house, there is no rice in that house, talk like that. We began to see *kkotchaebi* on the streets. Then rumors began to spread about where to get food and money in this or that area, including China.

Life is not lived alone. The subject that narrated the oral accounts was always a "we." The subject was always in relation to others, real or imagined, and always in relation to the nation. The busy years were about getting through things together, survival of the nation and, with that, the survival of the society.

2

COHESION AND DISINTEGRATION

Life is not lived alone. Our relations with others support our lives through mutual help but also burden us through duty and attachment. In times of extreme stress, social relations grow strained. "Everything is annoying, isn't it, when you're hungry?" Sun-hi Bak (53) asked rhetorically when I turned our conversation to how social relations changed in North Korea. This chapter explores aspects of social cohesion in North Korea. Collective coping methods and ways of viewing life helped bind people in a strong social unit, but this binding was also restrictive. Social cohesion is not something new to North Koreans, but during the famine years it took on a more earnest and determined visage. It is natural to adapt to difficulties through preexisting networks of relationships, such as within a community or through the guidance of the leadership, which had material consequences. Mutual suffering sometimes results in a stronger bond, and the years of the famine were marked by the endurance of suffering and working to overcome suffering. The proper response was not depression or melancholia but action. Rather than focusing on what was lost and what was lacking, people turned their attention to getting by. Part of this meant making sense of the difficulties in a way that generated hope in saving the collective.

The phrase *irokke saratta* has no object or subject of address (lit., this way lived) but was a common phrase used by interviewees to describe the pattern of daily life in North Korea. A collective way of living is identified through context. In social relations the same collective is suggested. The expression "my" husband would be a cultural and grammatical oddity in Korean. Pronouns are expressed through social relations that are inclusive and open but always relational. In the Korean language, expressions such as "our country" and "our language" are ubiquitous in reference to nation and language, and they do not smack of jingoistic chauvinism as they would in English. In Korean, subjective relations are constructed through contexts of who is speaking or writing as well as the addressee to whom one speaks. The expression "our" husband is correct. It assumes a unit of relation that surrounds the pronoun. When the subject does appear in language, the plural subject always already accommodates a web of social relations. The subject is situated—in fact, it is identified—via the world of relations. A friend's mother is not "Mrs. Kim" but rather "Jung-eun's mother" and so on. Social and filial relations shape what kind of speech is possible, which in turn shapes what kinds of relations are possible. Language maps existing relations and networks of relation, establishing relations of exchange, whether in speech or behavior, that are acceptable or possible. Language shapes and reflects social dynamics. This web of relations is clearly demarcated in language, from the most direct and intimate relations within the family unit to the leadership of the country. So the expression *irokke saratta*, the way that was lived, without overtly saying it bound the collective in one way of life.

In North Korea the leadership figures in daily life, profoundly ritualized through statues, plaques, historical sites, gifts, walls adorned with portraits, and, of course, text media where the names of the leadership sometimes even appear in larger-sized font. The constellation of the leadership is so complete as to be referred to as pieces of the sky, meaning that there is nothing greater but also nothing else that can be seen or known beyond the leadership. The leadership is framed within popular discourse as the father, or as Suk-young Kim smartly observes as the mother of the nation.[1] The timing of

Kim Il-Sung's death, the weakening of agricultural capability, and the floods marked a distinct before-and-after for many North Koreans, who consequently placed recollections of pre-1994 as "not that bad," while the Kim Jong-Il years were identified as harsh. Kim Jong-Il's rise to power was mentioned as the historical turning point for the downturn in economic and food security. Not all but many interviewees mentioned that there were few problems with access to adequate food before the death of Kim Il-Sung in 1994. In the oral accounts, people made connections between the failed food situation and the change in government leadership. The combination of the collapse of the Soviet bloc, the floods, and other weather problems were often eclipsed in importance by the death of Kim Il-Sung. Kim Jong-Il was inevitably inadequate in comparison with his father.

However, none of the oral accounts indicated a critical understanding of how choices made by Kim Il-Sung, many years prior to the famine, primed the country for intense vulnerability to natural disasters and political isolation. Geographically, the country was already on precarious footing regarding self-reliance. The terrain of North Korea is 80 percent mountainous and roughly 18 percent arable land. Prior to the partition of the Korean peninsula, the northern portion had always imported rice from the southern portion. Coarse grain from northeastern China was also imported.[2] In this geographic situation, self-reliance is a recipe for disaster.[3] In the oral accounts, negative events were correlated: Kim Jong-Il's taking power, the natural disasters, and the visual spectacle of societal changes, behavior formerly unknown in North Korea.

Young-chul Kim (58) lived fifty years of his life in the country. He remarked that when Kim Jong-Il came to power, he saw the emergence of beggars. "Socialism is a society without beggars," he said, perhaps echoing what he had learned about capitalist South Korean society, a place supposedly overrun with beggars. "With the death of Kim Il-Sung, as the Kim Jong-Il era came in, the food problems, the famine and, along with it, the many starvation deaths . . . there were lots of beggars, and we saw many who died." The emergence of things deemed nonsocialist, which he had been educated to believe were archetypical of capitalist society and evidence of its inherent corruption, was incongruous with both received ideology and lived experience. North Koreans lacked information about international issues, and they lacked the necessary mechanisms for adequately knowing or judging their government's response to international events. These limitations meant that local information, rumors, and misinformation were used to make sense of emerging problems, which were linked only with the inabilities of Kim Jong-Il and not also to the unrealistic aspirations of Juche ideology.

For Chung-su Om (69) and Sun-ja Om (67), there was a strong connection between the rise of the famine and Kim Jong-Il's rise to power. They saw the famine as starting from 1995, shortly after Kim Il-Sung died. "There were no people—none—who died of hunger before the death of Kim Il-Sung," Chung-su Om explained. Some of these stories about Kim Il-Sung are reminiscent of North Korean propaganda narratives in that almost superhuman powers are attributed to him. Perhaps the severity of difficulties that Chung-su Om and Sun-ja Om faced when Kim Jong-Il came to power threw the strengths of Kim Il-Sung into sharp relief. To quote Chung-su Om more fully:

> Kim Il-Sung did quite well. When Kim Il-Sung was around, he would say, "I intend to see this entire country. I will see it all. Where they are living well and where they are not living well, I want to see it all." Then he went and did that. He saw where they weren't living well, and he fixed it. He would say, "Where is it I need to go?" Then he would say, "Prepare the car" and go there. He went to Yanggangdo, and there he went into one particular house. What I'm saying is that Kim Il-Sung went right into that house. There was an old lady in that house, with a child of about five years old. Kim Il-Sung went into that house and asked the child where his mother and father had gone. He asked the grand-

mother where they had gone. The tiny child, who had no idea who Kim Il-Sung was, began to talk. He had no idea who Kim Il-Sung was. The child said, "My mother has gone to look for rice with my father. We are hungry, so they went to find some rice." The child had no idea that it was Kim Il-Sung, and he said that his mother was hungry and went to find some rice. That's how it was. Kim Il-Sung went back later and the child was gone too, and he asked the grandmother, and she too replied that they had all gone to find something to eat. (Chung-su Om, 69)

Chung-su Om (69) repeatedly emphasized the child's ignorance of Kim Il-Sung. His words carry a blush of shocked embarrassment at the child's seeming irreverence to speak so directly and without care to Kim Il-Sung. The directness of the child's speech is unusual in the daily experiences of life under Kim Jong-Il. Chung-su Om saw the child's direct speech as ungracious and unorthodox but sweetly truthful. Certainly there are issues of age at stake here, but above that is also the fact that the child spoke directly to Kim Il-Sung without knowing the grave importance ascribed to him, or the gravity of what he said since he was indirectly criticizing Kim Il-Sung's leadership.

Chung-su Om repeatedly stresses two things: the child didn't know Kim Il-Sung, and the speaker was a child. This effect is achieved through repetition and then through elaboration when the grandmother speaks directly, just as the child had done. The juxtaposition of these statements creates a tension between our awareness through an unspoken moral code, that the child should not speak to Kim Il-Sung as much as anyone, and yet the child continues to do so directly. With the unstated moral code in place, Kim Il-Sung's response to the child is highlighted as even more gracious and benevolent in the face of the child's inappropriate behavior. It is through the child's speech that the problem is exposed. Kim Il-Sung is presented as quick to see where needs are unmet and unflinching in the face of struggle: "I want to see where they live well and where they do not live well." He resolves to ameliorate the suffering of people with humility and haste. The account continues:

> Then Kim Il-Sung said, "I had no idea it was like this!" He had gone and seen how things were. He knew how things were. "If I hadn't gone, how might things be? How much worse might things have become? I had no idea about this." So, with Kim Il-Sung there was no starvation, we all lived. We were given lots of rice, lots of meat. We even received many frozen pollack [fish] as well. When Kim Jong-Il came, everyone starved. (Chung-su Om, 69)

This section of Chung-su Om's account relies heavily on anecdotes of what was seen, said, and done. The narrative emphasizes the confluence of hearing and seeing the suffering of others in order to reach a solution. Later, in the time of Kim Jong-Il, this structured contingency between what is seen and what is said gets inverted. It is through not seeing, not speaking, not telling that the problems of living are resolved. Here, Chung-su Om shares his recollections of Kim Il-Sung's concern, care, and benevolence. His account mimics the abundance of care attributed to Kim Il-Sung. The speech and actions of Kim Il-Sung and Chung-su Om's detailed description given to the theme of concern is startlingly asymmetric to that attributed to Kim Jong-Il. Only the final sentence of his narrative brings in Kim Jong-Il, and yet the entire contrast is achieved through this small insertion. The attention and even the amount of words allotted to the two men are starkly disproportionate, almost mirroring the perceived benevolence of Kim Il-Sung and malevolence of Kim Jong-Il. Kim Il-Sung is active, agentive, he is with the people. His speech and behavior are powerful. He listens. Kim Il-Sung is immoveable; he can accept and absorb the direct, critical speech of the child and grandmother. The last few sentences of this account reveals the attribution of the difficult times, "So, with Kim Il-Sung there was no starvation, we all lived. We were given . . . We even received. . . ." But this is startling because the previous sentences depict hunger, and a hunger that gets worse, not better, after his visit. In fact, Kim Il-Sung's grace and benevolence can be depicted only because he stands ready to ameliorate the hunger and suffering of the people. Kim Il-Sung's curiosity and awareness seem to have removed his culpability, as if his compassion alone was the panacea. The narrative only indirectly suggests a nutritional resolution to the crises, and certainly not a structural one. In the account, Kim Il-Sung actually does nothing but ask, listen, and talk. It is Chung-su Om who attributes benevolence to him. We then arrive at the coda: "When Kim Jong-Il came [took up leadership], everyone starved." The deep contrast between the two men is clarified.

Another interviewee told of how neighborhoods were temporarily supplied with materials to host a visit from Kim Jong-Il. It would all be arranged beforehand, Sun-hi Bak (53) told me. Rice and other foods would be put into the houses so that he could look and remark on how well people were living. "But when that was over they would take all the provisions back with them," she explained. "Kim Jong-Il is dishonest to the people, but also to himself." It is difficult to estimate to what extent the positive recollections of Kim Il-Sung and the negative recollections of Kim Jong-Il are representative of how people thought while still inside North Korea. However, the extent to which Kim Il-Sung is lauded in the accounts certainly identifies a shift toward the negative with the loss of Kim Il-Sung; the three-year period of mourning may have been in earnest, and since the narratives of Kim Il-Sung place him at such a height, Kim Jong-Il was set to disappoint. So how was the great difference in the two leaders reconciled, particularly during this period of extreme deprivation?

There is some anecdotal evidence that the internal reception of Kim Jong-Il was indeed deeply fraught. In 1996 a coup d'état was planned by No. 6 Corps based in North Hamgyong Province, Cheongjin. The group was planning an uprising in North Hamgyong Province first, before taking Pyongyang. Before the revolt could be implemented it was picked up by the Defense Security Command, and the entire corp was dismantled. Around forty people were executed and three hundred severely punished. The coup was foiled by North Korea's triangular monitoring system where political committee members, military commanders, and national security agents mutually cross-check each other. The whole system is monitored via wire taps. According to Monique Macias, a student in Pyongyang in 1989, around the time of the Tiananmen Square protests, rumors circulated about a student protest at Kim Il-Sung University.[4] In 2005 the group Free Youth Comrades or the Young People's League for Freedom posted antiregime declarations in the 1.17 Factory in the town of Hoery-ong and under a bridge on the way to Daeduk middle school, both in North Hamgyong Province.[5] The failed coup of 1996 had a ripple effect through North Korea. It was a substantial effort, demonstrated by the number of dissidents executed and the number of related individuals punished. It might be that these executions and punishments severely discouraged any aggregate numbers of people who would have called for overthrow of the regime, yet there have been reports of antagonism between ordinary people and police.[6]

There were other social factors at work that encouraged people to endure the dreary leadership of Kim Jong-Il. Symbolic conceptualizations of power, duty, and obligation likely facilitated the acceptance of the fallible Kim Jong-Il as part of the Kim dynasty. Charles Armstrong observed that the development of symbols, language, and rituals in North Korea's ideology had by this time largely moved from a Marxist-Leninist style to a distinctly Korean familial style centered on the Kim family.[7] This symbolic material produced a nationalism inherently rooted in blood and land, which, unlike the abstract language of socialism, used a discourse of familial connection, love, and obligation. In interviewees' recollections of Kim Il-Sung, the "family scene" is apparent. Kim Il-Sung cares for the family as if he were a grandfather. Kim Jong-Il was part of this greater family unit; he had a connection to the benevolence, if not in his actions at least in his lineage. Armstrong attributes the survival of the North Korean regime to this network of familial symbols. Emotional and physical adaption during the famine years reflected this quasi-family rhetoric. As Suk-young Kim observed, North Korea remains deeply rooted in

Confucian tradition, where the collective is held above the individual, and where family operates as one organic body that is the basis of a universal structure.[8] This is not only a feature of cultural history that predates the existence of North Korea. Even after its formation, the postcolonial nationalism of North Korea situated itself within terms of family kinship. This literalness was strongly routinized, and from these the paternal leader emerges. This family union was prioritized over other socialist values.[9]

Alongside these symbolic bonds of filial piety, the material expression of the leadership's promise to society identified through food, wages, and other material needs was supplied through the Public Distribution System (PDS). This system of distribution was struggling to distribute sufficiently, and the existing triage of goods grew more extreme as resources dwindled. Resources had to be siphoned off to prepare for war. Although in 1995 Kim Jong-Il appealed to the international community for aid, interviewees reported only learning that North Korea had requested aid once they crossed into China. For them, there was no sign of aid as far as they knew. Those who said they received aid explained that they were expected to receive and then return it. They had visits from the United Nations and received relief, but it was taken back once inspectors had left. Interviewees who had been in military service during the famine years also described intense hunger and no signs of aid.

There were aspects of life that could not be assessed by international aid agencies because of their enforced dependence on the North Korean government for operations and information within the country. The elaborate smokescreen that obfuscated their access to the real situation could not be assessed, understood, or challenged. Restrictions were placed on these agencies because foreign relief efforts in the country were viewed as potential imperialist weapons waiting to strike.[10] International food relief was not mentioned once in interviews as a means by which individuals survived the famine. A high percentage of North Koreans believe they did not receive aid while in North Korea.[11] It was understood then that food came from the leadership or the efforts of the people but not the international community, and this is significant.

Pitirim A. Sorokin, a sociologist who survived the 1921–22 famine in Russia, observed that people's political loyalty transformed according to their source of food. He wrote, "They bowed to Kolchak, Denikin and the Tsar, and they kissed the hands of the princess and the countesses; but when their food supply began to come from the international sources and communism they then became ardent 'internationalists' or 'national internationalists.'"[12] North Korea's strict control over how relief was distributed within their country was guided by the perception that sources of food supply alter worldviews and change political loyalty. This is logical when food gifts are received from the leadership, given the connotations of exchange and duty with which such gifts were typically framed. Donor countries and agencies naturally wanted to see how their relief was being used. They were sometimes placated.

> So Canada, America, and other countries, when they send their relief, they want to see how it is being used, they want to see those people who have received it. They are curious to see if those people for whom the relief was sent have received it. So because they want to know, they send someone to come and take a look. To show how it was all being used, I was given a ration, I was given money, and I was given a particular task to perform, in order to show them how the relief was used. They showed the agencies Pyongyang. They couldn't show them where the farmers were hungry with nothing to eat, that would be an embarrassment to the country, so they couldn't show them that, they showed them Pyongyang. (Sun-ja Om, 67)

Hyun-woo Kim (42) discussed how the United Nations came to his neighborhood (in Yŏdŏk District, Hamgyong) to do an inspection. The food was given and then taken away.

The area where they came, that area was given rice and meat. It was beef from America given in preparation for the inspection. Then we were all told what to say and so on. They ensured that the people would know what to say. When the UN came they thought we had everything. But we hadn't been given anything. It was just talk, lies. That's it. So the relief that the UN and ROK are giving isn't getting to those who need it. (Hyun-woo Kim, 42)

I have not heard of rice, let alone meat, being part of food aid operations, so mention of this in the account is intriguing. Rice and meat are too easily sold on the black market for a high price, so aid agencies never provide such items for relief; it is likely that the government officials provided these items to show the inspectors how regions outside of Pyongyang were faring. Andrew Natsios documented the triage of food shipments from the World Food Program in the mid-1990s. Although 33 percent of the population lived along the eastern ports, and they should have received the bulk of shipments, only 18 percent of food aid reached them. North Korea had shut off food aid shipments, ensuring the area was chronically food insecure.[13] The function of power relations is clearly delineated in Hyun-woo Kim's account. Not only did the government triage relief but individuals were encouraged to deceive the international community. An atmosphere of fear pervaded discussions of relief activities, particularly due to the lack of information provided to the population. The government's geographic restrictions on aid caused one level of trouble for the population, but the lack of accurate communication between the population and those international workers delivering aid placed North Koreans in a perplexing situation. Suk-ja Park (84) described the type of food they were permitted to keep:

We got corn. But the corn would be mashed up and smell rotten. We would get that. But if we didn't eat that, then there was nothing else to eat. So we would wash it over and over, cook it over and over. Finally we'd just eat smelly, mold-infested corn. It was really too much. When we ate it, we wondered how China could send us this rubbish. But it wasn't so. North Korea gave it to us. (Suk-ja Park, 84)

North Koreans had to maintain practices and actions that demonstrated belief in the government. Otherwise they risked severe criticism, imprisonment, torture, or execution, depending on the severity of their crime. Therefore, the ideology represented in the North is not a system of "real relations which govern the existence of individuals, but the *imaginary* relation of those individuals to the real relations in which they live."[14] Reality is made material through the actions and practices of those who live within that imaginary relationship to truth. As Suk-young Kim identified, the embodiment of North Korea's elaborate and obsessive theatrical presentations, though in stark contrast to economic reality, is a sociopolitical necessity.[15] It is a mode of entertainment and a means to mobilize the masses to the point of distraction.[16] The continued material manifestation of ideology is enforced through the punishment of those who transgress and through imaginary relations maintained between real relations. This serves the ideological apparatus because, as some people engage in a seeming belief relationship to Juche ideology in order to avoid punishment, it is difficult to discern who does and does not genuinely believe.

Having a connection to friends or family in China made the difference between life and death for North Koreans. Sometimes, however, the exchange of foreign items and information did not have the expected response in North Korea.

Since we heard from our relatives in China a lot, we knew how China was and how South Korea was all from stories. In our country, they put out propaganda that "because the U.S. put on an economic blockade, our country is like this" and say things like that because the U.S. and our country are enemies and South Korea is also an enemy, so "they continue to pressure our country." They say, "That's why our country is like this." Because North Korea connects it like that, whenever they report something, they say something similar to that.

It's not that we don't know the U.S. is rich. Relatives in South Korea, China, and other places know all that too. In Chosun [North Korea], people who know, know. If you go to America you live well, and in fact we see all these foreign products. What is there that comes from our country? Chinese Koreans come out to sell things, from toothbrushes to toothpaste. It's all Chinese products or foreign products. And when we go to Wonsan, there are Japanese ships too at the harbor. When you go to Wonsan when the Japanese ships come, from soap to everything, people use all Japanese products—soap, shoes, TVs, refrigerators, washers, and especially a lot of bicycles come to Wonsan. You see a lot of Japanese products in Wonsan, and they are so cool. "Wow, there are things like these!" But why is our country so poor? About that people say, because the U.S. keeps placing heavy pressure, and since there is only one socialist country left, they try to destroy us. That's what the propaganda says. So we don't know much about the U.S. or international politics. Whatever the country says, we believe as they say. The country tells us about international politics, but they polish some little bit of whatever is good for North Korea by changing the basic point. They change the stories like, "We're not doing anything, but other countries do this." So for us, that makes us think that the Americans are bad, makes us hostile toward them.

We believe that. But even if people don't believe that and know the reality, whether they know or not, whether the U.S. was like that or not, life is difficult. People say "good president" if they're fed well. But because life is difficult they think badly about Kim Jong-Il. Inside we think, "Damn this country. Something has to happen," they curse and all that too. But what could they do? Are they going to start an uprising or what? If they can't do anything really, they just live on quietly and maybe another time. They just live like that. (Jung-ok Choi, 21)

Although the foreign products might be good, and although they indicated a higher standard of living, a Manichean worldview emerged as a means to make sense of the unintelligible: our country cannot produce products like this because of our enemies. So the very items that might have planted the seed of doubt about socialism's superiority, as it did in East Germany, for example, in the case of North Korea fostered feelings of hostility, inequality, and injustice: the moral economy attached to foreign goods. The control of information, particularly information concerning nonsocialist countries, is highly regulated. Thus materials from outside, into North Korea, were described according to these imagined relations. Material goods from other countries, via China for instance, are interpreted according to what was ideologically acceptable. Or, to echo the words of Tzvetan Todorov, the fact of the foreign product did not come with its meaning attached.[17] A nice bicycle made in Japan can be bought and sold in North Korea, but the fact of the bicycle (that it is well manufactured) does not arrive with the meaning intact (that it is well manufactured because it competes in a market economy). Since the fact of the object, but not the meaning, transfers it is easy to attribute a local meaning; the foreign products are better because those countries are not sanctioned as we are sanctioned.

The late Hwang Jang-Yop, former member of the Politburo, and the highest-ranking defector in South Korea, reported that the government increased propaganda efforts during the worst years of the famine; new slogans included messages about having more to die for than to live for, as well as making sacrifices for the next generation.[18] One of the clearest indications of the intersection between Juche ideology and the body in North Korea is manifested in the high numbers of people who, according to the oral accounts, starved to death waiting for distribution to arrive. Each interviewee witnessed someone reach that stage. North Korea attempted to engage another level of loyalty to the nation through increased propaganda messages that incorporated welcoming death as a sign of loyalty for the nation. Death is not too high a price to pay; in fact, it is not a price at all but an honor. As a demonstration of loyalty, death is not new to nations, religions, or ideologies as is historically evidenced by the kamikaze, the soldier, and the suicide bomber. On December 29, 1998, in the high-profile North Korean newspaper the *Rodong Shinmun*, Chŏnghŭi Kim, a Party official, wrote a piece about the "New Sprit for Suicidal Explosion" that shares similarities with the thinking behind suicide bombing.[19] Dying from starvation was not a problem for North Korea, but individual acts of self-preservation involving border crossing, theft, and illicit trade were a problem because they threatened to corrupt the North Korean way of life and possibly erode government order.

Opposition did exist in North Korea, but it was designed by the state. Its type and target were manufactured in a way consistent with the nationalist discourse—we must oppose the outside enemy—so it strengthened national sovereignty but created greater vulnerability for the population. The North Korean government's response to both the famine and to the manifestation of famine coping strategies in the lives of its population demonstrates not only a negligence to uphold the basic human right to food through acts of omission and commission, but also the willful deception of its population so as to reduce the likelihood of uprisings.[20]

The government remained consistent in its message of dutiful loyalty although the conditions of many North Koreans differed. Youngchul Kim (58), who worked at a light industrial factory, demonstrated an awareness of the extent of the problem and the government's indifference. When I asked how he figured the number of famine dead in the population, he answered with reference to the factory's production of shoes.

They know. The government knows how many died. It is the government, so they keep statistics on their population numbers. The government doesn't publicize these figures, so other people don't have any idea how many have died of starvation. When I was in North Korea, because I studied economics, I was working in light industries where they make shoes, T-shirts, hats, the things that people use in daily life. We made those things, and for that amount of production we need to plan according to how many people there are. In North Korea each person is allotted four pairs of shoes per year. So I could tell how much the population was going down when the country's plan for the number of items came out. "Ah! The population is dropping, the population is dropping." You could know that, couldn't you? From 1995 the population continued to decrease. How could I know? Before that we used to make one million or more pairs of shoes, and then it declined steeply. . . . People were disappearing. So if you looked at it carefully you could see how many were dying. So we knew, but if you let on that you knew you'd be snatched away. (Young-chul Kim, 58)

In an effort to get a grip on its population numbers during the confusion of the famine years, North Korea issued new identification cards to the people.[21] Aid received, siphoned off, or never seen was not something North Koreans depended on for survival during the famine years. Having some kind of connection with extended family, particularly in China, was often the lifeline. Having a "China connection" helped ease the transition from famine to somewhat sustainable existence. Market selling was a means of survival, and those who didn't try it were most vulnerable. Interviewees reported that large numbers of the intellectual class died during the famine. Loyalty to the government motivated a sense of certainty that the Public Distribution System would resume delivery of food again. A failure to moonlight through capitalist-like coping strategies was not unusual within this group. Other people began to fend for themselves, unable or unwilling to rely on the government. Most North Koreans' understanding of the famine was scripted according to what they were told caused it, and initial responses were particularly informed by the social need to maintain familiar lifestyles.

The accounts reveal that the government explained the famine as caused by nature, namely the flooding which came in 1995, but also from activities of Western and Japanese imperialist interference. The government's recourse to mythology is not usual; as Claude Lévi-Strauss pointed out, the use of a binary, opposition, or mythology is useful for understanding the world.[22] It is common to all peoples throughout history. But how did North Korea populate this narrative? Who were the main actors? The famine problem was a result of imperialism, and the solution would come from Juche ideology. These two stood as combatants within an already familiar narrative of national identity developed and repeatedly delivered through education and the state media: the triumph of good over evil. The social behavior generated by this narrative was not unusual because it was in keeping with nationalist narratives of war readiness. It tapped into the sense of solidarity and collective persecution within the country. It classified behaviors that were unacceptable. The social atmosphere created by this helped to keep chaos at bay during the famine. It was understandable that this narrative involved suffering, sacrifice, and endurance. The political body represented by Kim Il-Sung that took shape in the 1960s emphasized the suffering nation and the suffering of Kim Il-Sung himself in exile in 1938.[23] So within this narrative it was without question that the people of North Korea would also suffer and endure their grief for the sake of the common effort, duty, and collective survival.

The response of intellectuals and the vast majority of the ordinary population was prescribed by the government, but many would likely have tried these methods without the government's advice— namely, the procurement of famine foods from the mountains, the restriction of the diet to two meals a day, and the nutritional supplement that came in the ideological message that this famine was an arduous march against imperialism. Interviewees explained that local government officials taught this message of coping strategies to the community. Famine foods were collected from nearby mountains. The roots, grasses, and weeds were mixed with cornmeal, flour, and other items to make a palatable meal. Hye-jin Lee (23) hated eating the roots and grasses.

When the food downturn came, it wasn't possible to have a full meal even once a day. I almost died. Weeds were mixed with the corn, like porridge. I wouldn't have it. My mother made porridge from the corn and weeds. I had one spoon of it. There was only one spoon each, no kidding. Other people were in exactly the same situation. One spoon of weed porridge, that's what we all ate. The porridge was made from seven spoons of the greens taken from the mountains. I hated to eat that. Really I did. For days we had to eat it. There was no seasoning, there was no soy sauce, and even salt was precious. There were plenty of houses that had no salt at all. There were many people who died. (Hye-jin Lee, 23)

Interviewees went into great detail about the daily effort to find material for their meals and the elaborate process by which they tried to make them edible. Nicer food items such as tofu and liquor were for selling rather than eating; the dregs left over from making such items were eaten instead. Soon things became so bad that the only weeds available were those deep underground.

We pulled those out, cleaned them well, dried them and [by pounding] made a flour of them. Then there are bean husks, you take the bean out and you have the husk. We dried those and made flour out of them and ate that. Then we also had the bark of trees such as pine trees, we'd mix that with the flour made from corn. People began to wonder whether they would die of starvation if the ability to farm secretly in the mountains were taken from them. There were people in charge of controlling the mountains. "If they take this away from us, we'll starve to death" and they would say this and again go out to farm the plot in spite of it. People were without clothes, starving, no shoes, no clothes. They are just crying out, "Give me something to eat," crying for rice, the children crying for food at night, like the sound of mosquitoes buzzing, like that sound. Even if you're dying there is nothing you can do. Absolutely nothing. And the house, the house belongs to the country, doesn't it? Since it's given to you by the country you can't sell it to get enough to eat. So you are hungry, you are starving, you are hungry, there's nothing that can be done. You go out and catch some frogs, you eat those and survive. (Sun-ja Om, 67)

In the village where I lived there was a lot of liquor selling. When you make liquor, after you take the liquor out there are the dregs left behind. We ate that. And with tofu, tofu soup, we'd mix a bit of flour with the dregs of that and eat it. The tofu we sold at the market. We only had a little to eat. Just the dregs left over after making the liquor, it was like *makkŏlli* [a raw rice wine]. What's left behind is a bit solid. We'd buy some saccharine and mix it together. I ate acorns the most, and the dregs from raw rice wine and the dregs left from tofu. Then in 1996 things really got bad. There were many days when I went with absolutely nothing to eat. (Hye-jin Lee, 23)

Swindling also occurred and, while this ensured individual survival, it often made things more difficult and undermined the collective. In his autobiographical novel *This Is Paradise*, Hyok Kang writes that "in everything they produced for the collective, the farmers had got used to slipping in incredible quantities of stone to keep to the quotas, which were measured by weight."[24] In the markets, "American" cigarettes that were just rolled-up paper were sold instead of tobacco, and colored sawdust was substituted for chili powder, and nails were put in mushrooms to increase the weight.[25] Farmers and sellers in the markets were not the only ones swindling buyers. Gangs of starving soldiers are said to have looted houses and stolen chickens and other domestic animals at night.

I had lots of friends who died from hunger. Because we worked on the farm cultivating, though things were bad, we could manage to eat and survive at a minimum. Members of the farm collective could also manage. But those in the mines, if they went hungry there was nothing for them to eat. They didn't have the strength to go out and pull weeds to eat. They would just lie down, waiting only for the day of their death. While at the very same time there were people eating tofu soup, liquor, and acorns. Then there were those who had close family in China, who would send things from China, those people lived well. (Chul-su Kim, 23)

Indeed, thieving was a growing feature of society. Where there was commerce and trade, people were drawn to opportunities to satisfy needs that couldn't be met elsewhere. Shipments of food from China, according to Sun-hi Bak (53), were accompanied by thieves and beggars, which lead to the perception that society was growing more corrupt as a result of outside stresses.

In the border town where I lived there was a lot of commerce going on. That was in Hyesan. We provided logs [to China] and in exchange we got food. There were many beggars, especially in Hyesan. Those beggars, about thirty of them would go to the food truck entering from China. When food trucks had rice and corn, beggars would stab the bags of food with knives. The bags would open and the food would flow out while other beggars got ready to catch the food. The image of thirty beggars climbing on the trucks and stabbing the bags, and putting the food in their bags . . . I saw that so many times in Hyesan. (Sun-hi Bak, 53)

Changes to ordinary social life were interpreted as signifying the depth of degradation reached by the people. Divorce, prostitution, and the abandonment of children were cited as examples. Efforts to maintain a proper North Korean lifestyle are sign-posted throughout the accounts. There was a strong reluctance to change former ways of living or engage in behavior antithetical to the norm. And yet, during famines, wherever they occur, most of the population will be involved with some kind of crime connected with nutrition.[26]

> The country is filled with thieves. At night they would come into the markets and steal what they wanted. Continuously the thieves were thieving. How was it possible to live? It wasn't possible. (Hye-jin Lee, 23)

> Human compassion comes from the rice bowl. If there is an abundance to eat, there is harmony, if there is nothing to eat and only a little work, there will be quarreling. It's incomprehensible. As times got more and more difficult for people, trust broke down; this is obvious, no matter the country, the story would be the same. (Chun-ho Choi, 43)

Interviewees reported a general hardheartedness that emerged in their local areas toward people who had died of hunger. The experience seems to have had a particularly strong impact on younger North Koreans coming of age during the famine and on those who witnessed the deaths.

> At the beginning, when we saw a dead person, or a beggar, our hearts would thump with compassion for them. "What's this going on? What in the world?" After that there were so many dead to see that it was like it wasn't real but like a dream. Just like it wasn't real, and then, "Well, if even Kim Jong-Il can't do anything about it, in what way can I do anything about it? I, too, have to really think about how I'm to survive." That's what I thought. Yes, they were so hungry they died. The sound of the children crying out for something to eat in the evening, they were like frogs croaking, crying. (Young-mi Park, 65)

In our family, well my grandfather died before I was born so I didn't know [anything about] death. Because of the famine, fear grasped me. I remember there was one family, they all died of starvation. Father, mother, two daughters, a son, and one of the daughters had children, and they died of hunger too. At any rate, there were eight of them and they all died of hunger. They lived in the house behind us. This was in the Onsŏng region, an area mostly mountainous, but this was the part that was flatlands, all open fields; it was not possible to farm there, mostly rock. (Hye-jin Lee, 23)

A frequent comment from interviewees was that upon waking in the morning they would wonder who had died, and would go around and check to see who had died the previous evening. According to Chung-su Om (69) and Sun-ja Om (67), 1996 was the worst period for them, every time they went to bed and woke up the next morning someone had died in the night. Many interviewees reported changes that occurred within themselves as the famine progressed.

When this famine problem reached its most extreme state, men and women took flight in all directions. You had to move to live. You had to move to live, and so families were broken apart, orphans started appearing, and you started seeing instances of the elderly starving to death in their homes. (Jae-young Yoon, 45)

People were on the move in order to survive. Catching a ride on the trains meant saving time and energy in walking, but this could be a dubious form of travel. The trains were dangerous not necessarily because of the guards but because of how people had to ride them to avoid the guards who asked for travel permits or bribes. People climbed onto the outside of the trains in order to ride them without a ticket. At the train stations people climbed under the trains, grabbed on and held themselves up against the tracks that passed beneath once the train got going. "There is a high tension wire under the train, and yet people would crawl under the train to catch a ride on it and then bang! they were dead, because they had touched the wire; there were lots who died that way. I heard a lot of those stories." In-sook Lee continued:

Because I had relatives, and relatives from here and there came to our house looking for food, since they didn't have any, I knew the problem was throughout the country, but I didn't think that it was a worldwide problem. Because I was young, I didn't know that it was a worldwide problem, or why that was so. I just thought, "Oh it's difficult to live." People go on trains, go to places, with no particular plans, go on and sell things out of their bags, carrying their bags from bamboo sticks. When they get on a bad train with strict screening, it's hard for them to get a travel ticket, so it becomes very difficult.

Our trains, you can't even imagine. It's like trains from 8.15 [Korea's independence era]. People get on the top of the trains even. My sister was on a train with her family in Cheongjin. Holding a small a baby in her hands, they got on the train, but the space between the connecting cars was wide, and while the cars rattled out of Cheongjin the guards were screening the permits. You must have a permit. If not, you are sent to the labor education department and forced into compulsory work at a labor camp. My sister was asked for her permit. As she put her hands in her pocket, to take out the permit, the car rattled and the baby fell from her hands through the gap in the cars. There were train conductors, safety guards, and even police, but they didn't stop the car. The train kept going. Because it had just begun to depart the speed was slow. As the baby fell, she dropped to grab it. My sister fell underneath the train and just before the baby's head was about to get broken by the wheels she grabbed him and threw him out from under the train.

People watched as the train carriages just went on. They were saying, "Oh what do we do, the baby and the mother? Did that mom and baby survive? *Aigo* [gosh], no probably died, couldn't have survived. When we get to the next station, let's follow the tracks and clean up the bodies." (In-sook Lee, 51)

Trying to get around the countryside to find a way to make ends meet, Sun-ja Om (67) used to ride the train, but she rode without a ticket, which she accomplished by pretending she was mentally disabled.

They were sure to rough you up, drag you off the train, and ask, "Why are you riding without a ticket?" they would tell you to go. I would ride the train and when they came to me I would act as if I were mute. I wouldn't talk. Just mumble. Then two security officers came and roughed me up, so I pulled at my clothes. (Sun-ja Om, 67)

Some interviewees stated that North Korea deals harshly with its disabled population. Sun-ja Om explained how she would talk incoherently and rend her clothes. She would pull off her clothes because the guards would look through the travelers' clothing to find tickets. However, a partially undressed woman proved a formidable traveler. While there is no clear evidence that there were gendered aspects to the consumption of food, there are indications that the selling and purchase of food, particularly in the black market, was dominated by women. Sun-ja Om explained a coping strategy she used, which many others had also mentioned in their narrative: "I too went out into the streets to find any way to live; I even went as far as selling my blood. I sold my blood several times." Interviewees, both men and women, reported that women were less embarrassed to take more extreme measures to survive. Selling in the markets was an activity dominated by women. "The men easily lost face," she told me, but also the women were less likely to be bothered by the soldiers, less likely to be asked why they were not at the factory working, less likely to be viewed as a threat to the social order.

Sun-hi Bak (53) explained how factories became defunct, operating only as check-in places where workers were turned away and told to find money for food elsewhere. Some people in her community learned to trade safely and ensure their livelihoods through different means. Searching out other opportunities, she described how she and many other women managed to trade across the Amrok River.

Since the government stopped giving out distributions [PDS], we no longer got the distribution tickets, and there was nothing to produce at work. Everything was paralyzed, so you just get a stamp on your time clock card at work, then you would go to the marketplace to see if there's any daily jobs available. Hyesan had the Amrok River. We had things like jewelry and other precious metals such as gold, silver, and bronze. Those items were traded secretly through the river [items wrapped in cloth and tossed across].

So after giving the items to China, you get the money and buy food. People from Hyesan referred to men who wouldn't smuggle as stupid. People who are stupid didn't smuggle, and everyone else did. Even girls did it. So the strategy was that men imported through secret channels via the river route while girls did laundry at the Amrok River. "Doing the laundry" was a way to send goods across. We would put stuff under the clothes in a big bowl.

[We traded things like] metals, like gold and bronze. We put them under our laundry, already wrapped. We wrap them and label them with their weight. Since it's shallow people would cross the river from the other side. We'd hide it before they'd come. We would pretend like we were just doing laundry and the people from China would take it from where we hide it. They'd just take it without saying anything, but then afterward, they would be like, "Okay this has the person's name on it and the weight. . . ." They would pay us after checking the weight in China. They don't hand us the money with the rock or anything, but throw it to us saying, "There you go!" When they say they're going to give us the money at 12, it's not just one person getting their money, but a crowd. So around 12 o'clock, a lot of people would come out and gather. Then they'd call us and throw each person a rock. Then we'd go back home with the money.

Different portions of society and different geographic regions coped in ways acceptable to their position. Sun-hi Bak explained that the security police in the region were "pitiful" enough to be bribed by the traders at the river. Since the police were only given food twice a day and were expected to find a third meal on their own, they were susceptible to accepting bribes. "That's probably why they watched out for us," she explained.

After a period of what North Koreans referred to as needing "patience" (*ch'am ta*) and "endurance" (*ch'amŭlsŏng*), coping strategies emerged and developed along with greater evidence of government inefficiency. This provided opportunities for ordinary North Koreans to witness a disjuncture between what their lives had been like before the famine, the indoctrination and ideological education about life in North Korea, and the reality they saw around them. These opportunities ran the gamut of black market activities to public executions for the crime of grain theft. People identified disappearances as directly linked to the discussion of starvation-related deaths. Furthermore, although they could not speak directly about the starvation deaths they witnessed and heard about, these deaths and their causes were clear. No amount of ideology could nourish a starving body, and if it did manage to nourish their patient endurance, it could not bring them back to life if they died waiting.

Relationships between people began to change on a local level as well as on a state level. Children were newly required to bring rabbit hides to school, as Sung-min Noh (19) explained, and would suffer self-criticism sessions if they fell short of the quota. Relations between students changed too. Children with more to eat ate alone. There was less talk of play or schoolwork and more talk of what to eat.

Because of the March of Suffering the school had a regulation. It was the rabbit regulation. We had to catch rabbits and bring their hides to school. We had to bring at least five in one year. The rabbit hides were used for the soldiers. They were sent off to be used for belts. It was very hard for people to do this during the economic difficulties. The students would come to school and have to self-criticize that they were not successful. "I will have it by tomorrow, I will do it by next week," they would say. Then they wouldn't have managed and again they would have to self-criticize. It was really horrible. I got it too. Because of that I hated attending school.

More than study, we would talk about being hungry at school. "How are you managing?" we'd ask. "What are you eating?" We were worried about that, so we talked about it. "What are you eating?" "Have you eaten?" Then we would go out after class hours and get grasses and weeds. We didn't talk about studies, we talked about what we would eat; outside of that there was no talk. Playing was not pleasurable. Before the food shortage came, we would play with pleasure. Just like here in South Korea. Skipping rope, drawing straws, kicking a ball. After the food shortage came kids didn't have any energy to play. They would just sleep, and when they weren't sleeping they would talk about food. They never talked about studying, and even though there wasn't anything to eat they would go to the agricultural station all the time [where in ordinary times food was given out].

Those who had something to eat had family or friends in China. People with rank were eating. The soldiers in our area, their families, were eating. Those who lived well stayed to themselves, and those who didn't live well stayed to themselves. Most of the well-off students had lunchboxes. In the past, they would sit together and share out the food and eat. But after [the famine started] they would sit together but they would eat alone, they wouldn't share out their food. They couldn't do that. You have your pride, no? North Koreans have a strong sense of pride. (Sung-min Noh, 19)

Because of the famine, relations between people became difficult. Hye-jin Lee (23) said that those who were in positions of leadership had trouble adjusting to ordinary people with new money and new power. "There were some ordinary people who were good at selling in the markets. They would get the boss to give them easier jobs through bribes; they wouldn't get stuck with the difficult jobs. In that way, things changed. Those with power managed, and those without power were in an even harder position."

Sung-min Noh (19) talked about the changes that occurred after he left school. He had not seen his teacher since he graduated, and one day he saw her in the market selling Korean vodka and cigarettes. "We were all just people in that situation." But he said that he most regretted seeing his respected teacher making ends meet like that. Interviewees shared information about family breakdown in North Korea. There was mention in the oral accounts of increased separation of husbands and wives and a rise in prostitution.[27] Changes that were contrary to former ways of living were occurring, showing that the hardships shifted from the maintenance of former ways of life to efforts to sustain life. Although North Korea does not now have an official Confucian ethic (there was a history of Confucianism in the past), North Koreans reported behaving in ways contrary to such unofficial ethics. In his autobiography, Chol-Hwan Kang expressed his conflicting feelings about the hunger he experienced, and filial piety:

Ceding to hunger, acting like an animal; these are things anyone is capable of, professor, worker and peasant alike. I saw for myself how little these distinctions mattered, how thoroughly hunger alters one's reason. A person dying of hunger will grab a rat and eat it without hesitation. Yet as soon as he begins to regain his strength, his dignity returns, and he thinks to himself, I'm a human being. How could I have descended so low? This high-mindedness never lasts long. The hunger inevitably comes back to gnaw at him again, and he's off to set another trap. Even when my grandmother was suffering from pellagra, the thought of bringing her soup only crossed my mind after I devoured a few rabbit heads. What leftovers I did bring her she pounced on with avidity, searching furiously for any remaining strands of meat. Only after she had eaten her fill did she stop to ask whether I had eaten.[28]

Some families grew stronger under the strain, as Hye-jin Lee (23) mentions, but others gave in to the pressure.

There was the food ration downturn, but despite that our family didn't suffer collapse—there were other homes where there was lots of fighting. Well, because you have a downturn in food rations . . . Who's to blame? That kind of thing, that's the way they fought. I didn't have that experience of fighting in our house. My mother and father really brought me up . . . since the time I was born in North Korea I never once saw my mother and father fight. Arguing, fighting, I never saw that. The famine, the food downturn, even then . . . together they worked hard, they tried very hard. They collected weeds and greens from the mountains. My mother would go out and get what she could, and we took care of each other. Even if my parents didn't have something to eat they always ensured that my siblings and I had something. (Hye-jin Lee, 23)

Although abandoning children was unlikely to be an early response to famine, many survivors reported seeing orphans as a defining symbol of the famine and social collapse. Kyung-hee Kim (45) also saw the orphan children in her town of Danchon:

From the 1990s I saw these kids starving to death in front of Danchon station. Parents abandoned their children, even on New Year's Day. They would clean them good and do everything a parent could do for the last time and put them out there. They'd be really clean. Sometime later if you go out to see, the kids would be crying, you see tear marks and snot on their faces. Then, next time, they are lying down. And the next time, they're dead.

People who passed them here and there may have given them something to eat. So they live like that, but even if they take what's given, it's not enough to live on, and they die. At that time, I had to live. It hurt to see that. I am a mother, I have two children. Even if I took one of those kids, could I feed him? Clothe him? No, I couldn't. People who left their children, they did that to survive. How could you take on someone else's kids in addition to your own? Maybe I could take on one kid once in a while, but not thousands. Who do you take on, who do you care for?

If I had this kind of mentality back then, maybe I could have taken on one or two kids. But back then I wasn't like that. So I didn't feel anything. I thought: "I should be calm. I shouldn't be moved." Over there, people live like that, and here people live like this.

Grandmas and grandpas, dying is just dying. But to see kids die is awful. Don't you think? At an old age, people have lived long enough. So the first thing I thought when I came out of North Korea after crossing the Tumen River was to set up an orphanage. (Kyung-hee Kim, 45)

Sun-young Kim (43) also saw the kids,

I went to Cheongjin Market because I was hungry. I went, but I was crying inside. The merchants sat in the market next to the railroad tracks, the noodle merchants. There was a kid. His face was dark, no shoes and dirty clothes, his hands and feet were black, his hair was dry. "I can't just die sitting here, if I come here and do something to lift the mood, maybe I can get some soup or something left by the customers." Must have thought like that. And after the customers eat noodles there is some soup left and the kid says, "Please give it to me, don't throw it away," and he got it. When I saw that, I thought, "Yes, do whatever it takes to live. You must do whatever it takes to live. Even if you have to steal. Live. Good job, good job."

You know how we carry our kids on our back? I saw this little kid on his mom's back and gave him a snack. Then I saw this elderly senior take the snack from the baby because *he* was so hungry. How dire is that? The starvation situation. I got snacks and gave them to kids near the train station. I gave some to a child and the older kids took it off him. They stole it and ran away. I thought to myself, "Yeah even if you have to be like that, eat and live on." Even old women were saying it, "Good job, good job." So eating like that to live is good. They are better than dead kids. (Sun-young Kim, 43)

Sun-hi Bak (53) gave this account:

People here in Seoul don't even know their neighbors, but not in North Korea. Those of us in the *inminban*, local authority leaders, live harmoniously with plenty of interaction. When we make rice cake for holidays, we would share them and talk amongst ourselves even if it's trivial, but it doesn't happen here [in South Korea]. But then, because we didn't get food anymore from the country, none of us were free to do whatever we'd been doing in the past. We couldn't talk since we were too busy earning money only to use it all up in a day. So everyone started to grow apart and lost laughter. Before in North Korea, when people are building, they delegated us into federations. Then ladies from *inminban* would go work, have a good time, and come back, but by the time we left, it wasn't like that anymore. People no longer smiled. They are all deep in thought, and no one just wanders around aimlessly like here, but all have bags on their backs and have their destinations. The changes in relationships occurred since no more food was distributed and it was so hard to live, for everyone. We were all hungry so we couldn't afford to take care of relationships on top of the burden we carried.

In North Korea, everybody knows what is going on with everyone else. There was a sharing of things. Even when the food was given out, it would be shared. If we had a piece of rice cake, even if it was the one piece, it was divided and shared between us; the relations between people were good. You could talk and discuss what was on your mind. And then when the food wasn't given out, when the food shortage came, people were. . . . When could they sit around chatting with each other? They couldn't. So the relations between people grew further apart. Laughter and that kind of thing also disappeared. Along the roads you could see all the doors shut tight. There wasn't anyone who didn't lock their door. Everything was so difficult at that time. There wasn't any more getting together between people . . . the laughter just vanished from the roads. From the time the food distribution didn't come, the relations between people became quite strained. So it was that everything just. . . . When you're hungry everything is annoying isn't it? It was all like that. (Sun-hi Bak, 53)

What happens when national narratives engender a sense of alienation and reflect back an entirely unmatched experience that discounts personal experience? What does this mean on a collective scale? As Nancy Scheper-Hughes observed of Brazil, the hungry body is a truthful body; it does not maintain the gap between reality and experience.[29] Worse, it threatens the dominant discourse doled out by the government. The gap that emerges between lived experience and ideology has been observed elsewhere. There have always been efforts to eliminate the appearance of the gap though camouflage, seen most clearly in language. To live within the truth is dealt with harshly. Havel, writing about communist Czechoslovakia, explains that living within the truth is dealt with harshly not because it has power but because it has potential to ignite a trend of living in the truth, and thus the potential to transform social consciousness.[30]

> I saw a lot of difficult situations. Since I was little I went to many places on the train. I went to Gangwon Province, Pyongyang a lot, by the train. Going to relatives too . . . my sister also got married and moved there, so I visited my sister a lot too, especially Gangwon Province. When I go to the market at Wonsan, there are corpses in the corner. Beggars and bums died on the streets. There are these places near the entrances of apartments. If you look underneath those places, there are corpses like that. At least it wasn't that bad in Cheongjin. But when I went further in [into North Korea, away from the coast], it was even worse. The corpses were out in the open, with no one to claim them. Even now, it's so appalling and scary. They didn't die because it was cold. It was summer, so they died because they couldn't eat and starved. They wandered around with no home, lived like that and starved to death. (In-sook Lee, 51)

The life people saw around them increasingly contrasted with ideological messages of the utopian future that was to come for North Korea. How people communicated about these incongruities is crucial; the next chapter explores this in detail.

3

THE LIFE OF WORDS

Living was tied to speaking. To live well, particularly in the famine years, one had to speak well. Choosing the right words, knowing the right words, was a feature of life that was learned through subtle lessons of daily interaction. Speaking properly could result in a comfortable life and decreased vulnerability. Although the body endured hunger and the mind may have desired to voice its complaint, society was collectively going through what Kim Il-Sung had endured for the sake of North Korea, the March of Suffering. Individually they should not be so weak as to pull the whole structure down now. Therefore, it was pointless to complain, the voice could not speak of hunger, and the body could not need what the state was unable to supply.

At this stage in the oral accounts it was clear to people that a disconnection was present between discourse and reality, but a socially developed ambiguous discourse operated and enabled people to communicate despite contradictions. It wasn't as if everyone was ignoring the famine and pretending the consequences weren't there; rather, a way of thinking guided by education, historical narrative, and social norms contributed to a resolution that getting on with things was preferable, and perhaps inevitable. It wasn't a time to stop and ponder the enormity of the difficulties but a time to busily work collectively toward a solution.

This collective movement toward solution in the face of suffering is traceable in the language habits that were common at that time. These language habits can be identified, for instance, in the jokes, turns of phrase, and dominant metaphors that emerged in the oral accounts. The surfacing of such linguistic habits indicates not a singularity of use but a wider web of interlocutors in North Korea who also used and shared this style of outlook and communication. Language is relational, evolving, adaptive, and time–place specific. The appearance of humor, recurring metaphors, and turns of phrase in the oral accounts are not incidental but instead indicate a further layer of relation within North Korea: that of the people to their collective spoken discourse on the ground. To live without trouble from the state, one had to speak without trouble. Rather than a collective and deliberate effort to avoid "speaking truth to power," I observed instead an interpolated normalizing of what is and is not proper, sensible, and helpful to say. Instead of speaking truth to power, it was about speaking in ways that were subtly empowering. Speaking in North Korea is in many ways akin to creating things, performing, as John L. Austin might say, new relations of power.[1] In the context of its real-time unfolding, speech was part of a predetermined structure, but speech could also carry within it an individual intentionality and opportunity. People were therefore not just repeating things they had learned to say, but their speech was infused with both the customary styles of acceptable speech and individual desire.

As previously mentioned, official state terms for the famine were carefully designed to shape public experience along historically convenient interpretations. What was commonly referred to outside of the country as the North Korean Famine was inside known as the *Konanŭi haenggun* [the March of Suffering], which refers to the 1938 defeat of Japanese imperialism by Kim Il-Sung's guerrilla army in Manchuria. It remains the most common term of reference for the 1990s famine. Among the interviewees, everyone, without exception, used the term. In fact, when I used the Korean word for famine, I was asked to clarify, "You mean the March of Suffering?" Or they would say, "Ah, you mean the March of Suffering." North Korean official literature—for example, the leading newspaper the *Rodong Shinmun*—also made use of the term "Red Banner Spirit" (*pulgŭn ki chaengch'wi undong*) and, for a time in 1998, "Forced March to Final Victory." Each of these historical references are characterized by national usurpation of foreign powers.[2] Terms loaded with cultural and historical significance are not used arbitrarily but are part of the cosmology geared to maintain or reinforce preexisting norms while discouraging the emergence of threats to those ideals. Speech that departed from these norms put the speaker in great peril. Therefore, the body and the voice were locked into a twisted relationship where the latter could not reveal the truth of the former. The voice could not, for instance, give accuracy to hunger felt by the body.

As a result, people also learned what not to say. At least on the level of language, this created registers of reality that could and couldn't be spoken about. People engaged with one world but linguistically at moments accessed another. The world of subjects and objects was unmoored from the words once used to describe them. Language in turn grew attached to other less accurate things. In some ways this mooring and unmooring is the development of an argot designed to speak precisely about hunger and the starvation deaths without actually talking about them. Language shielded the speaker from the culpability of speaking the truth. New ways of communicating were achieved through misspeaking.

Direct language about the famine experience was not acceptable. Interviewees reported restrictions on speaking about hunger, food shortage, or famine deaths. This implicit control over speaking about hunger and its consequences was consistent with government-sanctioned discourse, which took a historical tone and avoided implicating the state.

If someone had died of hunger you couldn't say that they were so hungry they died. You would say they were in so much pain they died. When you were working you would always feel hungry, to work without having eaten, argh! There was no way you could say, "I am hungry, so I can't do it." "I'm in pain," you could say. "I'm hungry," you couldn't say that. (Jae-young Yoon, 45)

Already characterized as an absence or inaccessibility to food, famine became doubly absent and inaccessible in language. By removing overt discussion of famine from personal and public discourse, individuals and the state participated in strengthening alternative linguistic registers for discussing reality. This created an awareness of the contradiction between state ideology and the world people experienced around them. What emerged was a discourse that recognized the failures of the state but continued to operate and live within those failures. Indirect speech provided the chance to more accurately address lived experience.

As previously mentioned, famine and starvation in other contexts have demonstrated the absence of resistance, as it is understood in the classic sense of revolution, and an increased attraction to social authority.[3] Social relations among hungry groups, such as soldiers, have shown that mutual respect and congeniality survived despite mounting difficulties with food resources. Higher ordering of power and shared ideology may have strengthened the expectations of mutual respect and honor or at least the sometime performance of it toward these authority figures.[4] Therefore it is not unusual that the speech patterns of individuals would reveal elements of loyalty, either genuine or performed.

In the following account, Young-shik Kim (45) demonstrates how he learned to bend his speech to the wishes of an actual or potential listener; indeed, he also explains how he then took this lesson and taught his family members to do likewise. There was awareness that direct speech could result in the speaker being severely punished. Young-shik Kim shared the following scenario with me. Although it is unclear from the account whether it is told from his direct experience or whether it is anecdotal, the underlying message is that levels of communication were guided and controlled.

In North Korea there isn't even one person who died of hunger. Why? Take this as an example. My father has died from hunger. When I'm drinking liquor with my friends I say, "Yeah, I had so little rice that my father died of hunger." If I just say that, the next day the secret police will find me.

[Here he imitates a knock at the door]

"Comrade Kim, come out please."

"Yes," you reply, and you go out.

"Sit," they say.

"Yes," you say.

"Comrade, your father has passed away?"

"Yes, he passed away."

"What age was your father?"

"He had just turned 70."

"Oh, he was quite an age when he died then."

"Yes, he was."

Already I have an idea what the secret police are getting at.

"Did your father have some kind of illness?" they ask me, and I say, "He had high blood pressure."

"Ah! He died from his blood pressure going up. Comrade Kim, comrade, don't go around saying that people are dying of hunger. Do you get it? Why should anyone be dying of hunger in a socialist society? Comrades speak intelligently [*tongmu mal ttokttokhi harau*]."

They frighten the life out of me. So I pull my children and my wife aside and tell them not to say grandfather died of hunger, because if we say it they'll take us away. So if someone has died of hunger you cannot say it. (Young-shik Kim, 45)

Here we can see that speech in North Korea is performative speech par excellence. An individual accomplishes something, does something in the world, through the mere act of enunciating.[5] As with earlier definitions of performative speech, the speaker, the audience, and the context all combine for the action of speech. The words go out into the world, doing. Therefore, not only could someone manifest famine and starvation through merely speaking words about those things, but speech also had the power to undo manifestations. The invisible, voiced word was an actor in the making and unmaking of North Korea. The voice, something that cannot be seen, had the power to eliminate, to disappear the speaker. But, if this is the case, it must hold that all speech in North Korea is performative, all speech acts in the world bringing the speaker closer to or further from vulnerability, along with her listeners and those she speaks about. When Young-shik Kim gets a knock on the door, he is asked, "Why should anyone be dying of hunger in a socialist society?" This question simultaneously recognizes the failure of North Korean socialism and obliterates recognition of this failure. In North Korea, where the regime emphasizes the "primacy of correct thought," the way that a person speaks reveals whether or not his thinking was intelligent, as the police officer in the previous scenario explains.[6] This aspect of articulation was observed by V. N. Vološinov in *Marxism and the Philosophy of Language*, and it is reminiscent of Lev S. Vygotsky's classic text *Thought and Language*, particularly in the demonstrated link between silent inner speech and oral language.[7] Vološinov explained that the psychology of a person or group could be traced in their utterances, and that these revealed political aspirations or loyalty.[8] Vygotsky identified that where people live in close psychology their speech is typically abbreviated because they often share similar thoughts, just as inner speech is characterized as abbreviated and incomplete. When the thoughts of speakers are shared, the role of speech can be reduced to a minimum. Participating in the correct way to speak meant producing oneself as a "smart" North Korean within a system and within all the relations that entailed. What Young-shik Kim describes is how this correct way of speaking was ritualized.

Speech revealed whether or not the interlocutor's thinking was, as the police officer suggests, intelligent, correct. Utterances were invisible but linked the internal world of the speaker and the external world of his political life as a subject in North Korea. The context in which an individual speaks had the power to implicate him. That space has a set of conditioning moral norms, and he cannot stand apart. Instead he is directly vulnerable to these norms. When he speaks, it is not only his own story that is told but rather the story of a set of relations. Not only is his relationship to his deceased father evoked but also, and more dangerously, his relationship to the leader, Kim Jong-Il, to the state, and to socialism. By proximity, his family is brought into this too.

"You never knew," interviewees told me, "who was listening, and who might inform on you." The general suspicion between people was so strong in cases that some individuals left the North without saying a word to family and friends. The dialectic exchange about defection was conducted without words but rather through *nunchi*—a Korean word that can be translated as having an unspoken sense of social atmosphere. Speaking openly about dissatisfaction with life was "kept in the mouth," to quote my interviewees, not only to avoid punishment but also to avoid implicating the listener. Therefore, speech was a manifestation, genuine or performed, of an individual's mental political proclivity. North Korea is a landscape where a seeming descriptive comment becomes an act. Therefore, "He died of hunger" is not a description of how a man died but rather a generative act where both the individual and the state are made to behave in ways totally uncharacteristic: the one has died of hunger and the other has maliciously permitted the death. The sentence that performs the act thus creates the starvation death and implicates the state.

Young-shik Kim's account explains three different levels of communicative context. The first is public while he is drinking with friends, where in a moment of unguarded speech he speaks his mind and he is informed upon. The second is semiprivate, literally at the threshold of public and private (I recognize the complexity of these while still employing the binary). When Young-shik Kim gets a knock at the door, as if knocking on the door of his unconscious, he is reminded to engage with the ritual of proper speech. He is reminded of how his father died. He is reminded that if he is to exist within the norms of North Korean life, he must speak intelligently, as comrades do. The local official "frightens the life out" of him but reminds him to engage in the ritual of how to speak properly. Young-shik Kim demonstrates that he is willing to participate in the ritual by providing an answer to how his father could have died. Through this he shows that the message is received. The third context concerns the private sphere of his home where the two earlier contexts come to inform his directive to his wife and children, where he reiterates the instructions of the local official clearly: Do not say grandfather died of hunger. With the official's unspoken clarification that people who do not speak carefully do not speak at all, he tells his family to obey or "we will be taken away."

Here language is concealing *and* revealing reality, but beyond that dualism, it also responds to context; it is a mutable actor. Speech is producing knowledge, and knowledge is producing speech. Just as other aspects of North Korean life are organized, regulated, and an object of power to be maintained by the state via local government agencies, so too speech is an object of power that needs proper modeling for best use. In learning what was impossible in North Korean society, the contradictions between speech and experience were confirmation of the existence of those things. Although censorship was a feature of society since its early days, with the famine a host of new topics fell under the unwritten law of smart speech. North Koreans reported disappearances during the famine times, and there was an awareness that this could happen to them if they did not speak carefully. As Young-shik Kim (45) explained, "I could not say that my grandfather died of hunger because if we say that they'll take us away. The Party will have my family and close acquaintances banished." In North Korea, the exact location of "off somewhere" is understood to be a reeducation center, prison camp, or death. For those who knew of them, the prison camps regulated behavior among the population, as it predictably does in totalitarian regimes.[9] Whether in the factories or in the fields, people could not discuss hunger, but they could discuss hunger as pain. This linguistic shift was not without signification.

The art of knowing what not to know grew commonplace in North Korea. After witnessing the results of speaking out of turn, correct speech replaced genuine communication. I asked Sun-hi Bak (53) whether it was possible for her to speak her mind while she was in

North Korea. "That's right; truly you wouldn't let it out of your heart. Well, for that matter you wouldn't think about it, and you wouldn't speak of it. If you spoke of it you were dead. Your neck wrung. Banished. Executed. So because of that, it wouldn't leave your lips." Sun-hi Bak describes the containment of thought from the external world but also from the self. "You wouldn't think about it" because that might lead to speech and that would lead to death. The invisible world of the mind had the power to materialize self-destruction. The reality of experience then is kept within the heart but never voiced. Sun-ja Om (67) shared a cautionary tale about how she was advised on alternative ways of speaking, where pain was substituted for hunger.

> There was no way that the hunger could be spoken about. There was an elderly woman who was very hungry, she was about 80 years old, she went out saying, "Oh, my gosh! I'm so hungry. How are we meant to live like this?" And that very night she was taken off somewhere. This was in North Hamgyong Province. They weren't giving out PDS there. Usually they would give out about one kilogram of PDS, but they weren't giving out any, so the elderly lady was hungry. So she was asking how she was to live like that. She said that, and then she was captured and taken away. She was taken away somewhere. The police came in the night and took her away. You just couldn't say it. Even if I'm so hungry I'm dying, "I'm just so hungry I'm dying," I couldn't say that. "She was in pain and died," you could say that. (Sun-ja Om, 67)

When she tells me this, she does not begin with the disappearance story directly but rather with what the old woman had been saying the day before. Structured in this way, it is evident that for the speaker the old woman's speech and her disappearance are situationally linked in relevant ways. With the events juxtaposed, it is conveyed that the "antecedent event somehow gives rise to or affords the possible occurrence of the subsequent event."[10] This establishes the disappearance as an event naturally correlated to speech. Interviewees clearly identified what could and could not be said as well as the consequences resulting from speech choices. Ambiguous indirect speech enabled North Koreans to maintain existing ways of being, however fragmentary, faulty, and illusory. It enabled the maintenance of ways of being as a means to avoid becoming a threat to ways of life in North Korea as well as one's own life.

As Jae-young Yoon (45) explained: "Let's tighten our belts and forward march! This is the way they propagandized it." The imagery in his account is consistent with the values, history, and ideology of the North. The notion that these traditional, established values could pull the people through the crisis is not unique to North Korea. In the same vein, Alex de Waal observed that in Darfur in the early 1980s, people saw the famine primarily not as a threat to life but as a threat to their "way of life."[11] The Mursi believed that if people behaved "traditionally," then the extent of the hardship would not have emerged. According to de Waal, they believed that if they had accepted things as they were and not tried to strive to solve the problem in other ways, their material prosperity would have been assured. In a similar fashion, interviewees expressed the willingness to maintain the status quo rather than make more trouble by behaving in socially uncharacteristic ways.

The use of ritualized state-sanctioned discourse may have enabled the emergence of diverse, multiple, and unpredictable meanings in everyday life, including those that did not correspond to the authoritarian discourse. Just as the state manipulated language for national survival, individuals manipulated language for their own survival. In contexts different from North Korea's this has been variously termed "evocative transcripts" or "hidden transcripts." Hidden transcripts, according to James Scott, were used to make official discourse work toward the speaker's personal agency. Scott, working on colonial and class struggles, put forward the idea of a "transcript" whereby historical memory, which was not officially sanctioned, could be transmitted in spite of forces that dictated otherwise.[12] Caroline Humphrey, working on Mongolia, drew connections between socialism and what she called "evocative transcripts."[13] The evocative transcript acted as a tool that enabled people to express themselves without too great a risk because it used the language of official discourse to carry a double meaning in what was being communicated. The accounts show that evocative transcripts about the famine situation were embedded in language and were often totally forgotten unless jogged by asking questions about jokes and humor. I noticed that asking whether there was any humor about the famine was a provoking and evocative question, possibly triggering memories of things that were provocative in the same way.

Despite the difficulties of life, North Koreans had to carry on, live, and make do with what they had. The harsh realities of life can be heard in the humor they reported about the famine years. Like a kind of gallows humor, it may have shored up their hope that life would carry on. It shows a nuanced awareness of the contradictions between the expectations of the state upon the citizen versus reality and the painful life-and-death inequalities between people. Humor, like language, is relational. It requires timing, it hinges on contemporary relevance, and it evolves, adapts, and illuminates. It sheds light on how the human imagination works and, more so, the social, collective, and popular imagination. It emerges from real life; therefore, it must have something to tell us about life. It is wedded to notions of power.

North Koreans communicated their experiences and their ideas about events to each other in highly limited and ambiguous ways. Although witnessing the suffering of others is said to have a systematically silencing effect on people, the oral accounts show that the limits of this were breached.[14] The limits placed on the communication of experience, either by the impact of witnessing suffering itself or by the environment of its experience, methods of communicating achieved access to different registers of reality. Evidence of these highly specialized and refined tools of communication appear in the oral accounts. When I asked Jae-young Yoon (45) if he could remember any humor from his days in North Korea during the famine, he first told me he could not remember anything, but then he recalled the Worker's Department Store.

It's many years since I've come over from North Korea. I was in China three years and here [South Korea] quite a few. It's been seven years now. So a lot of the humor we used I've forgotten. A lot of it is gone, and I hate to think about that side, so most of the humor the people used is no longer in my memory.

Like the *paekhwachŭm* [department store]. We called the farmer's market the "Worker's Department Store." The area had a department store, but it was just a shell operating as a store, and if you went inside there wasn't anything you could buy. Of course, there were lovely looking bottles of alcohol, cigarettes, crockery, and clothes on display, but these were only for show, and you certainly couldn't buy them. Laborers and farmers would never have such a fate. The things the farmers and laborers could buy were at the markets, the black markets, that was the only place. So when we talked about the farmer's market we called it the "Worker's Department Store." (Jae-young Yoon, 45)

The humor of this comes across well in Korean since the word *paekhwachŭm* has a rather posh connotation, and the black market Jae-young Yoon refers to was likely a collection of merchants on their haunches, with their wares on a dirt road. The reality and the language used to refer to it highlight the sharp incongruity. The department store was devoid of purchasable goods, and this paradox was highlighted by the juxtaposition with the implicit notion of bounty, or even the possibility to purchase, when attributed to the black market. This shows not only the dry and black humor of North Koreans but also a subtle, evocative criticism of incongruities. The speaker of such humor is saved by the fact that the department store does exist, but the genuine meaning of the phrase is communicated because the interlocutor knows no ordinary person could hope to shop there; rather, they are referring to the market that cannot be named. Jae-young Yoon said this was a common expression, and because they used language that was acceptable to the government, and to anyone else listening, there was little chance that one would get in trouble for the various registers of reality embedded in what they said.

The intellectual contrasts exhibited here recollect the absurdity observed in the acquisition and allotment of food and other items. They not only recollect the absurdity but also describe how the inconsistent promises of the state were observed and discussed. As with the ritualized state discourse, which people used to constitute themselves, these expressions too constituted—identified—people in terms of activities and opinions. Within these evocative transcripts are two messages being carried in what is said: there is the acceptable message of the speaker referring to where he is going and there is the highly unacceptable message highlighting the incongruity between what exists and what is said to exist. Consider the following experience relayed to me by Jae-young Yoon (45) about his experience with famine foods. Again, this was shared as an example of humor.

It was called "substitute food products," so in place of food we had weeds, the leaves of trees, the bark of trees, lots of different things all mixed together, "substitute food products" officially. It was called "substitute food products," but between people when we spoke of it we called it "substitute fuel" . . . coal, gas, diesel . . . use substitute fuel. And when we spoke to each other we'd ask, "Hey, did you use the substitute today?" Oh, it's kind of funny isn't it? Fuel. Fueled machines, like cars, trucks, trains, this kind of thing. It isn't appropriate to use the term for people. We're living creatures, sentient beings, and physical entities, not machines, not equipment. Hmm . . . so, we used that metaphor, but there is no gas in North Korea. So, in the morning you'd go hungry, lunch you'd just skip, and for dinner you'd sleep. So, between those three meals, when would you have time to eat? There wasn't time. In the morning, you were just hungry. For lunch, you'd skip. For dinner, just sleep. So given that, when could you eat? At that time we'd say, "Hey! How did you manage to get by this morning?" That's the kind of way we talked about it. (Jae-young Yoon, 45)

Jae-young Yoon's account is almost nonsensical, particularly in its latter articulations of eating sleep for meals: "In the morning you'd go hungry, lunch you'd just skip, and for dinner you'd sleep. So, between those three meals when would you have time to eat?" The tone of this humor mirrors the ridiculous expectations the state had for the people to get by on so little, like machines without fuel. Jae-young Yoon explained to me that many old automobiles in North Korea, old pick-up trucks from the Soviet era, for instance, were converted to run on wood because of the shortage of gas. Like these machines, the body's digestion system was expected to undergo an equally creative conversion.

By contrast, Jin-sung Jang (33), a member of the elite when he lived in Pyongyang and an official poet of the government, shared the following joke that demonstrates some of the elements of "evocative transcripts." Jin-sung Jang introduced it as a joke common in Pyongyang. Since he shared it with me in casual conversation, the story is paraphrased here.

There was a rich family, and this family owned a dog. The dog would never come when it was called, so the family would give it some chocolate to encourage it to come. Whenever the owners called the dog, they would shout: "Hae-in-ah! Come and eat some chocolate," and the dog would come. Now in this same neighborhood there were lots of hungry kids and these children couldn't even dream of having even the smallest bit of chocolate. There was a poor family whose daughter's name was Hae-in and whenever the rich family called, "Hae-in-ah! Come and eat some chocolate," she would come. Hae-in was always downtrodden when she saw the dog getting the chocolate each time the rich family called her name.

Not able to stand seeing their child so distressed, the poor family paid a visit to the rich family and explained the situation. Mr. Kim Chŭlbim, of the rich family, listened to their story and then explained that their dog had gotten quite used to the name and it would be cruel to change it now. "Why don't you change your daughter's name?" he suggested. Hae-in's parents were enraged, naturally enough, and so they decided to rename their own dog, a mongrel, Kim Chŭlbim. [In Korean a mongrel is literally called a "shit dog" because they are said to eat feces.] Thus, each morning that day forth, the poor family would open the door of their house and holler, "Kim Chŭlbim, eat shit!"

Class stratification, privilege, and cruelty are articulated in this reportedly common Pyongyang joke. As a mode of expression, joking relates to social experience and categories of thought. It is not merely a rhetorical tool to contrast diacritically with seriousness, but rather it is about the full human experience.[15] Some jokes or humorous phrases from North Korea do generate laughter even when translated into English, but this was not always their purpose—hardly so. Often they were functional, permitting people to make connections to otherwise unknown resources or activities such as the black market. Other times, as suggested by the joke about the mongrel, they identify the social value attributed to elements and reveal the arbitrary attribution of value.

However, dynamics were changing in society, and value was an attribution that shifted. This resulted from people acquiring more social capital—for instance, by illegal selling in the markets or capitalizing on their official government positions. "Those who escaped into China and were captured would have to give money to the secret police, under the table. There was talk of that. That kind of talk went around. Then there were factions which were treated very well. They lived in Pyongyang; they had no idea at all that there was a food problem" (Hye-jin Lee, 23). Hye-jin Lee identified how certain sectors of the government, observed in local settings, took advantage of their position. These were known as the "secret police" and the "security police." The former focuses on the country and the later on the border. When I asked Hye-jin Lee whether nutritional discrimination increased during the famine, she explained that access to food related to occupational proximity to the government. "There was an expression to refer to it," she said, and then she shared the rhythmic, almost poetic quote with a laugh: "The secret police eat secretly and the security police just the same; the security police eat securely." Here in the limits of articulation but drawing on the lyrical connections between nouns (security police) and verbs or adverbs (securely), class stratification, political division, and the ability to access food are all linked and summarized.

In the phrase Hye-jin Lee (23) provided, the professional character is used as a means to evoke humor. The secret police and the security police have become so professionalized as to be self-dehumanizing in their greed over others who also need to eat. The repetition of words is significant in and of itself because the professional role and the abuse of power it enables hinge upon the unprofessional morals of the police. The moral elements are drawn out through repetition. Juxtaposition and asymmetry achieve a sophisticated critique of what is without "sense." The security police are secure in their access to food. The secret police eat in secret. The two are responsible for the safety and security of the country, but they only safely secure their own needs.

She did not elaborate the extent to which such an expression was used, but for a woman who was very young at the time of the famine to remember this phrase is an indication that such expressions had significant social currency and lasting power. Her simple phrase reveals the complexity of class division, political stratification, and the allocation of resources along professional lines. These evocative transcripts indicate that some people were not only aware of their circumstances but also aware that articulation of that awareness required clandestine and careful methods. Not only professional discrepancies but also gendered asymmetries of power were observed. Recall that famine exacerbates preexisting social inequalities in society. North Korea, like many other countries, operates on the unofficial and often unpaid economy of women. As the famine years progressed, the strain on women increased. As some families split up, as some men turned to liquor, as the country turned a semiblind eye to women selling in the markets, more and more pressure was placed on women as the sole breadwinners of the families.

Suk-ja Park (84) told me about her clandestine selling in the black market, but at the same time she told me about the gendered division of labor and social changes. "When they used to give the relief tickets, the men would get them and go stand in the line to get the food. But that wasn't happening. The women were in the markets selling. Women knew how to talk to sell the stuff. Women did that. In North Korea there is an expression that men are like daytime light bulbs. In the daytime you have no use for a light bulb do you? So they were daytime light bulbs." Men's role in North Korean society shifted during the famine years.

It is difficult to know how ritualized these kinds of expressions were in North Korea. Could they possibly be isolated expressions? Could I have found the only North Koreans with a sense of humor? Or are these evidence of what Freud identified as brief glimpses of play from the unconscious?[16] I judge them to be evidence of a complex discourse that identified registers of reality exchanged collectively, shared and repeated by different participants in different contexts. Interviewees explained that these were common expressions, and if so there must be a consensus of how they were generally used and viewed, understood and imagined, for the phrases to have currency, impact, and lasting power to pass from speaker to speaker.

On the landscape of words, this social gesture is a hyperarticulation of the otherwise unspeakable, unalterable experiences of life. These expressions identified imbalances of power and the dissatisfaction with existing power structures while living within them. These kinds of expressions carefully identified the paradoxes, absurdity, and discontinuities of life in North Korea, allowing people to have a creative, meaningful life in spaces of safety. By abiding with the limits of ritualized state discourse, the speaker was saved, and this opened the chance for other performative acts that were more expressive. Like survival, language is relational. Contexts shape the articulation of suffering at the time of occurrence and after the fact. People negotiated life with their suffering. The accounts point to a human need, regardless of conditions, to articulate observed incongruities and received confirmation of what is observed. This negotiation of safety within articulation, this maintenance of preexisting relationships with real or potential perpetrators through ambiguous language, is an observed aspect of speech for conflict survivors.[17]

These expressions demonstrate a few clear things: An active participation in ambiguous, rather than direct, forms of articulation that "affords the opportunity for realizing that an accepted pattern has no necessity" and that the "particular ordering of experience may be arbitrary and subjective."[18] Whether hidden, evocative, or ambiguous, the articulation of experience in North Korea is, and was at the time of the famine, precarious indeed. Of course there are plenty of social gatherings in North Korea, and there are clear categories of individual groups, but there is also an enormous elephant in the room: namely, the fear of who might inform on whom; this ensures that self-expression is never complete and the open exchange of ideas and opinions is nonexistent. North Korea's particular brand of Juche socialism resembles other socialisms, but it is unmatched in its degree of social control and longevity. Anyone could be an informer in these gatherings, and any one *is* an informer.

The relative sturdiness of ideology in North Korea encouraged a particular interpretation of things, shaping perception of the famine. The work of Václav Havel, in his analysis of socialist ideological stability in Czechoslovakia, and of Marcelo M. Suarez-Orozco for his analysis of perceptions of events during the Dirty War in Argentina, offer interesting insights to the North Korean case.[19] In "The Power of the Powerless," Havel explains that for ideology to function and ensure the security of the government structure, belief in the ideology is not an essential requirement because, among other reasons, the locus of power and the locus of truth are the same.[20] Ideology does not have to be truth-proof, in other words, in order to operate powerfully because truth is manufactured. There can be disjunction between reality and what the people are told about reality without threatening the government structure or its ideological buffer. Social control is exercised on a life-and-death level on those who attempt to harness power and truth themselves: They are dealt with harshly, if not fatally. North Korea's network of political and reeducation prison camps remind the population of acceptable norms and ensure that counter-ideological speech or actions are controlled before they evolve into something more effective. Such facilities encourage the population, as Havel expresses it, to accept living life within a lie.[21] Encouragements to live within the lie are strong, regularly reinforced, and strengthened by activities that involve large group participation in witnessing the punishment of wrongs such as crop theft committed by others.

In the mid to late 1990s, as North Korea grew increasingly exposed to exchanges with the international community through aid and other activities, scholars and journalists began to question the eventual dissolution of government as a result of this exposure. For example, Shin-Wha Lee argued that North Koreans

> increasingly perceive their regime itself to be the dominant cause of the famine. This change in people's perception appears to arise from increasing contact with the international relief community, as well as from years of an inefficient communist system controlling the economy and agriculture, and enormous military expenditures and the rest of the civilian sector.[22]

However, belief or absence of belief in the system of control is superfluous to its mechanism of operation.[23] North Koreans have explained that although their perception of things shifted, particularly after the death of Kim Il-Sung, they were mostly just trying to get by and live their lives.[24]

We went to the distribution center, and people were having hard times and were hungry, and we heard something from the back, "Kim Jong-Il, so incompetent, taking up the position, killing all people." They say that. When they are by themselves, they say he's incompetent; he's just taking up the position and killing all people. They say that so easily. When we went to the distribution center there were these women gathering around, talking about how life is hard and all that, and they said, "Man this country, hope it goes bust!" They said things like that. But you turn around after saying things like that, how do you know if there are spies among them? So you say, "The U.S. should go bust!" (Jung-ok Choi, 21)

As the distribution of food trickled out, slowed, and eventually stopped, Sun-hi Bak (53) explained that some people still did not complain.

North Koreans have a strong sense of pride. So even if they are really hungry, they wouldn't show. But what is the problem? They are only hungry because there's no distribution. Due to their pride issues, they don't say stuff like, "How come there are no distributions anymore?" or "I can't live because there's no distributions and I'm starving!" but say, "Why did the distribution stop?" There were food distributions for half a month, but because of the lack of food, for the next 15 days of the month, they would take out 5 days' worth of food and only give out 10 days' worth of food. Then there are people that say, "The distribution that was given every 15 days is now shortened. What am I going to eat for 5 days?" Little kids didn't know the situation so they would complain to their parents. But older kids couldn't really complain since they would be taken away for complaining. Still, people who are close to each other would nag about it. I don't know about the situation after we left, but when we were still in North Korea, we couldn't speak up about the situation, but only talk amongst ourselves saying, "How are we going to live if the distribution stops?" I guess there were people that got taken away because they were too rude when they are talking about the food distribution issues. (Sun-hi Bak, 53)

What is the internal result on people who live with an awareness of incongruities between their reality and what their government tells them to perceive? Suarez-Orozco calls the result of living under such conditions "percepticide."[25] Hye-jin Lee (23) expressed a determination to survive that was kept personal to her. It is not possible to know how many other North Koreans spoke to themselves in the way that Hye-jin Lee describes. Is this a characteristic of border crossers and defectors, or is it also common to those who stay? "No, just to myself, I spoke to myself that way. I would work hard at the farming, and in the future I would sell in the market, and I would throw off the famine, throw off the poverty. I had those kinds of thoughts all the time" (Hye-jin Lee, 23). This was her way of encouraging herself to work harder and look forward to the future. Censorship, already a fixed aspect of communication in North Korea, ensured that discussion of the famine, hunger, and any direct criticism of food resources were implicitly understood as forbidden. State media helped the process along by framing discussions of the famine according to proscribed language. Hye-jin Lee explained,

> They did not use the expression "Famine" nor did they use the expression "hunger"; rather, they used the term *shingnyang t'agyŭk*, food ration downturn. Starvation [*kum jurim*] was a term we really didn't use. I had been taught that starvation was happening to the beggars in South Korea, and in that instance we used the term a lot. But for the situation we were going through with the food, we didn't use that term.

These twists of phrase were the earliest coping strategies of the government. Through linguistic controls, an imaginary relationship to the real was maintained. The terminology used to express the situation needed to be inaccurate—it needed to transpose the imaginary onto the real. Accurate articulation of lived experience dissolved this imaginary; those who articulated lived experience accurately were disappeared. The built structure of ideology required constant maintenance under conditions that tested its declarations; without this maintenance the structure would crumble.

Omitting the words "hunger," "famine," and "starvation" from spoken vocabulary during the famine and using instead "pain," "illness," and "food poisoning" were substitutions that mirrored other inadequate substitutions during the famine years. Yet, to say one was "dying of starvation" could prove more life-threatening than starvation itself. The skill of knowing what not to know in such circumstances can be a lifesaving coping mechanism.[26] The oral accounts demonstrate the skill of perceiving registers of reality in which they lived.

People referred to the famine period as the March of Suffering, a term with such currency and lasting power that if I used the Korean word for famine (*kigŭn, kia*), it was either not understood—the word was originally Chinese—or it was understood and the "famine" being spoken of was regarded as another topic entirely, as something that happens elsewhere. The term "food problem" (*shingnyang much'e*) was uncomplicated and used commonly in discussions about the March of Suffering (*Konanŭi haenggun*). This same term was used to refer to the liberation of Korea from Japanese colonialism, a point that was explained to me repeatedly by interviewees. The war metaphor is linked within this term to Kim Il-Sung's 1938 defeat of Japanese imperialism.[27] Linguistic terms are not incidental or arbitrary, in spite of how incongruous they may in fact be. North Korea was engaging with the famine, on some level, as if it were war and thus deserving of collective war-stance rhetoric and ideology, and a fight to the death. These historical ties reaffirm the term's militaristic and war connotation. Famine theorists have elsewhere noted the connections between time, place, and the names given to food shortage periods, noting the political motivation behind the labels given to those histories.[28] This metaphorical description can effect overall perception of the ongoing process of the famine as well as public reaction to the famine and how it would be spoken about after the fact.

Verification of information in North Korea was and still is extremely difficult; ambiguous communication provided a means by which to safely test and achieve some verification for one's perceptions. However, there was a context provided to the population by which to understand the famine. Culture can provide a "protective shield" through religion or "local cosmologies" by which to understand suffering, and from this will emerge appropriate ways of dealing with suffering that are locally embedded and reflect the moral fabric of the cultural influence.[29] Euphemism is a means by which reality is hidden or erased.[30] The euphemizing of famine history is nothing new. In China, what we know of as the Great Leap Famine (1959–1962) was officially called the "three-year natural calamity."[31] Likewise, the use of historical references to name the 1990s famine in North Korea was not incidental; for instance, in October 1997, as winter came, it was called the "Arduous March" and by the new year it became the "Forced March to Final Victory."[32] Although these terms might not be euphemistic, they were still a means by which to hide reality and rebrand the famine. Dr. Vollertsen, a doctor formerly working with Doctors Without Borders, told me that he saw death reports that recorded cause of death as food poisoning when in fact it was starvation or malnutrition.[33] I asked Hyun-woo Kim (42) what he thought of this, and he reported the same thing: "Yes, they wrote that the person had died of food poisoning, that's right. It was a lie, but that's how they wrote on the death certificates." This indicates a dominant discourse in North Korea that occludes the expression of observed incongruities between surrounding conditions in the community and the dominant discourse. As Nancy Scheper-Hughes observed of Brazil, the same might be said of North Korea: The transition from a popular discourse on hunger to one of sickness is subtle but essential to the perception of the body and its needs, essential to the perception of the state and its needs. A hungry body needs food. A hungry body exists as a potent critique of the society in which it exists. A sick body implicates no one.[34] "Sickness" is also idiosyncratic to the person; "famine" is systemic. Articulation of hunger as pain or illness demonstrated that an individual was keeping within the established discourse available for speaking about the famine. It also keeps within the expressed mentality established by the war metaphor: When fighting a battle, the soldier may experience pain, infection, or disease, but hunger is a condition that does not make sense. Hunger would rather indicate his softness and personal vulnerability. This is the way it was done in North Korea. To talk about the busy years, an element of performance was required. The voice could be used to share one's thought life, accordingly scripted. Isn't this a sure sign, then, that North Koreans are coerced or duped into a false consciousness? The "truth" of this is impossible to determine. Like anything, I am sure that some feel coerced, others duped, but also—as Havel mentioned of his years in Czechoslovakia—one had to get along in life. As Jae-young Yoon (45) explained it, "That's just the way we lived."

4

LIFE LEAVES DEATH BEHIND

With the floods of 1995, the famine grew increasingly deadly. For-merly, famine dead had appeared in the northern cities of Cheongjin and Musan, for instance, but now they were in Pyongyang. Whereas formerly select social groups such as the old and the infirm died from hunger, now average sections of the population became vulnerable to starvation death, sometimes whole families. These realities were im-possible to overlook or ignore as they might have been in the past.

People knew there were starvation deaths but acted as if they didn't know. In places like North Hamgyong Province, Ryang-gang, in those areas, they put the worst people; by that I mean they put people who were considered to be against the govern-ment, and there wasn't a small number who were against the gov-ernment. As you know, you could shoot them dead if they didn't support the government. [There,] Kim Jong-Il knew they were starving to death but just quietly let them slip away. So long as the military and the people of Pyongyang could live, that was enough. (Sun-ja Om, 67)

In the late 1990s in Pyongyang, interviewees reported seeing bod-ies. As the famine worsened with the floods and failed crops of 1995, the effect was felt in formerly untouched parts of the country.

In 1997, when I was living in Pyongyang, I was leaving the house for work one morning and there in the front entrance of the building was a woman and a child, dead from hunger. It was morning. It was December. Seven o'clock in the morning. When I went out it was bitterly cold. Everything was fully frozen. . . . So I went back into the house and phoned what we call the district administration office, "Ah! here . . ." I gave them my address and said that on the first floor at the entrance there were two people who had frozen to death, and would they come and take care of them. I said that. And then, "Alright," they said, and put the phone down as if it were of little importance. But I was thinking two people are dead, and how could they just be careless like that, so I phoned them back. "Yeah, a comrade has died, how can you just reply like that?" Then he said, "Sir, who are you?" "I'm the one responsible for the area," I said, to which he replied, "We've got lots of dead people. So far this morning we have dozens of people who have died. You've called us, but we have many places to go to collect the bodies. We will come and collect them." So then, "Ah! So a lot of people are dying." Then I knew. Our area was an upper-class neighborhood, so I hadn't any idea there were that many dying. So, then I went to work at the Northwest office, "Ah, this morning I came out of the house and found some mother and her child frozen to death outside!" And they replied, "You're just starting to notice that now? Outside of the Unification office we have been seeing dozens dead every day." Ah! And then I knew. I had been abroad and had friends who helped me with money, so I could live without worry over eating. So, because of that, I hadn't any idea. So, through the policy of the government these numbers of people were dying of starvation. (Dong-hyun Lee, 54)

In this account, death could be openly discussed, so long as the cause of death, starvation, was not identified. This pattern is emblematic across the interviews. Dong-hyun Lee begins this portion of his interview by telling me unambiguously that the mother and child had

died from hunger. Then he describes the scene, focusing on the extreme cold. He uses direct quotations (reported speech), to describe
his phone call with the local authorities in which he explains that the
two had frozen to death. The phrasing ensures no one is implicated in
their death, whether state or individual. Hunger or starvation death
was not possible in the sociopolitical context of North Korea, so it was
articulated as death by freezing. At the local government office, Dong-
hyun Lee's interlocutors are similarly engaged in an act of obliteration,
not over the fact of multiple deaths in the city that morning ("We've
got lots of dead people. So far this morning we have dozens of people
who have died" and "You're just starting to notice that now? Outside
of the Unification office we have been seeing dozens dead every day")
but rather in the meaning ascribed to the deaths ("two people who had
frozen to death and we have many places to go to collect the bodies.
We will come and collect them.") The facts behind their deaths—that
they were starving and thus more vulnerable to freezing to death, the
aggregate of bodies at specific locales—get muddled and instead the
cause is attributed to cold rather than government negligence.[1]

Coded communication could be exchanged with great care. The
articulation of experience was restricted, and this likely influenced the
recollection of things after the fact. Coded ways of speaking while in
North Korea continued to appear in interviews, making complex and
almost indecipherable the meaning attributed to survival in North
Korea. As observed, accurate expressions could spark disapproval or
violence; thus, ambiguous expressions were necessary to maintain
safety. The following account from Hyun-woo Kim (42) demonstrates
how the safety net of indirect and ambiguous speech can continue to
obfuscate, confuse, and baffle the listener beyond its original context.

Hyun-woo Kim shares his metaphorical reference to a body destroyed by frostbite to explain the famine. He describes the whole
famine landscape through the metaphor of an individual bodily experience. He switches into this metaphoric description easily and sus-
tains it until the end of his explanation of the famine. Echoing an

observation of Elinor Ochs, the events are narrated to convey that the antecedent event (chilblains) gave rise to the occurrence of the subsequent event (death).[2] The prevalence of this conversion from hunger to cold (or pain), from starvation death to freezing death, repeats throughout the oral accounts across the spectrum of survivors I interviewed. Connections between cold weather, dropping body temperature, and hunger are invariably intertwined at latitudes such as North Korea's. Famines kill principally through making a population nutritionally deficient enough to then become vulnerable to disease, illness, and inclement weather. People perish more quickly through these than through starvation alone. But were it not for starvation, the vulnerability of freezing to death would not arise.

When a person is cold, the freezing starts at the end of their fingers and then their feet freeze, later it comes to about here [points to mid-chest]. Why? They are far from the heart, the heart is far away so the blood that comes out at first is hot, but it cools as it goes out. It gets colder. So the fingers freeze. In North Korea, likewise, we call Pyongyang the heart. Near to Pyongyang they are giving out the food relief [the government's Public Distribution System—PDS]. Then, further away at the tips of the fingers far away in North Hamgyong region, Yangkang region, and so on, from 1991, 1992, they weren't giving PDS. Then by February of 1996, little by little, they weren't even able to give out any PDS in Pyongyang, the blood was starting to freeze; by about February 1996 the relief had stopped even as far as Pyongyang. So if you think of it as a person, if they are frozen up to here, to the heart, then they are going to die. Then at that time the warehouses were nearly run empty and Kim Jong-Il took a countermeasure against it. From that time on, Kim Jong-Il was telling the population, "Yeah, because of our natural enemy, the bastard Americans, we are unable to farm and so there is no food, so it is difficult to give the PDS." (Hyun-woo Kim, 42)

Hyun-woo Kim's account mirrors nationalist discourse about how the famine is best understood and interpreted: as one national body suffering in concert. The progression of the famine in North Korea is depicted through the metaphor of a body (the nation) gradually overtaken by chilblains (the famine), where only the heart (Pyongyang) is scarcely saved (to save the whole, as a consequence, unnecessary extremities must be sacrificed). On one level we have the associated articulation of the national experience of suffering. On the other we have the articulation of an individual experience of suffering. Both of these pain expressions are separate from starvation experience; instead chilblains is selected as a metaphorical carrier, perhaps because it provides the handy convenience of drawing a relatively clear image of gradual, inevitable, and fatal exposure to "the elements." The propensity for the idea that the scientific/biological are inevitable finds itself a place in the history, policies, and leaders of communism, and in the supposed inevitability of communism itself.[3] The experience of the individual in starvation is extracted from this metaphor; reference to the famine appears in the form of cessation of food ration delivery, and then it is draped in the metaphor of blood flowing from the heart. It might not be possible, from this metaphor, to say that the famine was a shared experience since the notion of the inevitable and wholesale loss of nonvital parts is explained as a biological, scientific, and therefore logical process.[4] Countermeasures against the food shortage were to shape the perceived source of the problem, reinforcing interpretations of the suffering as inevitable. If we take Hyun-woo Kim's metaphor to its ultimate end, the treatment for most severe chilblains would indeed be to cut off the affected areas so infection does not set in and destroy the entire body. A partial death is unfortunate— it is complicated, there are inconveniences, one ought to have taken precautions in the first place, and so on—but it is preferable to total death. The causes of famine (nature and external forces) and the inevitable survival methods (sacrifice of nonessential parts for the good of the whole) were rationalized and understood through roughly this type of narrative structure. This type of narrative always ends in the same way. Under threat of total death, parts have to be sacrificed. In times of war, or war-readiness, North Korea evoked such economics of survival and justified its rationality.

The analogy of chilblains only appeared in my interview with Hyun-woo Kim. Although he takes the story to a pitch unprecedented among my interviewees, it is consistent with the general theme I found in the accounts, namely, in the abstraction of cause and effect for the famine. Hyun-woo Kim's account does not offer the self-awareness seen in other interviews where speakers revealed their knowledge of incongruities in lived experience. This may be due to his being a resident of Pyongyang where there was, indeed, a more palatable reality well into the 1990s while the rest of the country suffered severely. Hyun-woo Kim was also a former government figure who sought asylum while abroad.

The ideological apparatus of North Korea maintains a rather liberal relationship between language, meaning, and truth.[5] It should naturally follow that similar types of communication appear in the language of those who lived within such ideology. Intentionally or otherwise, Hyun-woo Kim's metaphor communicates the government mentality that pervaded the sociopolitical space: it explains government inaction and the countless lives lost as the result of a scientific, organic failure. Given how far the metaphor moves from the subjective experience of starvation, it is interesting that the body is mentioned at all. But the body was essential. The means by which North Korea attempted to manage the famine manifested itself most clearly in how it managed the bodies of its population: how they farmed, where they farmed; the food and nonfood they ate; where they lived, migrated; how they spoke, what words they used to speak. Furthermore, the use of human anatomy to explain political structures, in particular the Juche idea, is standard in North Korea.[6] The people (the bones and muscles of this metaphoric national body) execute the orders given down by the nervous system (the Party) and the brain (the Great Leader).[7] When the body appears in metaphoric articulations of the famine, particularly in ways of managing the famine, it is not unusual for it to appear the way it does. The control of people through the control of the body is central in North Korea. Bodies passing in and out of the country; the control of verbal communication between bodies; the control of criminal bodies in prisons and reeducation facilities; the displayed execution of bodies as a means to teach criminal wrongs, where bullets are shot into bodies; the tying of gags, the filling of mouths with stones—all of these are regulated and the details intentional and sociopolitically significant. Types of violence are rooted in a "pattern and ideology of behavior," and memories from the famine reveal the enduring structures of violence that justified suffering.[8] The fact that Hyun-woo Kim chose to speak about the nation undergoing famine as a body experiencing extensive, agonizing suffering is not incidental. The kinds of narratives that were available to people for making sense of their experiences characterizes the culture of North Korea.[9]

Given that the voice, embodied but invisible, can perform acts in the world, it is worth examining how distinctly silent yet unmistakably communicative the corporal is in North Korea. The body cannot keep its promise of loyalty. Although there are efforts to maintain loyalty through speech, the body is vulnerable to complete betrayal of the state because it requires more than ideological nourishment. This complexity was eloquently observed by a survivor of China's Great Leap Famine, Zhang (1994), when he said, "To be hungry was counter-revolutionary";[10] similarly, Jin-sung Jang (33), a North Korean poet, wrote, when in the South, "our very lives were illegal." The body, to ensure its survival and continued service to the state, requires something from the state. This places the body in a precarious position vis-a-vis a state that expects its citizens to get by on next to nothing. This was taken to a scientific level when the government began producing ersatz food, a practice that continues. The BBC reported that North Korea developed a "special noodle" that keeps one feeling full longer.[11] Use of ersatz food is common in socialist systems.[12] It is a feature of the shortage phenomena of classical socialist economies and is emblematic of the nation's desire for a citizenry who requires next to nothing for survival.[13]

The treatment of bodies, dead or living, bore significance. Treacherous bodies, those who betrayed the state through defection, theft, and other criminal activity, were similarly marked. An elaborate message is communicated through the punishment of bodies. While the animate cannot speak openly without considerable wordplay, the inanimate does. In this atmosphere of speech registers, the body is brought all the more fully into communication. The most spectacular example of this can be seen in public executions, where the criminal body and its method of killing are staged for the education of an amassed audience. The previously mentioned poet, Jin-sung Jang (33), a graduate of Kim Il-Sung University, lived in Pyongyang and worked as an official poet to the Party. He continued to write after arriving in Seoul. The precipitating factors that led to his departure from the North are detailed in his memoir, *Dear Leader: Poet, Spy, Escapee*. It is possible to infer that driving around the country, a detail that is prefaced in his poetry, afforded him the dubious privilege of observing harder lives. Strictly speaking, Jin-sung Jang did not suffer starvation, but he was a witness to the famine and the government response to the changes taking place in the country. In his poem "The Notices," the poet highlights the connections between famine, violence, Kim Jong-Il, and language. The notices he refers to are posters pasted up around the country informing citizens that crop theft was a state crime met with capital punishment. The poem begins by describing the roads and alleyways as inundated with these posters, threatening the people with their very presence. The poem anthropomorphizes bullets that speak, and turns the citizens into objects that neither speak nor breathe: "Bullets hurl words in these times. / Though you are hungry, 'I am hungry' are words citizens cannot say." By the close of the poem, the scene of a public execution is implied. As the executioners aim and shoot, the bullets give the final notice "in three syllables" that shout from gun barrels: "Kim Jong-Il." Each bullet punctuates a syllable of his name.

Jin-sung Jang's poem links the omnipresence of social control with the notices placed around town. The atmosphere cannot be misinterpreted: Day and night the potential for punishment is ever present and inevitable. Both action and deed are regulated. The end of the poem reveals the mimesis of North Korean life, where bullets hurl the words that citizens cannot. While citizens must hold their breath, hold the bomb that is the heart, the ultimate act of violence in the form of public execution speaks in place of the victim and citizen. "Bullets hurl words in these times," he writes. The only word they speak is three syllables: Kim Jong-Il. Just as the mass graves of victims can point to the crimes committed against them, and possibly to the criminals, likewise the violence that is perpetrated against the body simultaneously claims and unites the victim and perpetrator: *bullets hurl words in these times*. But what is being said, and how is it interpreted? Are we intellectually and emotionally cut off from this wordless, purely corporal and terrifying discourse? My interview with Hye-jin Lee (23) answers this question.

Hye-jin Lee reported witnessing a public execution at a young age. She saw two men executed for crimes that were famine related but were deemed economic crimes by the state. The point I wish to highlight here concerns the messages communicated through the public execution. Her narrative is provided here at length.

Because of the famine, people were doing all kinds of bad things—how couldn't they? For instance, there were the farmers. They were having a hard time getting by with nothing to eat. So there was this threshing floor. . . . Well, I saw this wretched thing. These guys were put to death for what they did.

This kind of thing happened. As you know, North Korea is a country devoid of human rights. So, if one person dies, it's not a big deal. So, in North Korea they have a lot of shootings. I saw a public execution once.

The execution took place in Onsŏng. Onsŏng is a prairie area. From my house to Onsŏng was about an hour-and-a-half's walk. Many people had come. My parents, my siblings, we weren't allowed to not witness the shooting. I was just entering high school at that time. I had not seen a public execution until that time.

I was at school, suddenly we were all gathered into the outdoor gymnasium and the lead teacher spoke to us. We were all gathered in the gymnasium and told. . . . There were two high schools, we were joined together, and there were six years' worth of students there all together from each school. We were all brought together. In that area just outside the mines, they have the coal . . . well, they have that stuff, not coal but the stuff left behind that they cannot use. That's there like a mountain; we were all taken to that place. The students were all put at the front. So we are at that mountain-like thing. On one side we have the rice paddies, on the other side it's just flat, and up ahead the mound is high . . . so it was there they put the tree trunks into the mound. Right in front the students were stood, and then behind that the people from the village were brought to watch. They brought the students to see the public execution.

So that is how I saw my first public execution. Two brothers. They had worked in the mines. There were two others who were farmers. Those two who had worked in the mines, and they had taken bundles of the electrical wires that were used in the mines and brought them to sell in Sinuiju and other places to make some money. These two brothers had been caught on their way to sell the bundles of wires. So for that, they were receiving public execution. As for the other ones, the farmers, they had taken from the threshing floor. Corn, rice, and that sort of thing was piled high. They had taken some of this. Well, they hadn't taken a small amount. It seemed as though they had taken a large amount. They had taken it in order to survive. Four of them, they were maybe aged thirty, or maybe from their mid-twenties. Then the safety police came out and shot them. Twelve came out. To each person, there were three. . . . Each man got three men to shoot at him, three times each. So each man got nine bullets put in him. They came out quietly, and quietly like pow, pow, pow, they shot the men. These guys who shoot, they just do the shooting. They come in a private car and they go in the private car. Well, if the family or friends of those being shot knew who they were or could remember their faces they would retaliate, same with the safety police.

They put the bodies into the car; they didn't even give them to the families. That type of sack you see being used on the road, the hay sack. They put a few bodies in each sack. How inhumane. The two had damaged the county's collective property, the brothers who took the electrical wires. When I saw [the execution] I got quite a shock. The people needed something to eat, but there was nothing like a proper economy. People weren't stealing anything. They knew that stealing was a bad thing to do. Though they knew this, sitting indoors and starving to death, eating only a little and starving to death . . . kap'sŭn katchanayo [isn't the price the same]? Escaping into China had the very same price. If you stay, you die. If you go, you die. The dying was all the same, right? So you had to make a venture, hazard something. All of us, because of the famine, we all had to hazard something. So they brought the students up front to see the example they were making of those men. "If you do as they did, you'll be killed like this." That's what they wanted to show us. (Hye-jin Lee, 23)

The brothers had stolen electric wire that they intended to sell to get enough money to buy food in the market. She identifies feeling shock at witnessing the execution, and later she explains that they wanted to show what would happen if you commit such crimes, how such acts and their punishment should be understood. The sociopolitical value ascribed to ideology will play an influential role in the types of death meted out to a population and will simultaneously proscribe the appropriate response to witnessing such deaths. However, the bodies of these brothers were brought into an unmistakable discourse with Hye-jin Lee (23) wherein the message was not simply: "If you do as they did, you'll be killed like this." Instead, the message was also about the limits of the body and the limits of death. To paraphrase: If you stay, you die. If you go, you die. The dying was all the same. They had to hazard something. This opened the spectrum of choices such

that the vulnerability of the body interpolated a sense of freedom because of its vulnerability.

Interviewees reported witnessing public executions for what could
be called famine crimes, such as the theft of grain or saleable goods.
Since these were seen as capital offences, the punishment was death,
and public execution was being used for crimes not listed in the North
Korean penal code. According to a 2006 white paper report by the
Korea Institute for National Unification, up until 1996 there were
posters announcing that theft of grain was punishable by execution.[14]
In a speech given by Kim Jong-Il at Kim Il-Sung University in 1996,
he stated that farmers had been stealing grain. That same year the
government arranged for the army to guard the fields against theft
from the starving population.[15] The famine was taking shape, and as
the worst years took hold, the government applied social control at
its most extreme level—that of life and death—for famine coping
strategies.

When we consider contemporary famines that emerge within complex sociopolitical dynamics, the issue of what constitutes a famine
death can be complicated. Famine deaths demonstrate that human
rights violations are always plural phenomena. The response to famine
coping strategies was extreme and often fatal violence by people acting on behalf of the government. The legal strategies available to the
population for survival were so limited that virtually the only way to
survive within the prescribed methods was to require no food for sus-
tenance at all, to be a biological anomaly. Thus, the increased hardships
of life expanded within the restrictive prescribed methods of coping,
but thresholds were reached and people began trying other means to
survive. The behavior of individuals and communities can indicate
the extent of hardship in a particular region, where such behavior can
lead to increased likelihood of death through accident. Deaths were
not accidental but deliberate, since they took the form of punishment
for crimes. Many of my interviewees witnessed public executions that
were punishments for crimes against the motherland (theft, for instance). The majority of these crimes could be classified as nonlegal

entitlement efforts, famine coping strategies. Theft of food, stealing of goods for sale, and discussing the food situation were all methods of coping or finding methods to cope, and they were dealt with harshly.

Men and women were publicly executed for crimes that were in fact famine crimes—and the punishment of these individuals took the form of a public spectacle as an example of how such unacceptable behavior would be treated. However, the way that this violence was carried out suggests that there was another message aimed at regulating the individual's relationship to herself. It was not enough for the criminals to be killed, they had to be killed and mutilated in the killing, in a particular way.[16] Dozens of interviewees reported that criminals had their heads completely shot off, describing in detail the clouds of air that rose from the hot blood into the cold winter air. When I asked why the entire head was blown off, I was told it was because the criminal's thinking was wrong: the criminal was thinking like a capitalist. It is not coincidental that the characteristics of this violence echo the sociopolitical values of North Korea; in fact they not only echo these values but reinforce them at the level of life and death.

Crimes related to famine increased. Criminals were caught and punishments enacted. The punishments were intended to instruct citizens on correct ways of behaving that did not undermine socialist ideals of community, equality, and selflessness. Sang-chul Lee (67) explained:

Woman, man, either could die. So long as there was a body for the bullet to go in to. "Shoot the head! Drive that bullet into the head!" [Mimicking the executioner's voice.] Because their thinking was wrong it had to be driven out, so they got nine bullets in the head. Nine bullets. In the head. When they did that, whether it was a woman, whether it was a man, the head would be totally gone.

These individuals were publicly executed for stealing corn from a field. Hunger that started in the body and threatened life is in fact a problem of the mind if it leads to coping strategies deemed criminal. The government controls the population through punishments against bodies. When the traumatic experience is bodily, memory is often held in both the body and the mind. Seeing others experience physical pain had the potential to affect a kind of shadow experience of pain for witnesses. Violence inflicted on the bodies of others sends messages to those who witness it, and what is left behind in the form of wounds, scars, and disabilities are both evidence and message. As Broch-Due explains, violence is not enough; mutilations are also necessary, perhaps because they are carried into other social spheres where they can reverberate carrying messages to others.[17] The public execution is a reverberating spectacle that most North Koreans have witnessed.

Physical and structural violence in North Korea is interrelated. The body was physically punished. Control of speech enabled a further level of invisible punishment—control through restricting individual articulation of the experience of hunger, for instance. There are cultural elements to the forms of torture or punishment in different societies that can be influenced by tradition, religion, or style of government.[18] Some scholars caution the application of notions of culture to situations of extreme violence, terror, and uncertainty.[19] I suggest that tendencies exist within all cultures that influence the direction of and preference for some types of violence over others. Punishment is intended to provoke and encourage normalization that is culturally described. Therefore, punishment is meaningful in the messages it carries to witnesses. There are also culturally specific tendencies in selecting the targets of punishment and the way that punishment is performed. Punishment is often shame based; although shame is a concept that differs across cultures, forms of shaming are often richly culturally bound. Thus, some anthropologists have referred to "cultures of violence," "a grammar of terror," "terror as usual," or "cultures of fear."[20] Gendered violence emerging in times of war, for example, is not a social anomaly unheard of in times of peace but rather a continuation in larger and more abundant scale of the smaller form of the same kind of violence in times of peace.[21] In short, violence is not a rootless act. In the same way that an emergency—that which "involves human suffering and includes violent disruptions of ways of life causing hunger and death"—is not something beyond the norm but an "accelerated and traumatic manifestation of social and economic change," so too violence is the manifestation of preexisting values at heightened and extreme expression.[22]

Most violence is not without "reason." Institutionalized punishment has a rationality that can be seen through its aims.[23] These aims center on division and unification of identities operating through a "grotesque cultural logic" where identities are constituted through the exclusion of others such as criminals.[24] Preexisting cultural models of appropriateness influence the way a community or an individual copes with violence. Violence has immediacy to it, but this proximity does not reveal the systems of power that deliver and create violence. The target of violence is often not the "chief enemy" but rather those objects that are nearest.[25] Likewise, that which delivers the violence is abstracted from the sociopolitical mechanism that created it. There is also, inevitably, the invisible level on which power operates and hides. Nordstrom and Martin conclude that systems of violence are "no less powerful by virtue of their intangibility."[26] For instance, symbolic violence is important in structuring and ordering relations of domination and subordination because it demonstrates the template by which violence in times of stress may be meted out. When individuals are publicly executed in North Korea, their mouths are gagged—an example of symbolic violence. Whether or not the "criminal" would speak without the gag is irrelevant because there is always a gag. Its symbol conveys the ultimate structure of power, which silences eternally.

Chun-ho Choi (43) became estranged from a friend of his. After seven months had passed, the friend's wife came to Chun-ho Choi's house in tears, saying her husband had been caught for robbery. "I asked her what he had been arrested for, and she said that at night he struck someone with a club as the person cycled by to snatch the bicycle and sell it. 'Can you save him?' she asked. My eyes grew cloudy. How little I had known. The friend whom I had believed in could do nothing but that. . . . And me with my healthy frame" (Chun-ho Choi, 43). His friend was publicly executed for his crime. "This is how things are done only in North Korea," Chun-ho Choi explained, "It is criminal punishment by example."

In North Korea, coping strategies led famine victims ever closer to increased violations of their human rights because of the tight restrictions on social control and the need to set examples on correct behavior.

In North Korea the pigs are kept in an individual's house. That is how they are raised. Then there were some men who didn't have any land who traveled miles at night to steal a pig from a man's house. They went into the house and stole the pig. That kind of thing, whether it was a dog or a pig, it was taken and eaten. They couldn't have done it alone, so there were a few who did it. Those men were publicly executed for that. At that time they did the public executions outside, they publicized the day, time, and place. "There will be the public execution of so-and-so, for such-and-such" and they made sure everyone came. It was in Hyesan. Attendance was mandatory. I was the representative of our area at that time, I had to go around to people's houses and bring them to watch the execution. We all gathered at the bottom of the mountain. Three men were tied to wooden pillars. They read out what crimes the men were guilty of . . . so-and-so did this, so-and-so did that, they were explaining the crimes, but it wasn't the truth at all. They were saying that one of the men had stolen many pigs, that that was his crime. Another had stolen a cow, which as you know in North Korea is used for farming. . . . And to stop any of them for speaking out against what they were accused of their mouths were gagged. They were each shot three times [she indicates the head, heart, and stomach]. (Sun-hi Bak, 53)

Their crimes were read out, but Sun-hi Bak explains that she believes they were not true. The convicted had their mouths gagged to ensure they could not, if they would, speak out. However, the message carried in the act of killing these men publicly and brutally, and pinning these crimes to their deaths, is clear. There might have been some in that community who had thoughts of stealing in order to make ends meet. Sun-hi Bak's (53) testimony shows that agentive resistance to the famine in terms of coping strategies that could have assured survival was dealt with at the most extreme level of social control—namely, that of life and death.

There were some people who went to the mountains secretly and planted corn. "Some people tried to hide the food, but if caught you would be punished," Chung-su Om (69) said. I asked how he knew that people were punished for hiding food. He replied that they had seen those people who had stolen food receive their punishment. "It was unspeakable," he said. Then he added, "Theft of food is an economic crime, and for that you could get one or two years in prison." The coping strategies that were deemed a crime against the state were dealt with harshly. Chung-su Om (69) once worked for the North Korean military in the arsenals division. He shared the following story.

There were some people who were so hungry they had taken some sprouts. They had taken them from the field to eat. They had hidden them in their shirts. They headed out of the fields like that, and they were shot. They were so hungry, there was nothing else for them to do, so they went and took those sprouts to eat and on their way out the military shot them. Two lives were exchanged for two potato sprouts. They were killed for two potatoes. I crossed after I saw that. Shot for being so hungry. The field was defended by the military. It was a potato field, a corn field, and a bean field. There was a fleet of military defending it is what I'm saying. Now, why would that be the case? We are hungry again and again, so again and again we will try and steal to eat, and if you steal from that you will most certainly be killed. You will absolutely be killed.

Chung-su Om identified the spectacle of two people getting shot for stealing two potato sprouts as the moment when he decided to leave. He knew the hunger would continue and with it the killing. This calculus is what brought many of my interviewees to the final decision to cross the border into China. The cost of staying was weighed against the attempt to depart.

5

BREAKING POINTS

"That person who defects has reached the point where their very existence is dead . . . by the time they arrive at that point to put their decision into practice," Jae-young Yoon (45) explained; to make the decision to defect, one had to already be dead in a sense. The people who shared their stories with me are exceptional in the sense that they represent a tiny minority of people who have left North Korea. Regardless of the varied factors that precipitated their departures, the mere fact of their crossing into China places them in an infinitesimal class of people in relation to the rest of the population of North Korea, the vast majority of which remains and possibly will never contemplate leaving. Just looking at the numbers, choosing to leave for any reason is an exceptional act. The estimated 26,124 North Koreans now in South Korea are exceptional, adept, and lucky, which does not exclude those who remain in the North from these same characteristics.[1] In the history of the divided peninsula, the total number of defections has never been so high. However, if we consider that the population of North Korea is about 24 million, then the number of defections to South Korea and further afield is minuscule.[2] Although defection is on the rise, particularly since the famine, the majority of people stay put.

In defecting, the risk to life is great. Travel into China without a legal permit is deemed punishable by up to five years of labor reform under Article 233 of North Korea's Criminal Code, and deemed an act of treason against the nation under Article 62 of the Criminal Code; however, former North Korean officials report the existence of a shoot-to-kill policy that dates back to the early 1990s.[3] China classifies North Korean migrants as illegal and economic, not as refugees. As such they are not provided legal channels to access refugee status. Getting through China and other countries to South Korea or elsewhere means risking everything. Even before the act of crossing from North Korea into China, the most typical route of defection, an exceptional decision has to be made. This chapter explores the resistance to this ultimate decision in the oral accounts of interviewees, and the threshold of physical and mental suffering at which it is made. The argument here is that defection was an option for an exceptional minority, but increased thresholds of suffering led to intranational choices for many others. I caution against the interpretation that increased suffering—albeit a measure not strictly or universally quantifiable—will lead inevitably to increased likelihood of defection. From this cautionary observation another follows. We cannot assume that those who defect are necessarily those who were worse off.

Could the vast majority of North Koreans have stayed because they are under duress? We may be quick to guess that people stayed for reasons of social pressure, coercion, or threats of violence and imprisonment, but the oral accounts suggest that the decision to remain inside North Korea is informed by more complex, nuanced factors. Some cannot leave because of geographic restrictions in areas that are so mountainous, remote, or isolated that they cannot safely depart. Others believe their country is the best place to live and do not want to leave. Even among my interviewees, a majority expressed a longing attachment to home, often because they missed family, friends, and community. Some missed what they called the purity of the North, attributed both to the landscape and the character of the people. The decision to cross the border, even if initially a temporary reprieve for present difficulties, was not a decision made easily. The practical difficulties of crossing had given pause, as had the web of social attachments.

Why did some people stay rather than leave? This may seem like an unusual question to ask, particularly if we perceive the North as a totally inhospitable country or a veritable prison camp where people are desperate to escape, but the vast majority of people remain despite the difficulties. It is important to acknowledge that although the number of people choosing to migrate out increased during the famine, the majority stayed.

Interviewees identified border crossing, along with returning home, as a means of ensuring their livelihoods in the North. North Koreans were reluctant to leave their country, and though they might have traveled to China to get supplies, they were determined to return home. In the oral accounts, interviewees explained that their main reasons for leaving the country were driven by economic necessity. They did not link economic and political aspects of life in North Korea when it came to border crossing. Instead, their reasons were connected to being unable to endure the hunger and related problems any longer. The most common refrain was "I never would have left if I had not been so hungry or so ill." In migrating to China, they might encounter border guards who could kill them for committing the treasonous act of border crossing, or guards who were open to receiving bribes. If they were lucky enough to have the opportunity and the means to do so, bribing guards with cigarettes, alcohol, and money meant that they could pass into China without risking death or imprisonment.

Of course this was not a fail-proof plan. Rather than suggesting a softening of authorial lines of power and a weakening of the political system within the country, these tactics reveal the ambiguity of power relations and the arbitrary ways that power was sometimes exercised at the level of life and death. Instead of a certain line of power and control that is obviated by uniform, occupation, and stature, uncertainty takes the place of certainty and generates an arbitrary delivery of power. In such cases, the value attributed to bribes and the resulting power manipulation of bribes is unclear. Bribes are by nature difficult to regulate and ascribe value. Approaching guards to exchange bribes for favors invariably involved a risk that could mean the loss of one's home country and one's future host country, all at the unknowable whim of a border guard.[4]

Remaining was the choice of the collective majority; departing was the choice of the individual few. Decisions to cross into China were connected with ambitions to return to the North and live more comfortably afterward. Departing the North without the hope of return was rarely described. At heart, departure was an individual act, and the breaking point leading to the decision was often negotiated at the level of the self, often deliberately excluding others from discussion and debate about the decision because so few could be trusted.

As previously mentioned, the appearance of humor and jokes in North Korea is evidence that at least some people were aware of the arbitrary attribution of value and power within society. It might be possible to say that discrepancies between day-to-day life and ideology generated a lack of confidence in the political apparatus of the country overall. Kong Dan Oh and Ralph C. Hassig observed that North Koreans are politically disengaged, emphasizing the lack of necessary energy to become politically engaged.[5] I think it is more accurate to say that the busyness of daily life in North Korea may only allot opportunities to engage with dissatisfaction on the level of creative linguistic channels and, further, that political dissatisfaction may only materialize when daily life improves enough that people can begin to solve problems other than the most basic.

By way of contrast, consider Soviet Georgia. There people engaged in something called *Keipi*, collective social feasts that provided opportunities for large groups of people to gather. It was typical at such gatherings for people to sing songs and share proverbs and folktales. Through these methods of oral communication people could speak more freely than usual. Written communication, by contrast, was controlled.[6] The *Keipi* were collective avenues where the public could engage clandestinely with dominant and minority opinions. However, even in the limited circumstances where such meetings occurred there remained multiple layers of observation and supervision within the social structure that hindered communication from becoming totally free. The balance between accepted and unacceptable views had to be delicately negotiated.

It is evident from the oral accounts that self-talk was a way of expressing dissatisfaction internally but also a way of generating encouragement to continue. Opportunities in North Korea to share opinions, suspicions, and doubts where such thoughts could be safely explored and challenged appears nonexistent. Instead, even the most minor of frustrations could, if voiced, result in life-or-death punishments. Having seen others take this risk and gain nothing, people often deemed it better to leave. So while there is evidence in the interviewee accounts of sociopolitical dissatisfaction in the North, there is no means by which people can transmit this information to each other safely. Still, it was explained to me, even if it was clear that your family felt as you did, nothing could be done. The sense of impossibility, defeat before trying, was a refrain that echoed through the interviewee accounts. It was as if the population had been preemptively disarmed and dissidence squashed before it could be imagined.

Keep in mind that while revolt and revolution are born in the same family, their lifespans are rarely the same, and revolt does not always become revolution. While it is arguably true, as Foucault says, that there is no authority "capable of making it utterly impossible" to revolt, to generate change revolt needs longevity, revolution, and staying power, and none of the coups in North Korea achieved this.[7] They were crushed by authority. Interviewees shared anecdotes of revolts in an unidentified prison camp in the northern province of North Hamgyong where several prisoners rioted but were all killed in their uprising. Revolts or struggles were rare but not nonexistent. Revolt or struggle is not in question, to confirm Foucault's earlier point, but the likely success of it is. The individual act of leaving the North, while not personally identified as political or resisting authority, was the only way of generating the possibility for positive change in an individual's life trajectory. These revolts happened internally, and the risks and benefits were often those of the individual alone.

North Korea promotes the idea of collectivism in everything from factory work to farming and self-criticism sessions. Where the famine was concerned, there was a distinct lack collective action in the form of rebellion, common dissent, or mutual complaint. Instead resistance took a very individual form, and it was toward resisting hunger itself rather than the political apparatus that facilitated the famine. Avoiding hunger in North Korea was a complex operation. Trying to contain the capitalist behavior of individuals was also difficult for the government. Resistance to hunger will not always or necessarily take the forms we expect. The circumstances in North Korea were such that the priority of national sovereignty dictated government response to the famine. This resulted in the strict regulation of coping strategies as well as the interpretation and expressions of the famine because these activities were presumed to be forces that would dissolve the imagined self-sufficiency of the government system. The capture of North Koreans crossing into China and the subsequent treatment of these individuals in detention centers are among many indications that the North Korean government placed national sovereignty above the well-being of its population, all the while failing to provide a legal means of sustaining life. During the famine period, supposed traitors of the nation faced torture, imprisonment, and public execution. Yet, if my interviewees are any indication, loyalty to the government was not always in question. Many crossed into China to ensure survival and had every intention of returning. The government willfully neglected the population's most urgent need for a legal means of acquiring sufficient food. Instead military resources were prioritized over humanitarian need, and migrants leaving the country were targeted as traitors.

Breaking points were present in many ways in North Korea. Sometimes they existed within individuals, where hunger reached extreme starvation and the individual perished. Loyalty and belief in the government system motivated people to wait for the famine to turn around. The increasing numbers of people who died waiting served as a warning to those who remained. Kyung-ok Park (63) eventually decided to depart, but—as with all interviewees—there was the earlier phase of choosing to remain. This deferral and delay is remarkable, particularly since Kyung-ok Park had lived in Japan and recalled her former life there.

I guess it was between 1992 and 1993, and then in 1994. Things got very busy. There were people in North Korea who simply decided that they could not live any longer and killed themselves. From 1994 onward, people didn't have enough to eat. They would go to the mountain and eat grass. Worse than animals. It's really unspeakable. When I think about it now, it's so ridiculous, I am speechless.

I didn't plan to leave. When my daughter said we should flee to China, I did not object. "Fine, you go ahead. I'm going to stay here and starve to death. Do whatever it takes to get out of here." That's how I sent my kids away. She promised she would come back to get me, and I waited for a bit to see whether or not there would be some news. But nothing came, so I was concerned if I could really flee to China.

My husband and mother-in-law were dying. We would have died like that. So we decided. During that time, many people were going into China. Many of them succeeded. "Let's flee to China now," I said. My daughter had gone first. I could not even walk properly. She said, "I'll come back for you with good news." She was sorry about leaving me. The poor people died of hunger and beatings, they all died like that.

At last a man came and took me, telling me not to worry, so I went. When I arrived in China, after crossing the Tuman River, I suddenly got nostalgic for Japan. "I'm actually in China," I thought, and then I realized I had finally got out of North Korea. When I got to China I ate food every day. I had a banana for the first time in forty years. We had nothing like that in North Korea. When I was eating the banana in China, I thought, "I am actually eating a banana!" I was so well treated and I thought of how my siblings were doing back home, but I couldn't stay in China indefinitely. I heard that they come and arrest you in the night, so I couldn't sleep after that. I fled here and there. I couldn't live like that. In China there was a contact route to Japan. "I have to go to Japan," I thought. I went to the embassy and got connected. I got to Japan safely. It felt like a dream. I took a plane for the first time. I had succeeded. (Kyung-ok Park, 63)

Her account demonstrates reluctance in the face of the difficulty in crossing to China. One needs to be physically up to the task, as she mentions she had trouble walking. Many North Koreans cross out of North Korea on foot. She saw the fate of her in-laws dying of hunger, what would be her fate. Even at this stage, although she makes her decision, it is not followed by action until a man comes (a broker, sent by her daughter) and assures her not to worry and helps her leave. Kyung-ok Park is an ethnic Korean who grew up in Japan and moved to North Korea in the 1960s at a time when Japan-based Koreans were encouraged to return to the homeland.[8] That history was one marked by regret and confusion, which doubtless led to the tamping down of frustrations. It is only when Kyung-ok Park is in China eating a banana that she seems to allow herself for the first time to remember her life in Japan.

Some people decided to defect to China after getting severely ill in the North and being unable to find the medicine they needed. Many came to this breaking point when they saw that they could not continue living inside North Korea, either because they lacked essential medicines or because there was no longer a possibility of securing enough food and they saw death around the corner. Although the consequences of the decision were political, the reasons for making such a decision were rarely expressed as such. Nearly every interviewee reported that ultimately the decision to defect was a practical one prompted by the death of a family member or friends, by witnessing killings, or by their own imminent death. None expressed their defection as an arbitrary or incidental decision, or one where they intentionally resisted the government. Rather, it was a decision they were compelled to make, one that was made reluctantly.

North Koreans reported that they would not have left if they had had enough to eat. Hye-jin Lee's (23) loyalty to North Korea was unwavering. Although she was very ill and needed medicine she couldn't find in North Korea, she was reluctant to try crossing because such a journey requires strength and physical endurance. She explains how, prior to departure, she tried everything, such as buying medicine in the black market and seeking local medical attention to fix her condition:

> In a place like North Korea, there are lots of contagious diseases going around. The majority of people have measles or other kinds of contagion. So I was in that situation, I had completely lost consciousness. It was like any day I would be dead. There was nothing to eat. My hair fell out. I had a high fever. In North Korea the treatment that they give you is free, but even if you go to the hospital there is no medicine. Patients buy medicine elsewhere and take it to the hospital, where it is administered. Sick as I was, eating and selling were very difficult things to accomplish. You have to have money to buy medicine. It was a complicated situation. I was just at home, getting more ill.
>
> My father knew a doctor, knew him personally. I was in a lot of pain. My father put me on his back and brought me to that doctor. We went at night. I was given an injection and had a boil lanced. The doctor couldn't see very well because all of this was taking place in the dark. There was no electricity to see what he was doing. So the needle wasn't put in right, and I got worse. I was close to dying. I would die in a day or two. I was at home like that, dying.
>
> My brother had been going to China a bit. So when it seemed like I was going to die my brother put me on his back and brought me to China, all the way to China on his back. That was our motivation for going. We crossed the Tuman River. It was my great

fortune that my brother had been going back and forth to China in order to eat and live. I lost consciousness. My brother put me on his back and carried me. It was pouring rain, so much water poured down. We were down in the Tuman River, my brother was in the water with me on his back. We were crossing into China. The reason we went to China was because of my illness. When we got there we had every intention to return, but once we got there we decided against it, and to just go on to South Korea. (Hye-jin Lee, 23)

The relationships Hye-jin identifies with her father, the doctor, and her brother are key to her survival. She identifies the country's limitations, such as the lack of electricity and the need to travel at night for the safety and security afforded by clandestine timing. She identifies these, but she does not criticize; rather, she indicates how they placed her at a disadvantage. She knew this and articulated it clearly. She identified the worsening of her illness with the damage done to her in the unlit makeshift surgery room. She identifies the compounded difficulties she must negotiate just to stay alive: In order to eat, to be well, she must sell in the market for money; to be cured she must have money to get medicine so that she can eat to be well and sell in the market. Only on a subtle level are the state's failures identified as causing her failure to recover. Instead, her representation of this near-death experience is rendered in rather banal terms: *eating and selling were very difficult things to accomplish* and *it was a complicated situation.* There is little emotion expressed in this portion of her account; it seems devoid of emotions and instead focused and determined. The mechanically represented experience—"I was just at home, getting more ill. . . . I was at home like that, dying"—more readily recalls the steady, watchful response she had to her illness. She describes being taken through the motions as her father, the doctor, and her brother all try to get her the help she needs. It is truly engaging, then, that after all of this, she and her brother do not initially question their desire to return home to North Korea. But after arriving in China, they decide against it. I asked Hye-jin why she wanted to return to the North in the first place. This is what she told me:

I received education (*kyoyuk*) about South Korea that it was a country with many beggars. They were our sworn enemy. That is how we were taught. The ideological education was very severe. So, in North Korea I was a person who thought like that. We were completely shut off from the outside world. So because of that, the thought of going to South Korea hadn't even occurred to me. Because of my illness we went to China with the intention of getting treatment and heading back to North Korea. Our family was there, but then . . . but then . . . the situation was such that we were unable to go back. Well, if we went back we would die, or get caught and dragged back by your nostrils. They drag you back by a hole they make in your nose. That's what they do. So we couldn't go back. So after being in China for a few years, well, we couldn't go back! After a few years we decided to go to South Korea. (Hye-jin Lee, 23)

In identifying her reasons for wanting to return, Hye-jin begins by explaining the education she received about the South and how cut off she was from knowledge of the rest of the world. The concrete factor she mentions that makes her want to return to the North is the presence of her family there. What stands out in this account is the presence of a largely nonnegotiable barrier to departure and return. In the description she turns herself from subject into object, giving the listener a sense that she very much stands outside of that experience now: "In North Korea I was a person who thought like that." The self-objectification identifies the past and present selves, signaling an internal fracture between her identities then and now. She reflects rather firmly how her present self and past personhood differs. She did not say "I once thought" or "I thought that way" but rather "I was a person who thought like that," identifying her former self as external and other but also identifying a way of thinking that grouped her as a person among others who thought the same. The act of departing is difficult not only because of the threat to life but because it is a departure from how the self is identified and what the self is bound to for identification.

Her physical survival was driven up against her unchallenged education about the superiority of the North over all else. To consider that another country had the means to save her life was a test to her former beliefs. The two could not survive together; one would have to lose to save the other. It is a terrifying act of completion. Relationship to the homeland is forever transformed by crossing over. In her account, Hye-jin Lee also highlights the role of rumors in her decision to remain in China and try to continue toward the South. Her almost unbelievable description of the way North Korean illegal migrants are rounded up and deported home is something I heard many times in the interviews, described precisely in this manner. The noses of individuals are pierced and the collection of migrants strung together and dragged back in a humiliated, agonized mass. I cannot verify this method of refoulement, but the rumor had such currency as to be a factor in her decision to exit China and continue to South Korea.

The price of defecting and the price of staying were described as equal—if I leave and get killed, it is the same as if I stay and die, so I may as well die trying. This cost assessment was commonly articulated in the oral accounts. However, reaching this conclusion took a considerable period of time during which key elements of the social fabric fell away. Trends in the accounts suggest that, for these interviewees, the difficult decision to defect was made through a series of shattering realizations. These followed a chronology that began with the death of Kim Il-Sung and the floods, which eventually lead to witnessing things deemed incongruous to socialist society. The inflow of rumors from people who had crossed into China for trade, selling, and other resources met with a growing community of citizens who were increasingly anxious about how they could continue to survive on so little. With strictly controlled access to media, telephones, and even open communication among themselves, North Koreans had only the briefest of opportunities to learn from rumors and to corroborate what they heard. Although they could not be verified, rumors provided an alternative explanation for why the country was in economic turmoil with no end of food shortage in sight. This altered interpretations of their suffering. The rumors did not instantly change people's ways of thinking but brought in the element of doubt.

People who were regular border crossers carried information about China, South Korea, and other countries. They explained that foreign aid donations had been provided since 1995, which came as a shock to many who had never seen such aid. An incongruity emerged between the messages from the government and the rumors of the border crossers. These stories provided alternative messages about the reality they witnessed and experienced in their daily lives. Jae-young Yoon explained:

> Around 1999, North Koreans started to learn that the food was coming from the international community. Before that they had no idea that aid was coming from the Republic of Korea or that medicines were coming from England. In 1999, a lot of defectors had gone to China, lived there, listened to South Korean broadcasts and so, "Oh! The international community is giving food relief for the benefit of North Korea." This kind of talk got around, not through the official media, television, or the central media [chungang] though. Well if you're embarrassed of something you don't want to broadcast it, do you?
>
> You see, North Korea as a society cannot be known. They can have the citizens dying of starvation, but they do not say anything about that to the outside world. So it was that crossing into China and back and forth that North Koreans came to know about how the international community [was] helping North Korea, and "Oh! We have been suffering with hunger for a long time, and the international community has been sending us aid for a long time." They came to know the truth. (Jae-young Yoon, 45)

The formation of an injustice frame was necessary but not sufficient to make the decision to once and for all abandon their country. Leaving North Korea without a legal permit is certainly bona fide defection according to North Korean law, but for many interviewees, leaving North Korea was not an intentionally political or legal gesture; it was not necessarily defection but rather a way of making ends meet. For some interviewees the decision to defect was made largely because they had no other choice in their given circumstances, particularly instances related to health, where the requisite needs could not be met inside North Korea. In some instances, the decision to leave North Korea permanently and continue through China to third countries came only after learning about the difficulties to be had in staying in China or upon trying to reenter the North—as had frequently been their intention. Although some individuals were loyal to North Korea, the military measures taken by the government to ensure the capture and detention of border crossers kept people from returning. But, as greater contradictions began to appear between social groups, people felt a sense of betrayal.

I too never once saw food sent from the international community. North Korea wants to hide this, but [after a while] they could not because the USA trademark was stamped on the bags and you could see it in the black markets being sold. Republic of Korea marked sacks too are secretly taken and sold. Those who were strong and those who were weak were bit by bit more separated, and those who were weak had nothing but to die of hunger. All of this. Not only around the mid-1990s but until the start of 2000 as well. It became a destroyed society, as I see it.

But if the peasantry can't go out to work, they will just stay indoors and one by one collapse. I was just the same. That's how I lost my youngest. I lost him! And to live that way was so hard; I made the decision to escape to China. Of course, when I was escaping to China I told myself, "I will go and live a while, and never return to this land." (Jae-young Yoon, 45)

Stories about life in China provided ideas about alternative solutions to their situation, albeit perplexing and counterintuitive to North Korean ideological education. Jae-young Yoon's story about the loss of his son identifies that this loss was what created the greatest difficulty in continuing to live in North Korea. Others learned that essential resources such as food and medicine could be found in China. In some instances, defection became a default choice when loyal citizens had gone into China with every intention of returning after they had retrieved the necessary food or medicine. Many of these temporary defectors realized that they were at risk of imprisonment or worse if they were caught trying to return. Many remarked on how the elderly had just gone into their houses, closed the door and died. Such individuals were described as loyal citizens. Ways of dealing with suffering were influenced by locally acceptable ways of understanding problems.[9]

In a few cases the decision to depart was less individual and more a decision of the head of the family. Ji-young Kim (25) explained that her decision to defect was settled with her family; her account indicates the importance of good timing for the decision to defect. Many people were unable to tell even their closest family members that they were leaving because it would put them in danger. It seems that the idea to defect can sit a long time in the mind before it turns into action, preceded by a period of waiting and watching in order to ensure success.

We were living very badly off. . . . My mother had wanted to defect for a long time; she had made the decision long ago. It was like she had made the decision when I was very young. So there was talk of seeing our relatives in China, and it occurred to me that I would like to go and see China too, that's what I was thinking. I had heard a lot about China. One of my aunts lived there. Her daughter, once married, had moved to South Korea in 1994. We heard that life was good in China. We had also heard since early school days that South Korea wasn't doing well. In our school books it was written that the place was swarming with beggars and . . . filled with them. . . . But there is freedom isn't there, no matter how many stories you hear about how poor it is. . . . Knowing that, we escaped. (Ji-young Kim, 25)

A combination of factors resulted in each person arriving at the breaking point. The famine reached its worst stage in terms of recorded deaths during 1996–1997. Piles of deceased were reported in train stations around the northern cities of Cheongjin and Musan, and the capital city of Pyongyang was not immune either. Prior to the famine, this was a sight unknown in North Korean society, where needless death and suffering were attributed to capitalism. Along with the presence of the deceased, there were other manifestations of famine, such as internal migration, homelessness, orphaned children, and beggars. The motivation to leave North Korea came when all other methods of individual survival were deemed impossible. The country was no longer able to convince people that they could hope for a better day, proper and sufficient food, proper and sufficient medical care, and freedom from persecution for famine crimes.

Interviewees describe being pushed to the limit of their adaptive capacity within the country, which led many to make the ultimate decision to break with former ways of living and all they had known and to cross the border. This meant leaving the country permanently, though some thought they could cross back and forth. Many people acquired a new perspective on political and cultural identity as a consequence of their survival strategies, and out-migration exemplified this. Typically this act of crossing was a decision made much earlier than the physical act itself. The breaking point happened internally, invisibly, and often without direct communication. Instead, when individuals identified this transition stage in their accounts, they often recalled the use of self-talk.

There was a period of self-sacrifice for the good of the country, but interviewees saw others "giving up" on life, which meant giving up on individual survival, closing the door and waiting to die. Interviewees relayed such accounts, but for them over time the survival of the nation gave way in priority to survival of the self. Their hope for a better life in the North turned to hopelessness, and this drove many across the border. Jung-ok Choi's (21) narrative reveals that her family had a critical understanding of their precarious relationship to the state, given that they were from a less favorable class. As times got worse, her political vulnerability increased, making life more complicated. She told me about the day her mother told her about their hopeless future if they stayed in the North:

Because of the famine there were lots of people who died. They had given up on their lives. Those who had nothing to eat had given up. Even though it was hard for me, no matter how hard it was I didn't give up. I just had to think about the future. I thought, "In the future, I will not live this way. Right now it is painful, but in the future it will be better. It will get better." I would say those things to myself, just to myself. I thought like that. In North Korea I thought that if I just worked hard at farming or maybe I would sell in the market. I thought I would really be able to throw off the famine, really throw off the poverty in the future. I had that thought many times. I had no special skill, no method. I was only a student, after all.

But I could not have such hope. My uncle was in a political prison camp and because of that my family was categorized as bad, my mother, my father, my uncle. In North Korean law you are bound together, so in that situation being a *songp'uni nap'un kajok* (family of bad class), from myself to my mother to them, the effect would be on us all. I couldn't even dream that I would go to university or join the military in the future. What I mean is, in North Korean parlance *songp'uni nap'un kajok*, when you are a bad family, you know. I knew that.

When I was 16 I didn't have any special thoughts about what I would do. "What shall I study at university?" That kind of thought never crossed my mind. I couldn't go, so my mother had already made the decision to defect. But at that time, truly I couldn't have made that decision to defect. I was only 16.

One day my mother told me we had to leave. I didn't want to leave, but if you waited you would die. I had thought like "Oh, in North Korea so long as you work very hard, you can live well," but my mother was like, "We're going to China!"

My mother said, "You, we, have no chance of hope because my brother committed a crime against North Korea. You will end up like your mother, working the ground with a weeding hoe. Farming, that is how you will live," she said. My mother had gone to school. She had studied. When she was about 15 or 16 her brother was taken to a political prison, he was about 24 or 25 then. The whole family was relocated to a mountainous district. She told me about my uncle and how if we stayed in North Korea, apart from land, apart from farming, we would have to farm, she said, "No matter how hard we try to make it happen, it won't work," she said.

When I heard her talking like that, I saw there was no hope in North Korea. "How can I live in this land? I was born like this. How was I born into this world?" Those thoughts went around my head. So I consented to my mother's decision that we leave for China. (Jung-ok Choi, 21)

Jung-ok Choi and her family made the difficult decision to defect from home after realizing that there was no hope even for the return of their formerly ordinary lives. Her mother had been willing to live within those limits, but as the economic situation worsened, her mother saw that even that way of life was growing more difficult and impossible. There was an awareness of politically constructed class differences and the benefits or limitations these brought to individuals. The price of leaving and the price of going were equal. This calculus of survival helped in the decision to risk defecting.

In the book *More Frightening than Hunger Is the Loss of Hope*, written by two young North Korean siblings, Sŏnhŭi and Ch'unsik Park, who resettled to Japan, the authors explain that they crossed the Tuman River because there was nothing to eat, there was so much hunger in North Korea.[10] The book details much in their lives as hidden refugees in China, but there are moments when the siblings recall life in North Korea and the combination of precipitating factors that led ultimately to the decision to defect. Their father died from illness. After this, Sŏnhŭi and her brother, Ch'unsik, moved to their uncle's house. Life at their uncle's house was difficult too. There was only one bowl of cornmeal per day. Soon this became no more than half a bowl. Sŏnhŭi was sent out to collect weeds in a large bowl. She explains:

> Instead of regular food, we had to pluck weeds. Different kinds of weeds were gathered, shepherd's purse, dropwort, mugwort. At the beginning we would gather weeds such as these that were usually edible. But then it wasn't only us who were going out to collect the weeds, all our neighborhood was as well and because of that the edible weeds were gone very quickly.[11]

Shortly after this she spotted their aunt at the black market.

> One day my friends and I were walking near the market area, I spotted my aunt. My aunt said, "I'm off to sell something," and then wandered off. Then sometimes she didn't come back to the house. She took things to the market to sell and bought food with the money. She came home; we welcomed her with a happy heart saying, "Aunty, you're back!" and she said she was going out again. We could see in each of her hands a piece of rice cake and we could hear the sound of her munching on the rice cake. When I saw that, I thought my aunty looked like an animal.[12]

The young life of Sŏnhŭi was soon shattered. This all came during what she called the worst stage of the famine for her. In a chapter titled "One Dream Only," she explains what happened. The entire short chapter is translated here.

> I was always hungry. I even lacked the strength required to just stand quietly, I was so hungry. In spite of this, I still intended to

attend primary school in any case. There were other students who thought as I did. But they all had to go back home after an hour or two of classes. Of all these students, it seems that I must have had the least to eat of them all. I would stumble and stagger so severely that my close friends collected among themselves some corn and gave it to me. I couldn't have done anything like begging. I didn't even have the means to get money. So because I had so little food, I got quite sick. I would lay several days and endure the hunger pains in my stomach. I was aware that "I'm starving to death and there's nothing I can do, and if that happens then . . ." but I wasn't scared.

Even though I was in that situation, I continued to attend school because I was dreaming of my future. After entering college, I wanted to become a great doctor. That was my dream. My mother and father had contracted illnesses and at that time there was nothing I could do for them, this grieved me terribly. So because of that, more than any other student, I studied very hard. The result was that in my third year, I was able to skip a year, I became a fourth year student. But then, there was something new about the world that I came to know. Oh no! Study alone will not bring my dream! In that situation, studying to achieve your dreams is a terribly difficult thing.

If I'd had money I could have realized my dream through working hard with great determination and remarkable zeal. Still, I want to become a doctor. No matter what, I will do what is necessary to see that dream before me.[13]

Writing about the difficulties within their family, the siblings discuss the mixed feelings of receiving from fellow classmates what they could not have been able to provide for them if they had been in the same situation. They also write about tapping into a source of strength for survival in North Korea, which is about finding meaning in life, now and in the future, something that has been mentioned by other survivors of social suffering as a means of strength for the will to live.[14] The young authors elaborate their philosophy of survival:

There are no expressions to describe my feelings at that time [1996]. Having nothing to eat was a terribly painful thing. But more than that, the loss of hope was a far more painful thing. In this world, if the thing you wish to do most is taken away from you, life has no meaning whatsoever. Hope can shore up a life. If there is hope, no matter how hungry one is, it can be endured.[15]

The title "One Dream Only" sums up their experience. However, although the siblings survived, there is regret in the story. At the very end of her account, Sŏnhŭi explains, "We didn't escape from North Korea because we hated it. That is the country in which we were born and raised. I have so many memories that upon reflection bring tears flowing from my eyes. If I had been able, I would have lived in North Korea. It is regretful, but right now North Korea has no means by which to give us life."[16] This reluctance echoes in many of the stories shared by North Koreans. This same sentiment, the idea that perhaps it is possible to live elsewhere, that there is a hope for a better life, drove many across the border. They escaped the certainty of death in North Korea for the hope of life someplace else.

Defection came at a high cost and great risk. But the hopeless life many North Koreans saw laid out before them inside their country encouraged them to risk losing the little they had. The decision to defect was the final means by which to solve the countless problems brought into their lives by the famine and the strict level of control placed on coping strategies by the government. The North Koreans I interviewed also carried the experience of those Koreans, loyal to the Party, who died waiting for food to be delivered.

The decision to defect was not one taken lightly, and it was not necessarily informed by a desire to resist the regime or stand up against oppression. It was a practical act of survival. None expressed their defection as an arbitrary or incidental decision, or one in which they resisted the government. It was a decision they were compelled to make, one that was made reluctantly. Through a series of shattering realizations, some with overlapping chronology, the decision was finally made. The death of Kim Il-Sung and Kim Jong-Il's rise to power was frequently mentioned as the historical turning point for the downturn in economic and food security. With the death of Kim Il-Sung, whom every North Korean is taught to idolize, an emotional desperation seems to have linked any national failure with the nation's loss. It is also a demonstration that the collective experience of social suffering was understood to be mapped out on a national scale that incorporated the leadership at its center but not necessarily the center of responsibility.

Kim Il-Sung and Kim Jong-Il, their words are like two pieces of the sky, it was like that for me. That was all I knew. So, in that context, the issue of defecting is a very difficult one indeed. That person who defects has reached the point where their very existence is dead by the time they have arrived at that point to put into practice their decision to defect. (Jae-young Yoon, 45)

Jae-young Yoon, whose child died of starvation, describes his state of mind as he crossed the border, dead to the homeland, dead to existence, with a dead world left behind. Jae-young Yoon never expressed a desire to return to North Korea. He was free of it, dead to the North, a life elsewhere in China, in Thailand, in South Korea, anything but the North. There were breaking points with the relationship between the North and the loyalty of the people. When people learned about the aid, they realized they had been betrayed. The relationship between the state and the society lost the element of trust. When people grew ill and unable to remedy their illness in North Korea, their ill health forced a choice that, in pushing them across the border, widened their perspectives on their former lives and opportunities. When people lost family members to starvation, especially children lost to parents, it sometimes propelled defiant acts of border crossing since there was nothing left for them in North Korea anymore.

6

THE NEW DIVISION

What was it like to live an entire life in North Korea and then look at it from the outside? The picture was not simple. Defectors often carried a strong emotional ambiguity over leaving family, friends, and their homeland in order to survive. At each stage in a person's individual journey, particularly on the route out via China, daily life proved too fraught with anxiety and fear for many to gaze reflectively on North Korea. Nearly all interviewees reported equal and sometimes worse memories of their time in China. This could result from many real and imaginary factors, but at least in North Korea they were part of a community that was struggling together. In China they were alone and compelled to trust the kindness of activists of the religious or secular sort. Interviewees expressed confusion over volunteerism and distrusted it because it was so unknown to them. Christian religion on the other hand, which drove the practices of some nongovernmental organizations in China, bore too much resemblance to exalting Kim Jong-Il. The willingness of people in China who wanted to help, few though they were, was viewed with suspicion. For those frequent crossers, repatriated many times by the false promises of Chinese brokers, mistrust was a way to stay alive.

There were inevitably moments when new frames of reference set a jarring new standard for what life could look like, generating both anger at the Chinese way of doing things and regret that so many back home lived so poorly. The Buddhist group Good Friends, which has long worked in the border region helping North Koreans, published the account of a woman who shared her dismay at how well the animals ate in China:

> What we ate couldn't be called food. It was like a porridge mush. We'd put all kinds of weeds into the rice water mush, and a bit of flour, then stir it, boil it and eat it. But then, when I went to China, I saw a cat being fed that very thing. When I saw that I wanted to drag the cat away from it. . . . People inside North Korea are so hungry they are going around with their belts cinched tight.[1]

Leaving North Korea gave people the perspective they needed to view their former lives more critically. In the Good Friends account, a woman expresses a sense of shock at witnessing a cat eating porridge, but an even greater sense of injustice came when people heard stories about food being shipped into the North as aid relief, which they knew from personal experience had not reached the people for whom it was intended. Sun-ja Om (67) expressed her distress about the food shipments: "Hungry, without shoes, barefoot, no clothes on. . . . What is worse, that rice that was sent from South Korea and from China, that rice I'm talking about, where was it sent? The rice which was meant for the citizens, well, it didn't ever get sent out to the people at all, but instead was used to prepare for the war." When she lived in North Korea, preparation for war through the redirecting of resources to the military was understood as proper rationale for getting by on little and tightening belts, and such triage of resources as explained by the North Korean government was sensible. After some time in China, when she learned that the international community had been sending food to the North for the North Korean people, Sun-ja Om was furious at the bogus justifications she had heard, while so many people suffered with nothing.

For the Japanese-Korean interviewees, experiences of life in Japan before repatriation to North Korea in the 1960s provided them with concrete knowledge of how much better life could be. Also many of them still had memories of the shocking differences between their former lives and the promises of North Korea. Tessa Morris-Suzuki recorded Su-ryong Oh's memory of her arrival in Cheongjin on a February morning in 1962:

We sailed toward the docks. There were people standing there to greet us—crowds of people. When I saw the port and those people, I thought, *oh no!*

I think everyone felt that when they saw the scene in front of us—*oh no!*

There was a row of grim-looking warehouses. The wind was blowing hard and it was still cold. The people waiting on the dock for us were all wearing shabby, padded cotton jackets. We thought, "This isn't right. This isn't how it's supposed to be." I think everyone felt disillusioned when they saw it.[2]

Koreans who returned to the peninsula were typically resettled to the northernmost parts of North Korea. In North Korean culture, they were socially and politically questionable—sacred because they had made the decision to return to their homeland, but profane because they were oddly mixed with "the enemy" in ways that tainted their speech, manner, and outlook. As Morris-Suzuki documented, Koreans who left Japan in the 1960s were leaving a country that was on the brink of an economic miracle. But what was more significant and what only encouraged the North to view them suspiciously was the fact that some 97 percent of those Koreans originated from the southern part of the peninsula, during the Japanese occupation.[3] Though that history is deeply connected to Asia's Cold War history, with people merely pawns in the regional game of statecraft, many of the Koreans who left Japan shared resentment against the North Korean regime for fooling them into returning to the peninsula in the first place, to a country where they were outcasts and poorly off. This anger was targeted at the leadership and could only be fully articulated once they defected, at which time they gained a greater perspective on the culpability of the leadership for the North's failings.

> I have nothing but vehement hatred for him now. Does that bastard Kim Jong-Il think of the nation at all? Does he think of the people at all? The citizens? Really. Really. Kim Jong-Il! Exactly what kind of a bastard is he? I knew exactly what kind of bastard when I got here, since I got here and I saw the news and listened to the news reports. (Soon-ja Kim, 74)

This portion of Soon-ja Kim's account begins with her comment that she has nothing but vehement hatred for Kim Jong-Il. Then her sentences are punctuated by questions that rise in perplexed amazement at his cruel negligence. She ends this string of questions by asking, "Exactly what kind of bastard is he?" Can there ever be a good kind of bastard? This account highlights the evil nature of Kim Jong-Il and the absurd triumph he had over the goodness of the people. This section of Soon-ja Kim's experience highlights another feature of the accounts overall, which is the tendency to focus on the people's struggles while in the North and on Kim Jong-Il's failures once out of the North. The distance gave people an opportunity to test connections between formerly unconnected phenomena, such as political structure and economic welfare. For instance, defectors gained experience of other political systems and thus grew critical of the entire political system of the North, highlighting the inherent flaws of socialism as they saw it.

> It's a socialist country, so in that situation whether you work or don't work, it's all the same. Everything is averaged out, whereas in a capitalist system you get as much as your work is worth. Well, North Korea is not like that at all. Even if I don't do any work, I still get the public distribution. I still get my share of the allotment because the country gives it to me. There is no competition. In North Korea, even what a farmer grows is not his own. It belongs

to the country. In a socialist society, whether or not you work, it is the same. It is all equal. In a capitalist society it goes according to how hard you work. North Korea is not like that. Even if I do not work, I will still receive the food distribution. The country gives it to me. In North Korea, whether I plant the crops today or tomorrow, it is the country's crops; the country gives me food, even if I don't work hard. So we farm the corn, and there is a problem. Of course there might be a problem, but if it were my land, my plot I would work hard, right? That is the problem. Now you see China is a socialist society, the land is divided up to the people, and as a result it is very developed, right? There would not have been a famine if the country had let people have their own plots of land. That's what I think. (Hye-jin Lee, 23)

In fact, North Korea did permit private plots of a limited size and purpose. Although accounts testify that such plots grew better and were more attentively watched over, even this was not sufficient to solve North Korea's systemic problems with food insecurity. The critique of North Korea's political structure was hindered by overattention to symptomatic manifestations of its failures rather than the root causes. This is not a fault of North Koreans or defectors but rather a result of limited information. It is because North Koreans are denied basic social and civil rights that they cannot take full advantage of private plots, market selling, and cross-border exchange.

The social and personal arena was identified as the region where socialist systems find their weakness. The mentality of people was sometimes identified as the uncontrollable factor leading to trouble for all involved:

The idea of everyone sharing everything equally is wrong. Of course people might like the idea at first. In the beginning, farmers made this cooperative farming union to farm and distribute food. It seemed to work out well at first. Some worked really hard, but people are different. There were some who were physically strong, but some weaker than the others. Also not just about physical abilities, but the mind-set of people also differs. There are people who are diligent and benevolent, but also those who are opportunists. Opportunists liked it since they were sly and dodged hard work. So during the distribution, it didn't matter if some worked hard and some just played, since eventually everyone received the same amount of food. So they started to think, "Okay fine, I'm not going to work hard from now on. Let's just see how this goes. It's all the same in the end," and not do their work. So in that spacious field, instead of rice growing, it was all weeds. The field was full of weeds. The government allowed individuals to have their personal field, which was about 50 *pyeong* big,[4] but they were all nicely farmed since people worked hard on their own field. The corn is already small, but in the field that everyone should work together on the corn is even smaller because bugs ate them. This all happened because farmers didn't work and do their job. It was North Korea's policy that led to it all. (Sun-hi Bak, 53)

However, some interviewees—a minority of them, all from Pyongyang—only offered a critique of North Korea's structural failures and only if such criticisms were also leveled at other countries, like the United Kingdom, South Korea, and the United States. In such cases, the symptomatic manifestations of state failure, such as homeless men at Seoul Station or racism in the United States, were identified to demonstrate that all countries have their failings. At such moments I was asked by interviewees to concur that there were problems in other places. Perhaps the interviewee didn't want to harp too heavily on North Korea's misgivings; it was their former homeland, and it was embarrassing to talk too critically about the government. However, what strikes me in this dynamic is how the failings of other countries had to be mentioned first, if the failings of North Korea were to be mentioned. In a sense it was as if North Korea failed because that is what governments do, they fail people. It is not intentional but a by-product of a flawed mechanism.

In the accounts, interviewees were certain that North Korea was the purer of the two parts of the peninsula; this idea extended to both the people who lived in the North and to the land of the North. Their difficult experiences in the North had girded them up to be better prepared for a life that was far more difficult, building up their resilience, which their South Korean brethren couldn't handle. People in the South were softer and less able to cope with life's challenges. Lest we forget, many North Koreans once lived in small villages, nothing like the overcrowded, twenty-four-hour cities of Seoul and Tokyo, which are a culture shock in multiple ways, not only politically. It may be that the loneliness and social disenfranchisement experienced in South Korea and Japan encouraged a more positive reflection on their former lives than they might otherwise have had. Even so, a majority of the interviewees expressed a desire to reconnect to the North or to return to it, along with reluctance at having had to leave.

> Tell me, who, what person wants to throw away his hometown to live? But then, if you're going to die there, what are the options? We North Koreans in South Korea had no choice but to come here. If it were safe, would we not go back? Coming here there is so much to adjust to, right? Coming here has lots of effects on your life. We come because we have no choice. I did not come here out of choice. The best thing would be unification. That way I could be with my family again. You could live where you want to live. I often think of going back to the North, but how could I go now? (Hye-jin Lee, 23)

If basic conditions were better—enough food to eat, medicine, the ability to work hard and gain in social mobility—many wouldn't have left. Along with this was a tendency to forecast and dream of a favorable future for the North that would enable them to return or at least visit friends and family.

Being driven out of the North in exchange for food, medicine, money, and political freedom brings a mixed satisfaction for many.

Attainment of these provide enough comfort and satisfaction that an individual then remembers what was loved and longed for at home prior to being driven out by basic needs. When the host country meets North Koreans with suspicion, curiosity, or distain, it is natural that some of them would desire to return, but such a reaction is natural, obvious. The bond that comes from surviving a common peril is something that few others can share with North Koreans, and though they may sometimes view each other with suspicion, a connection exists between fellow defectors that is unlike the relationship to brethren in the South.

I still have lots of memories from North Korea. I want to go visit because I was born there. If they unify soon then I will go, but when will that be? Maybe ten years from now? When Kim Jong-Il's son succeeds, it will change. When that happens, how should I say this . . . there are many people who oppose Kim Jong-Il now, but since his influence is deep they cannot rise up. They did try a few times, though, but all failed. When the time comes for the son to take over, whenever the head of state changes, when the son takes over, things will happen. I guess that's what I think. Not because of South Korea's Sunshine Policy but because of domestic turmoil. The people are not stupid. They know the politics shouldn't be that way; they just cannot say it. When the time comes, I think something will definitely happen. They had communism, but who likes it? Of course the Party members do. The Party members praise Kim Jong-Il's leadership and say "Long live Kim Jong-Il," but the moment they turn away, they don't think like that. They are too busy living their own lives to care about Kim's policies and say whether it is good or bad. So unless one is stupid, they can see by looking at the way the country is going. Lots of people think that this isn't the way it should be. Now the problem is that they can't talk about it.

When I think of North Koreans, my heart breaks. Yeah, when I got to China I realized I had been deceived. I was deceived.

In China, even the dogs were eating rice. Eating better than the North Koreans, beasts! Then I knew that North Koreans had been deceived. They had said that the South Koreans don't live well. In China, I saw on the TV, they live well. It was a totally different world from what I had thought. I was angry. When I think of North Korea now, and how we were deceived, I feel sorry for my family still in the North. I always eat well here. Whenever I eat I think of them. (Mi-young Ahn, 45)

Did interviewees feel relief at having survived the famine? Were they content with their new lives in Seoul and Tokyo, eating well, wearing good clothes, and sitting in heated apartments where the elevators worked? Did they feel strange recollecting their former lives and now looking at North Korea from the outside? The answers to these questions are far from simple. There was a difference too in the experiences of interviewees in Seoul and those in Tokyo. All of them experienced the distinct and painful paradox that comes with the fulfillment of long unfulfilled needs for food and economic and political freedom, combined with an awkward guilt for how they had behaved and who was left behind. They missed home, family, friendships, community, the familiar, the routine, and the place of belonging. Considered this way, it may be more correct to say that they survived part of the difficulties brought about by the famine and its subsequent troubles, but they entered into a new phase of life where an additional agony emerged. They were called upon for a new type of endurance in the face of loss. The past was an experience that did not end but rather transformed itself on new ground. Post-famine life outside North Korea was characterized by a continuation of thoughts about life back home, ambivalent relief at having survived, and an individual, solitary repetition of the geopolitical features of division and separation typified by the Korean War.

The past continues as present in interviewees' accounts of internal and external triggers that evoke the emotion of the famine years. These triggers blend space and time such that North Korea exists in present-day South Korea and Japan as troublesome recollections, bringing the sights, sounds, and smells of the North into their resettled homes. These triggers splinter their present experiences with sudden and sometimes entire recollections of past feelings. These moments were described as haunting. At these points in the interviews, individuals shuddered to shake the feeling out, swayed against its presence, closed their eyes, wept, and sighed in exhaustion at the force of the past coming back. In other instances, a question transported them and they shook in revulsion at the reemergence of an image that surfaced in memory. Sometimes it was something else, the atmosphere of our talk, for instance, that provoked a sorrowful recollection causing interviewees to gaze in silence at something that occurred back beyond my field of vision. Their expressions reflected the grief of what they gazed upon. In those moments I was locked out, as if I held a photo and in the photo stood a man who gazed beyond the frame at something that had changed him forever. The difficult memories of life in the North act as phantom realities in present-day Seoul and Tokyo, where past and present exist within each other. In many ways the North inhabits the cities of Seoul and Tokyo. Sung-soo Lee explained that he still thought about the things he had seen in the North even though he was living safely in Tokyo.

> Yes. I think about it constantly. When I see children, the thought comes that there were children just barely alive. They weren't dead, but they were about to die. So they were put on the pile. . . . They were hardly breathing; they were with the dead bodies like that. (Sung-soo Lee, 42)

In this instance, I asked Sung-soo Lee how his former experiences impacted on his life in Tokyo. His account shows how his present experiences are overlaid with the past. It is almost as if there is no distinction between them. His narrative blends the ease of life today, where children are healthy and well, with the difficulties of life in the past, where children were left for dead, abandoned in a train station on a pile. The children he remembers from the train station back home are not dead, but "with the dead bodies like that," explaining that the traumatic aspect for him stems not only from the pile the children are placed upon, not merely from the proximity of the living with the dead, but also from the blurring of these two ways of being, how they no longer occupy separate spheres, but one. "They weren't dead, but they were about to die," and in the short time they had left the children were given to live among the dead. This experience lasts with Sung-soo Lee, as he explains; he thinks about it constantly. The contradiction of this experience, epitomized by the living heaped upon the dead, is a generator of other contradictions. Namely, the fleeting fragility of life witnessed in the dying children is transformed into a thought that is always on his mind. "I think about it constantly," he says. But what is this "it" Sung-soo Lee thinks about constantly? Since Korean is a language that largely omits the subject, and even sometimes the object of discussion, these must be identified through context. The transliteration would be "constantly thinking." The "it," then, refers to the atmosphere of that time in North Korea, which for Sung-soo Lee was connected to these children he saw at the train station. The most lasting and terrifying aspect of that atmosphere was a violation of basic norms: the abandonment of ill children, the proximity of the living with the dead, the blending of life time with death time.

For another interviewee, Min-ha Park (25), the sounds of train stations evoked difficult memories of life in North Korea. "Yeah," she said, "whenever I take the underground in Seoul I am reminded of the train stations and the dead. When I hear the sound of the train coming into the station I think of the dead people I saw." The sound of the subway train pulling into the station and squealing to a stop brought with it thoughts and images of home. Min-ha's synesthesia is evidence of the blending made of disparate times, places, events, and senses. This mixing of senses creates an overlap of past and present. The most disturbing experiences of home are easily, readily, and automatically recollected. The present environment, which is free of hunger and death such as she witnessed in North Korea, nonetheless evokes that other place of hunger and death through abstract similarities. "When I hear the sound of the train coming into the station, the thought that comes to me is the thought of the dead people I saw." The train enters the station, moving toward Min-ha, carrying its sound into the station. The sounds are like those of trains in the North, and because of this a transformation occurs in the mind of one individual who stands on the platform. Min-ha paints a sparse picture with her words: "I am reminded of the train stations and the dead." In the subway station of the South, the doors slide open and commuters get off or on the train, but for Min-ha the station is overlaid with the North, the sound of the train moves the North as a phantom nation into the South.

In the North people gathered around the train stations in the hopes of collecting scraps of food, catching an illegal ride someplace, or meeting friends and family. Sometimes parents abandoned children at train stations in the hope someone in such a busy area might find and take care of them. Train stations—with their train cars, their sounds and smells, their bustling activity—are potent image carriers for many former North Koreans living abroad. Sung-soo Lee (42), now living in Tokyo, shared anecdotal reports of abandoned train cars that were used to store the dead. "I met these young kids when I was in North Korea. They told me about a train carriage they had opened, looking for a place to sleep. When they got the doors of the carriage open they climbed inside. It was nighttime so they couldn't see that the car was being used to house dead bodies from around the area. The local officials must have collected them. The kids climbed right up into it and found them. They screamed. You can imagine their shock." Whether true or not, these anecdotes reveal the currency of rumors at that time. This narrative demonstrates the potency of the train carriage in Sung-soo Lee's recollections of the famine times.

Although safely settled into South Korean or Japanese life, many survivors said they did not feel relieved at their own survival. Sometimes this was attributed to the fact that so many family and friends back home continued to struggle. Once settled into life in Seoul or Tokyo, the memory of famine often haunts survivors, and if they lost family members and friends, it is that much more difficult. Some interviewees had come close to death themselves. This haunted many survivors, as did their ability to help others and their responsibility for acting altruistically. Some interviewees lived a relatively good life in Pyongyang, and some of them expressed guilt about how they had treated the less fortunate.

Kyung-ok Park (63) was not among the elite in North Korea and lived in relatively meager circumstances in Cheongjin, but she still felt very guilty about the children she didn't help. For her, the inability to help them was also connected to her inability to adequately articulate her experience. "That's right. I'm sorry I cannot explain it well. I wish I could have done so much more. I'm just a normal person. I feel very bad for the people." Other interviewees also expressed guilt. Jin-sung Jang (33), a poet who graduated from Kim Il-Sung University and a writer for the Korean Worker's Party, witnessed beggars in the city of Pyongyang and wrote about his experience in Seoul. His poems meditate on his self-confessed failure to act or speak to alleviate the suffering of others. His short collection of poetry is prefaced by the statement: "During the March of Suffering I walked along the road to and from work each day and saw bodies. I just passed on by." Jin-sung Jang's sense of guilt was strong. His poem titled "I am a murderer" identifies what he witnessed and his helpless reaction: "The begging hands of someone / . . . I pass him by like a mute rascal."

In the poem, Jin-sung Jang sees beggars on his way to work each day and ignores their pleas for help. He witnesses their begging, and he witnesses their deaths. He establishes a relationship between his daily work schedule, which is provided by the state, and the life and death of beggars on the streets. He gives the reader a sense of the city streets by talking about the main roads and the alleys. This creates a sense of the multiplication of suffering that is, he says, uncountable. Jin-sung Jang describes himself as a "mute rascal," implying his guilt, privilege, and greed but also his unwillingness to speak from his position of privilege to help others. He is also impotent to help those he meets on the streets. Why is he impotent? Several of my interviewees expressed confusion at the altruism, philanthropy, and volunteerism they observed in South Korean and Japanese society, viewing it with suspicion and explaining that it was unheard of in North Korea.

This is not always the case. Kyung-ok Park (63) spoke about helping many children in her community by giving them food and clothes. It could be that Pyongyang's environment was less open to altruistic acts. Perhaps helping the beggars would seriously compromise Jin-sung Jang's position. We are never told why he does not help, only that he does not and that for this he feels responsible. Jin-sung Jang's choice not to help the suffering beggar is informed by his desire to avoid the punishment that will come from such an act. Yet his inability to act is precisely the thing that later, upon arriving in Seoul, is the aspect of his former life that pains him most. In reading some of his other poetry, however, I get a different interpretation of his inaction. I almost wonder if he "failed to act" because to act would tamper with the material evidence of the state's failure. Perhaps Jin-sung Jang did not want to speak or act because the state was already so involved in its own undoing that it was speaking of its own failures loud and clear.

Aware of the nation's failures, people had little choice in how they reacted and coped. Interviewee accounts testify to the famine as generating trauma on multiple social, psychological, and physical levels that remain a part of their lives. This is true for those who have left, and it must be true for those who remained at home. The ongoing uncertainty of the food situation in North Korea was well known to all of my interviewees. Knowing that their friends and family are still living in this precarious state increases their anxiety levels. The result is a kind of double trauma: their experience of the famine and the full knowledge of what their friends and relatives are still experiencing.

Information about family and friends back home often comes as a mixed blessing for former North Koreans. Having contact with family back home doesn't necessarily mean having access to accurate information, even if it comes directly in clandestine mobile phone calls.[5] Mi-hee Kun (53) explained that even if she received a note from her daughter saying things are fine and they are eating well, she didn't believe it. "If my daughter says it, I might believe it, but I will ask her to tell me if it really is better, you know?" Then she says, "Oh, after the sanctions were lifted the food aid came in and they gave out food. Maybe it's true." The inability to verify information about conditions back home makes it all the more difficult to deal with the grief of family members left behind, blurring the past and present.

> My heart bursts in agony when I think of them. Seriously not knowing whether I would live or whether I would die, I escaped to China. My fate was good and I came here to Japan. I came here, but really of my siblings in North Korea what can I say? I lived that agony directly, like them, and because of that, what can I say? (Young-hee Kim, 67)

She blends her experiences with those of her family still in the North. While in the North she suffered protracted starvation. On the verge of dying, she managed to leave for China, but in Japan she linguistically identifies her corporal pain—"my heart bursts in agony"—as an expression of her sorrow over her family's continued suffering. She moves from the present moment after identifying her bodily pain. Perhaps this makes her recollect the physical condition she was in when she had to make the difficult decision to leave. In the next sentence she fully embodies this state: "Seriously not knowing whether I would live or die." Then she moves into discussing her family's experience, "I came here, but really of my siblings in North Korea what can I say?" Linked as they are, situated one after the other like this, there is a connection between the two thoughts and experiences. When she thinks of them she is heartbroken. She recalls her experience of that turning point between life and death and links it with recollections of what their life was like and what it is surely like now. How much harder it is for them to live than it is for her now. Strangely, in this portion of her narrative she ends with a contradiction: "I've lived that agony directly, like them, and because of that what can I say?" Her question was rhetorical, but the contradiction is strong. Surely her personal knowledge would enable deep description, but it does not: "There is no way to express it." Is she claiming to be, like the dead, unable to speak, or is she identifying with her family in the North who are unable to speak openly?

> Really, what can I say? There is no way to express it. It is hell, and there is no hell like it. After I came to Japan, a letter came saying that one of the children had died of starvation. My younger sister's child, my nephew, died. That breaks my heart. My family was part Japanese. If they could have survived, they might have made it to Japan now, but they all died of hunger and illnesses. How could they live like that? That place is not a place for a person to live. (Young-hee Kim, 67)

The hell that Young-hee Kim articulates is both the North Korea she knew in the past and the ongoing, incomplete agony of family members still residing in that environment. A letter arrives, delivering both an account of her nephew's death as well as an affirmation that although some people escape the famine experience, it continues to impact on her life even though her living is good. Her narrative also shows how kinship ties bind her current life to the difficulties of the past. Grief over the continued plight of North Koreans was almost exclusively identified in terms of family circles, rather than abstracted to the North Korean people as a whole. Young-hee Kim had the rare experience of being born and living in Japan prior to her family's return to North Korea in the 1960s. Her reflections take multiple geopolitically situated perspectives from Japan, North Korea, China, and back to Japan again. Her narrative explains that her traumatic memories are constantly with her, although she lives in a safe environment. Her account mirrors the narratives of other interviewees. She explained:

> You know when I was younger I grew up in Japan. I was able to eat and wear decent clothes. But when I was in North Korea, I would look at my daughter and think how her experience was nothing

like what I had growing up. I felt sorry for that generation, seeing my daughters growing up in such hardship. I was old, I had lived my life, but my daughters could not eat or wear anything good, so it made me sad. Eventually, all three of them made it out to Japan, but of the people we know who remained, such as my siblings, friends, acquaintances, many of them starved to death. Even now when I think about it at night I can't sleep because of this and that thought. Even if I'm watching something interesting on television, the interesting thing I'm watching doesn't enter into my mind. I'm always thinking about it. When I go to bed, I cannot sleep, until three or four in the morning I cannot sleep. My head hurts so much. It was like that when I was in China too, even now that I'm in Japan it is still there. My family is still in North Korea. Life is so difficult for them. (Young-hee Kim, 67)

It is not only that they experienced tremendous suffering as a result of the famine but also that their decision to leave places them in a position to experience afresh what many on both sides of the demilitarized zone have not newly experienced for decades, the physical separation from family and friends. This was true for those who settled in South Korea or Japan.

When I was in China I couldn't sleep from thinking about my friends back home. When I came to Japan, my eldest was with me, but her child and husband were still in the North. We were separated. My eldest would constantly worry about the situation over there. When she came to Japan, she tried very hard to bring everyone in her family out, but only she and her husband were able to leave. We were all separated. She was very concerned. When she was in China I told her, "Since you came out anyway, just come to Japan. You come here so we can bring the family out." But we couldn't. Some of the family is still in the North. Even if they were to come to Japan, they would still be concerned about those left behind. (Kyung-ok Park, 63)

Kyung-ok Park's account shows how the inability to access and assist in the outward migration of family back in North Korea is the key aspect of her concern. The fact that the family cannot be reunited, that their survival was contingent on this separation, is emblematic of the survival of both Koreas as sovereign nations. The reunion of separated families has intermittently taken place since 1985, an ongoing and fraught history.[6] However, while it may be feared that, with the passing of time, the emotional impetus for reunification weakens as the living memory of separated families passes away, each North Korean who departs the North creates a new history of separated families in the wave of defections since the 1990s. In recent years some of these North Koreans have saved money and brokered their own reunions by helping family members defect, and for many more the new wave of separations has taken hold.

The famine in North Korea, while not a product of the Cold War or Korean War, shares in the legacy of suffering emerging from these conflicts on the peninsula and the region. One of the lasting legacies of this history is in its continued division of the peninsula and the way this division binds the two nations together in an unresolved struggle for a peaceful reunified identity. The Korean War Armistice, signed on July 27, 1953, was designed to cease hostilities on the peninsula at the thirty-eighth parallel until a peaceful settlement could be found.[7] The armistice was implemented as a temporary measure against aggressive fighting, and in this respect it has been a success, but the war has continued to impact the lives of Koreans through other means. So while the famine was not caused by the division, the experience of the famine exists against and within this larger backdrop of history. Against this backdrop the Koreas exist in relation to one another. Defectors who arrive in South Korea first undergo approximately three months of interrogation by the Republic of Korea's National Intelligence Service, followed by a period of social and economic education.[8] While the Constitution of the Republic of Korea grants citizenship to North Koreans, they must first be questioned and interrogated because of the threat they could pose to South Korean national security.[9]

The armistice holds the conflict still—in the sense of continuance as well as in the sense of motionlessness. However, defectors frustrate the geopolitical conflict on the peninsula because they embody the porousness and slippage between the two states. They cross out of the North but make concerted efforts to maintain connections to family and friends back home.

Personal acts of defection agitate the incomplete aspect of conflict on the peninsula. As increasing numbers of North Koreans arrive in South Korea, this tension between the two sides will continue. Interviewees left the North with great reluctance, arriving in China, South Korea, and Japan in order to have a better life, but in doing so their individual acts of survival inevitably position them in vulnerability toward the political stubbornness of the North Korean government. Because each of the two Korean nations uses these individuals in different ways as a form of soft power, each nation is also implicated by the actions of these individuals. On the ground, though, defectors find themselves in South Korea and Japan physically divided from friends and family back home. There is no personal armistice to ensure that an individual battle to reunite with loved ones cannot be fought.[10] In the last five years increasing numbers of North Korean defectors have arranged for the passage of family members and friends to leave North Korea, resulting in what is colloquially called "the small reunification" (*jageun tong-il*).

When the first North Korean, Kum-sok No, flew into South Korea on September 21, 1953, there was no resettlement center or large-scale social policy in place for his arrival. Authorities assumed that when he left, he was motivated by "Operation Mullah," in which North Korean pilots were offered 100,000 USD to fly a MiG-15 across the demilitarized zone.[11] When North Korean secret agent Hyun-Hui Kim was arrested in 1987 for her part in the bombing of Korean Air flight 858, and when government official Hwang Jang-Yop, the highest-ranking defector, landed in Seoul, the South had yet to experience anything like the numbers of North Korean new settlers such as it has today.[12]

Since the 1960s, South Korea has offered legal protection for North Koreans fleeing the North.[13]

Today, with the reeducation center known as Hanawon established in 1999, all North Koreans undergo social, economic, and political education before they officially enter South Korean society. In recent years former North Koreans have arrived in a South Korea, which is trying valiantly to support, reeducate, and assimilate them through social, economic, psychological, and political integration measures.[14] In the last two decades, North Koreans who have left their country are not MiG-15 pilots, nor are they secret agents or government officials, but so-called ordinary people, and often 70 percent of them are women.[15] This feature of the demographic has brought greater strain to South Korean society both in terms of sheer numbers—there are now over 26,000 North Koreans in the South—and in terms of their limited skill set.[16] In the mid-1990s the majority of North Koreans defected for reasons of famine and food shortages.[17] In recent years the cause of defection has shifted to economic motivation, political dissatisfaction, and the social capital means to do so through the help of defected family members resettled abroad.[18]

North Koreans who cross out of their country threaten the laws of national security in the DPRK, China, and South Korea, all of which are shaped by the unresolved geopolitical complexities still in place from the Korean War. As such, defectors are more directly vulnerable to present-day hostilities left over from the Korean War. North Koreans who cross out are readily implicated by the present-day dangers of the Korean conflict far more than their South Korean brethren are, regardless of generation. It is almost as if they are resetting the clock on history, or as if multiple histories are co-occurring. They experience the split of the peninsula as new because for them the freshness of familial, geographic, and political division becomes new. As they emigrate they experience the division anew from the other side. North Koreans in the South experience anew what their grandparents experienced several decades ago, the immediate cutting off of family and friends that is a social manifestation of the physical division of the peninsula. They step from one side of the conflict into the other.

The act of crossing from North Korea into South Korea and Japan, by way of China and other countries, is not an act of individual freedom and liberation that resolves itself; instead it agitates an existing unresolved problem on the peninsula as a whole and the region. Each North Korean, through the act of defection, embodies a repetition of the traumatic division of the peninsula. A meta-repetition of the peninsular division gets repeated over and over again on the level of the individual.

Conflicts do not stay put but resurface in many areas of life, personally and internationally. How people reflect on their experiences and talk about them is a matter of how conflict on the peninsula continues in the personal, social realm.

CONCLUSION

IS PAST PROLOGUE?

A man in the back row of a small public lecture hall threw up his hand and asked, "Don't these people have any common sense?" It was the Q & A portion of a talk I was delivering to an audience in Los Angeles. North Koreans are not without sense. Whether their thinking would be comparable with that of Americans is up for debate, but the thought life of North Koreans is far from the static automaton, deeply victimized psyche typically attributed to them. What was deemed sensible in North Korea was to maintain the status quo, not to self-identify as a troublemaker, and get by as best you can. The components of a life must be understood but equally so the context of those components. As Mi-young Ahn (45) explained,

> The people are not stupid. They know the politics shouldn't be that way. They just cannot say it. When the time comes, I think something will definitely happen. They had communism, but who likes it? Of course the Party members do. The Party members praise Kim Jong-Il's leadership and say "Long live Kim Jong-Il," but the moment they turn away, they don't think like that. They are too busy living their own lives to care about Kim's policies and say whether it is good or bad. So unless one is stupid, one can see by looking at the way the country is going. Lots of people think

that this isn't the way it should be. Now, the problem is that they can't talk about it.

Mi-young Ahn identifies the component in the lives of North Koreans that she saw as holding the people back from living the lives they wanted to create. In the last few decades we have seen dramatic changes in the economic features of North Korea. Bribes, clandestine border crossing, and market selling have meant that formerly impossible things have become possible. The market may indeed set North Korea "free," but in this new life of economic exchange one thing remains at an absolute premium: No one, from the most elite to the most dehumanized prison camp detainee, can enjoy the ability to speak openly with impunity. This loss of the ability to speak openly emerged in the oral accounts in previous chapters in the form of jokes and other humor but also in careful phrases, metaphors, and repetitions that show an interpellation of the state and daily social life. Just as the absence of food and other resources found a new presence in the form of ersatz food and makeshift resources, the use of speech in North Korea seems to have long adapted to limitations.

When I met my interviewees in Seoul and Tokyo, the past was another country where things were done differently, and yet some of those differences were cherished. While volunteering at a nongovernmental organization (NGO) run by resettled North Koreans in Seoul, I had the opportunity to sit in on a discussion about our funding and how it should best be used. The discussion became heated. Our funder was a large well-known American organization represented by an American man who spoke no Korean. He sat at the table while our North Korean representative fumed. The issue was about the NGO using funds to facilitate the movement of North Koreans out of China to South Korea. The money had been given with the stipulation that it would be used solely for work in South Korea, but my co-workers interpreted the stipulation as mutable. During the course of the discussion, one of the key representatives of our group spoke up, and in Korean he said, "The difference is this. With us North Koreans, if our brother falls in the river we jump in to get him. But the South Koreans, they'll telephone the ambulance." We all laughed. The funding representative smiled curiously and inquired about the joke. After confirming it was okay to do so, I translated. He thought the analogy funny but insisted we abide by the rules. Otherwise the funding would be cut off. It occurs to me now that this micro-exchange embodies the American–DPRK and ROK–DPRK relations. The North Koreans didn't think the rules applied to them, and perhaps they did know better; time is of the essence for the drowning. South Korea was sympathetic to the North but was phoning in the help. The funders, the Americans, were very much in the dark, driving the ambulance.

Interestingly, at least in my experience, this did not stir up the anti-Americanisms my colleagues had learned in North Korea, though much of that discourse had been linked to the food shortages and nationwide suffering. In my experience, I sensed that the NGO really wanted to rely on North Korean solutions to North Korean problems. They were happy to accept funding and temporary housing in Seoul to conduct their work. But North Korea was a problem for North Koreans to solve. This could be symptomatic of the NGO that I worked with; other NGOs in Korea are a blend of both South Koreans and North Korean defectors. However, interviewees expressed something interesting during their personal narratives that reflect a retreat into culturally rooted North Korean ways of knowing. What I wish to highlight here is how interviewees returned to their collective North Korean experience that directly or otherwise locked out the listener. Jae-young Yoon told me:

> You haven't had this lived experience; this is my lived experience. Speaking from experience I can say no matter how I may appeal to you, you won't ever realize it completely. Rather, when reunification happens, when people go to see that place, "Oh, so in this country in the 1990s it was really perilous living," they'll say, convinced. Until then, all we can do is appeal to you and say *irokke saratta*, "this is how we lived." The situation is such that I too lack

the gift of eloquent speech, I can't imagine any expression for it; just "that's how we lived" is all I can say to appeal to you. (Jae-young Yoon, 45)

The starkness of that expression, *irokke saratta*, shows how some experiences strip down the finery of language. The suggestion is almost that any expression would be euphemistic; one must only go and see the land, as Jae-young Yoon suggests, when reunification happens. The silence that surrounds the phrase, the starkness of expression in the phrase "this is how we lived," calls out for evidence for proof of what the words do not provide. This may be a result of the heavy silence that was placed on the population around speaking about their experiences. Yoon's expression provides a space for the listener to drift into an imagined North Korea, to drift ahead in time to a reunified Korea when the details of life there might be known more fully.

It must be noted that Yoon and others may have struggled with articulation because of the trauma involved with their experiences. Interviewees spoke of *ch'unggyok*, a term that can be translated as shock or surprise. Psychologists working with North Koreans in Seoul observed occurrences of posttraumatic stress disorder. In the first large-scale study of posttraumatic stress among North Koreans in South Korea, Woo Taek Jeon and his colleagues found that 29.5 percent of the two hundred North Koreans assessed had the disorder.[1] There were twenty-five traumatic events listed in their research in order of highest frequency. Among these events, witnessing public execution ranked first, followed by witnessing a family member, relative, or close neighbor die of starvation. The types of trauma were divided into four factors: physical (receiving a beating), political (witnessing public executions), ideological (such as "agony over family background"), and family related (witnessing someone starving to death). Traumatic experience and its explicability have been the topic of research within the social sciences for some time.[2] Arthur Kleinman and Robert Desjarlais observed that trauma systematically silences.[3] Other elements can silence a speaker. The location where one speaks, to whom, and what one speaks about all contribute to the shape a story takes and what portions get told and how. It is not just the story that is told. Signposts appear, indicating whole portions that are cut off, not for sharing. Who could claim to have a perfect account of all that happened in North Korea during the famine years? Even North Koreans themselves repeatedly say that North Korea is a society that cannot be known, certainly not from the outside, but also not from within. As Judith Butler explains, "When the 'I' seeks to give an account of itself, it can start with itself, but it will find that this self is already implicated in a social temporality that exceeds its own capacities for narration; indeed . . . the 'I' has no story of its own that is not at once the story of a relation—or a set of relations to—a set of norms."[4] These oral accounts of life in North Korea were not so much autobiography but the biography of social life. And who could possibly tell all of that? The implication of the other, including those who remain, may be the variable that generates truncated, closed-off narratives. So while the act of eliciting and receiving speech may initially appear as a liberating inversion of North Korea's censorship, the rhetorical structure is not entirely liberated because it bears traces of discourse from the North and it acts and is acted upon by the interlocutory scene of the incomplete geopolitical conflict in both North and South Korea.

What a North Korean says about North Korea enters into the political realm of the South not only because of where she is from, but because of the incomplete nature of conflict between the Koreas. Her discourse about the North enters this conflict, however marginally or overtly. Speaking about North Korea does not occur in a geopolitical "state of conclusion" where the causes of the Cold War and the Korean War have achieved resolution. It is a conclusion neither on the individual nor on the international level but a scene where the conflicts have yet to find peace and where transfers of information, people, and loyalty are slotted into competing sides. This is evidenced most glaringly in the use of the South Korean *talbukja* (lit., escaped Northern person; defector) and the North Korean *paeshinja* (lit., traitor) to refer to those who leave the North. The relationship of North and South

Korea permits only a singular and uncomplicated narrative for North Koreans who cross the border. I have demonstrated that the narrative models available to North Koreans back home are highly limited; equally restricted—although different—narrative models meet them in the South. The narrative models in South Korea, intentionally or otherwise, make available a preponderance of North Korean defector narratives that focus almost exclusively on the most horrific aspects of life in the North. While there certainly are grievous atrocities in the North, such singular representations do not provide insights into factors other than violence that keep people in the North.

The tendency I observed among North Koreans to withdraw—not only during their oral accounts but also in terms of social engagement—may indicate a desire to return emotionally to the *ch'ung* (deep loyalty) and *hyo* (filial piety) they had with friends and family in the North. Deep loyalty and filial piety have been identified on a national level as two of the preeminent human ethical characteristics in Confucianism. When I consider this retreat in personal narratives as connected with loyalty and piety, it reminds me of Adriana Cavarero's paradoxical observation that "No matter how much you are similar and consonant . . . your story is never my story. . . . I still do not recognize myself in you and, even less, in the collective we."[5] This identifies the dissonance many North Koreans might encounter in the South, regardless of who listens. It is in such context that Jae-young Yoon's words—"that's how we lived is all I can say to appeal to you"—is at once an appeal for connection and an affirmation of our distinctness and our disconnection. It is an act of keeping the narrative to oneself.

Although famine is usually seen rather than heard or listened too, North Korea frustrated this tendency to visually sensationalize starvation. Because international access was limited, a paradigmatic shift was necessary in approaching North Korea generally but also in the study of those famine years in particular. The movement is from looking and seeing to listening and hearing. In this respect the distance between us is somewhat dissolved since listening is about participation, sharing, and permitting absorption.[6] This book shifts the typical approach to North Korea by identifying North Korean people as agentive. In the same spirit, the paradigmatic shift approaches the North not as a visual spectacle but as a discursive space.

The relevance of speech—its accuracy and its weight—is a complex political matter that is always at stake not only when North Koreans speak at home in the North but wherever they speak, to whom, and about what. Whatever gets done with that speech is political, but the way it is politicized may be determined by its emergence in differing geopolitical contexts. This is also true of written accounts, particularly of North Koreans who survived and escaped political prison camps of the North. These memoirs are in transit on a political landscape, used to convey different messages sometimes unintended by their authors, co-opted by national agendas.[7] Given this, Foucault's observation that the "verbalization of conflicts and domination is perilous" seems understated to say the least.[8] Speech is indeed, and writing too, an object, a site, of conflict.

This book is also unavoidably cast into that web of sociopolitical complexity. As the author, I perform an abstraction in transforming these oral accounts into written transcripts that are then transformed again in translation, and again through selecting and incorporating portions into the analysis. Intertextuality is inevitable, and this book in turn generates intertextuality. Indeed, even before we sat down for the interviews, the speakers engaged in countless exchanges, between us and among others. Rather than trying to organize the disorder inherent in the articulation of personal experience, I acknowledge the uncontrollable, imperfect aspects of research with human subjects, with memory, and with suffering. The book draws upon the information-rich sections of the oral accounts that provide inductive insights into the broader experience of life in North Korea.

Despite its intangibility, speech has the power to make and unmake the world.[9] Discourse is "controlled, selected, organised and redistributed according to a certain number of procedures, whose role is to avert its powers and its dangers . . . not just anyone, finally, may speak of just anything."[10] North Korea exercises a detailed control of the population, both in terms of physical bodies and in terms of what people produce—their labor or the product of their words. In the North the feeding, clothing, and housing of bodies is a state operation. The nonmaterial aspects of life are also the concern of the state: learning, training, and self-criticism, for instance. The state is interested in the management of physical bodies toward national service, and the minds of individuals must also be put to national work. As existing scholarship has shown, the North Korean government uses language in a particular fashion to achieve a particular result.[11] The reader will note that the national appropriation of discourse is not unique to North Korea. However, throughout the North's education and self-criticism sessions, standard nationalist narratives are ritualized and the "appropriateness of rearticulation is exercised between individuals."[12]

How can a researcher bypass habituated norms of discourse? What are the complications of using spoken discourse, once so controlled in the North, as a means of getting information? When North Koreans shared their experiences with me, the individual act of speaking was unlike the sociopolitical site of their original experience in the North. Previously, they had to choose from within their lived experiences those things that were acceptable to convey in language and those that they could not express at risk of death or other punishments, like the mundane social punishments that emerge from departing from custom and norm. They had learned to avoid wrong speech and action by witnessing what happened to others: threats, disappearances, public executions, or imprisonment. The privileges of correct speech were also learned. Aspects of speech, though perhaps state-controlled, were likely to have been so ordinary as to have gone unobserved and to have been absorbed into habit without significant duress.

In oral accounts, individuals recall experiences that at the time of their formation were typically voiced through coded and clandestine means, if at all. The very things forbidden to articulate in North Korea, things they had grown practiced at overlooking, camouflaging, or suppressing, are the very things the researcher in Seoul and Tokyo may call upon the interviewee to voice. The method involves bearing in mind that making use of oral accounts does not mean the natural inversion of sociopolitical contexts to which the survivor is accustomed. The initial experience occurred within a sociopolitical frame that necessitated ambiguous articulation because of social norms on one end and because of the threat of death on the other. It would be foolish for the researcher to seek unobstructed articulation or hope that the interviewee will speak "the truth" of her experience so that it can be captured and analyzed. Her survival once hinged on selective use of speech and silence. The interviewee that confirms experience is the same person who once could not give voice to those experiences she now confirms. This paradox is most troublesome: the researcher seeks articulation of experience when survival of the initial experience necessitated inaccurate, bungled, and altered articulation. These are the limits we must work within. Language raises the question of its own limits.[13]

When I elicit an account from an interviewee, if she speaks with words molded by the context that created her suffering, that language may also reveal how suffering was conceptualized, justified, and allocated in North Korea. The limits of her language are the limits of her world. Her words may show how she negotiated suffering within the limits of that context. This is quite expected, for in order to come into being, the initial site of suffering, atrocity, uses discourse to conceptualize, justify, and allocate suffering within a given population. When interviewees emerge from the context of rights violations, when they emerge from this discourse into a so-called neutral space, what sort of speech emerges? Let us recall that she experienced her suffering in a context that severely restricted how that suffering was communicated. Can we expect the former context of censorship to be inverted when she moves to a more neutral space? Imagine an open box containing objects that, once the box is upturned, will all fall out. If we invert the context, will the once unspoken words, the words she so desired to speak, will they emerge? Indeed, we run aground if we imagine an inevitable, pent-up desire to verbally "live within the truth."[14]

Though the survivor emerges from the famine with the language of that context, language operates as a linguistic package, providing insights into the structures that sustained and generated the famine. Another type of history is produced through the oral history of subordinate groups and their written testimonies because the narrative home is different.[15] (Within the field of psychology, the articulation of traumatic pain through narrative therapy is said to be an effective means of overcoming and resolving trauma.[16]) However, accounts from North Korea demonstrate the complex nature of oral accounts, the variety of positions from which a speaker speaks. Language, particularly spoken discourse, gives us a glimpse of the distillation of the state apparatus of propaganda, self-criticism, and social management: whether absorbed, how people conceived of themselves and others, and what they thought of the state.[17] The spoken word changes over time and reveals cultural habits, humor, and figures of speech more readily than the state's written discourse; its evolution is time and place specific.

The context into which an individual speaks has the power to implicate him. That space has a set of conditioning moral norms that he cannot stand apart from; the speaker is directly vulnerable to these norms. When he speaks, it is not his own story that is told but rather the story of a set of relations. Not only is his relationship to his family and friends evoked but also—and more dangerously—his relationship to the leadership, the state, and to socialism. In North Korea, the relevance of speech is always at stake. In this sense, all speech in North Korea risks politicization, the correct or incorrect type of politicization. Because of this ever-present risk, making sense of the world with speech requires careful skill.

The interviewee speaks of her own experience, and that experience of those who remain back home in the North. This speaking-about-others distinguishes one of the painful features of oral accounts from North Koreans precisely because of the continuance of suffering, and the inaccessibility of home. Suffering could be sparked by those who departed if they speak too directly or specifically. The control of language moves from North Korea to South Korea to where I sit in To-kyo writing this. I am compelled to change names, hometowns, ages, and occupations, to eliminate traces that could spark violence in the lives of others. This fragile involvement of those who remain in the North is inevitable. Fear of reprisals linger when giving an account. Ambiguous oral accounts may indicate a desire to ensure that friends and family back home are protected from potential danger. Because of the opposing natures of these two worlds—that of enforced silence and ambiguous speech in North Korea and that of encouraged speech in South Korea and Japan—the interviewee may not easily transition between them. The researcher may not fully appreciate the difficulty either.

In contemporary global discourse, leaving North Korea is typically framed as the achievement of ultimate freedom, the triumph of good over evil, the strength of the human spirit against all odds, but this framing is incomplete and not wholly accurate. Such framing situates life in North Korea as a monolith, the country as a veritable prison, and the mentality of the people as uncomplicated and oppressed: they hold their breath until one day they can breathe the fresh air of free-dom. It sets up the international community as the savior and North Koreans as those waiting to be saved. The framing situates those who stay behind as incapable of escape or unwilling because of their false consciousness. From this very limited perspective it is inconceivable that some may have opted to stay or may have weighed the option of leaving and chosen to stay because they see remaining as the best way to resolve the difficulties of the country. As previously mentioned, some saw the solution as an inside job. It is clear from the accounts I recorded that North Korean thought life is complex and nuanced and not pathological, as it is sometimes represented in the media. Certainly the population lacks information that could help contextualize and critique the political failures of their government. The day-to-day lives of people, as indicated by these accounts, demonstrate a negotiation of economic and social difficulties. If a small counterculture emerges that allows sociopolitical discourse, there will be a chance for change.

Historically there was an assumption that as famines and similar socioeconomic difficulties worsened, the population would rise up. As Sue Lautze noted, this was thought to be the case for the Chinese and Soviet famines.[18] Lautze explains that these views seem to be informed by Western models of democracy, where suffering would lead to the collapse of government. History and personal accounts of trauma have shown that increased suffering does not lead to increased likelihood of the opposition.[19] Furthermore, the idea that revolt is inevitable as situations worsen is historically unfounded. Rather, the opposite is true. As situations liberalize, people are more likely to have the ability to rise up. The French Revolution, the Russian October Revolution, the Hungarian revolution of 1956, and the Iranian revolution all demonstrate that it is not when oppression is at its most severe that violent revolutions occur but when the oppression is loosened and the system of control becomes slightly liberalized.[20] Similarly, the severity of suffering is less significant than the ability to conceive of another way of being, and being able to see other possibilities can motivate change.[21] We might have expected popular uprisings from North Koreans, given the presence of variables such as an easing up on suffering in the postfamine years. There was a let-up on the extent of suffering, a relaxation of social control of coping strategies such as selling in markets. One might have conceived of a different state of affairs by witnessing military personnel taking advantage of their position. Evidence that North Koreans were gaining increased access to foreign goods, particularly from China and South Korea, indicates that there may have been an awakening of what in democratic states we think of as oppositional consciousness and what Sartre calls "another state of affairs." But these variables were complicated by the presence of greater deterrents. Aggregate numbers of dissidents couldn't form because rebellious groups were crushed before their numbers could grow. The inflow of foreign goods did not necessarily arrive untainted by the orthodoxy of North Korea's ideology. In this nation where the collective is promoted, distinctly individual acts of survival were waged against the difficulties of the famine years.

Stories of pain and suffering involve complex relations of power in the telling because the pain and suffering came into being as a result of complex relations of power. How pain is experienced and the emotional attachment that emerges from it involves the attribution of meaning as well as associations between different kinds of negative or aversive feelings. It seems counterintuitive how repressive regimes get incorporated into the attitudes and behavior of people, with the consequence that citizens behave in ways that place the polity above individual interests.[22] Perhaps in North Korea, as in the Soviet government era, people lost faith not with the Party, but with particular leaders, with people in general, or with themselves. The death of Kim Jong-Il in 2011 sparked discussion in the international community: Does this signal the end of the regime or will the young leader Kim Jung-Un ignite a renewed faith that the North Korean government will fulfill its promise to build a prosperous nation?[23] But we have heard these questions before, when Kim Il-Sung died. North Korea continues to grapple with shortages of many sorts, and yet amidst these struggles to maintain its way of life there are signs that the people have long subtly managed despite the failings of the state.

APPENDIX

A SHORT HISTORY OF
THE NORTH KOREAN FAMINE

Surrounded on all sides by leading global economic powers, North Koreans endured one of the worst famines in the last years of the twentieth century. Arguably, North Korea suffered in silence for many years before 1995 (the year most commonly identified as the start of the famine), when a series of natural disasters devastated crops and the government requested international assistance. Since that time scholars and defectors alike report that the famine was in fact well under way by the mid-1990s, that North Korea used the floods as an explanation for the food shortage. The flooding did cause extensive damage, but when aid agencies gained entry to the country, they saw medical evidence of severe malnutrition that predated the floods. In fact, several agencies confirmed malnutrition rates in North Korea as among the highest in the world. The famine changed North Korea through the loss of roughly 5 percent of the population, the migration of at least 30,000–50,000 people out of the country, and the numbers who died as a result of punishments for coping strategies.

In some ways, the North Korean case resembles famines typical to periods prior to the twentieth century in the sense that they were triggered by natural disasters that left communities without enough food to survive.[1] While the view that famines are caused by natural disasters was still popular until the 1970s, in contemporary times, technical and infrastructure advances eliminate climate alone as a sufficient cause for famine, regardless of where it occurs. Increased capability of governments and international institutions can predict and respond to impending crises, so when famines do occur nowadays, prevention was always a possibility.[2] The famine in North Korea could have been avoided if the government had made certain choices, but many of these choices were antithetical to the political system.

North Korea's famine was caused by multiple factors: loss of Soviet bloc trade partners; bad agricultural reforms; broken, outdated, and irreparable equipment; unsustainable farming practices; natural disasters; insistence on self-reliance (Juche ideology); and mismanagement of aid and international assistance. The strict control of population coping methods by restricting migration and the cracking down on black markets and private plots probably led to more starvation deaths. In other respects, lack of free information flows inside the country led to misinformation about what had caused the famine and how best to deal with it. This delayed many people's timely response to the famine. What happened in North Korea has been described as a "priority regime" famine resulting from malevolent government and incompetent exercise of state power.[3] Similar cases have been identified in Ethiopia, Sudan, and Malawi and less well-known cases in Madagascar, Iraq, and Bosnia. There may still be technical failures in these instances, but the main problems are asymmetrically skewed toward political failure of local, national, and international response and accountability.

If the North Korean government sought any historical council on their decision making about the famine, they knew that wholesale national collapse was unlikely to result even if they deprioritized relief. Advisors within the government could have reassured the leadership that famines historically have never led to successful revolt or overthrow of state power, and they would have been correct. The leadership may have known that it is not when crises are at the worst that rebellions arise but just before or after. They may have known that preexisting social inequalities map the prognosis for increased inequality in times of famine, that the politically marginalized and economically impoverished are two features throughout history that distinguish those most adversely affected. In North Korea, these groups were preselected for nutritional inequality long before the famine anyway. Indeed, the habitus of North Koreans typically normalized nutritional inequality. Since famines rarely impact more than 5 percent of a population, they have not resulted in whole or even partial changes in political leadership anywhere.[4] What the North Korean leadership needed to be most mindful of was the period preceding and following the worst years of the famine. As Victor Cha observed, it is not when things are at their worst but when things begin to improve that the chances for social change arise.[5]

While it is wishful thinking to imagine that the North Korean famine would lead to political unrest or significant government changes, it was the first time since its early history that a potential threat to national sovereignty emerged from within, and in this respect it was a sensitive period. The famine was never presumed to bring collapse, but it brought a host of opportunities for the seed of dissatisfaction to take root. As a result, it was necessary for North Korea to cope the way socialist countries, long accustomed to hunger, had in the past. Punishments for natural responses to scarcity such as internal migration, crime, and vocalized complaints were dealt with harshly during the 1990s. Punishment for crimes such as theft, speaking freely, and border crossing were meted out on the level of life and death. In fact, the well-worn history of socialist hunger may have been the prescription North Korean used to draft its own solutions.

North Korea's famine was not a sudden event; rather, it was a process and the tail end of long-term vulnerability with multiple causal factors, such as a combination of agricultural reforms, natural disasters, and the socialist system, that provided the context for the "slow-moving" 1990s famine to emerge and progress.[6] Thus, multiple factors led to the economic crisis and food shortages becoming famine.[7] Between 200,000 and 1.5 million people died in the famine, but these figures are clearly very rough estimates. Low estimates represent North Korean government figures while high estimates are those of aid agencies; the former is not transparent in its information gathering while the latter are restricted by the North Korean government in their in-country information gathering.[8] No source offers a truly accurate picture of the famine's impact. Compounding these already complicated estimates is the number of people who suffered from famine-related disease and the people who died from punishments for coping strategies that were considered antithetical to the North Korean government.

North Korea's famine shows signs of entitlement failure not necessarily or only as a theory about the economics of famine processes but also in terms of politics and power.[9] Actually, it is not possible to speak of a failure of entitlement in North Korea but rather of "conditional entitlement," where a person is entitled to food on the condition that he demonstrates political loyalty. Several revolutions also played a role in normalizing inequality and preparing the people for vulnerability to food shortage. The ideological revolution involved the reeducation of peasants to put collective interests above personal ones. The technological revolution entailed irrigation, electrification, mechanization, and chemicalization. The cultural revolution necessitated upgrading the peasantry in terms of knowledge and skill. Added to this was scientific farming, and—like other high-modernist reforms[10]—a tendency to disregard traditional farming methods followed. Collectively, these revolutionary goals were seen to ensure the nation's food self-sufficiency and the population's loyalty to the state.[11]

Official sources report that Kim Il-Sung first shared the idea of Juche, the official state idea of North Korea, publicly on December 28, 1955, while making a speech to workers entitled "On Eliminating Dogmatism and Formalism and Establishing Juche in Ideological Work." The goal of the Juche Idea is to achieve independence in politics, economics, and military defense and to unify the peninsula under the Juche Idea. From the beginning, the Juche Idea was applied to daily life, from agricultural techniques to international relations. The analogy of human anatomy was used to educate the population about the Juche Idea.[12] The brain makes decisions (the Great Leader), the nervous system carries out those decisions (the Party), and the bones and muscle execute the orders (the people). The body and the nervous system are the population while the head is the leadership.[13] The Juche Idea requires loyalty of the people to the leadership.

The national deterioration in food production in the absence of additional imports resulted in food balance deterioration. As early as 1991 the North Korean government launched a gastronomic reform called the "Let's Eat Only Two Meals a Day" campaign.[14] Opting against choices such as opening to the international community and thus potentially losing control of its population, North Korea chose to reduce public consumption of food directly. The famine was already in motion, and only policies ideologically antithetical to the North Korean government could have changed things at this point; nevertheless the Two Meals a Day campaign was intensified. In July 2002 the government announced new measures in agricultural policy whereby state farm workers and members of production cooperatives were permitted to farm greater amounts of land. With respect to these changes, China is a likely influence. In some areas, individual families were allocated land from the assets of the production cooperatives, though we cannot be sure exactly which areas were allocated.[15] At the same time, the government ended rationing of rice, corn, and other basic foodstuffs, and consumer prices for these and other products were markedly increased. Wages, to a lesser extent, were also raised, but for many people the prices of foodstuffs were so high as to make money nearly useless.[16] In the early 2000s in North Korea, state consumer prices were hyperinflated and markets for all types of products have expanded nationwide. To some this indicated that the centrally planned economy of North Korea was dissolving.[17]

In the 1980s North Korea struggled with a lack of energy. The energy infrastructure of the economy received a blow early in the 1990s with the dissolution of the Soviet Union and the Chinese shift to demanding payment for supplies in hard currency. In 1990 North Korea imported about 2.5 million tons of crude oil from the Soviet Union, China, and Iran.[18] By 1993 crude oil imports plummeted to one-tenth of what they had been at the start of the 1990s. Given that 100 percent of oil in North Korea is imported, this decline had a major impact on transport and other sectors of the economy, including agriculture. Normal commercial exports collapsed with the end of the Soviet era.[19] In 1994–1995 China again reduced its exports to North Korea concurrently at a time of high world prices, making it too expensive for North Korea to import on commercial terms.[20]

The loss of trading partners from the former Soviet bloc adversely impacted the economy by reducing North Korea's access to imports. This became increasingly significant in the coming decade as it was more and more difficult to raise enough hard currency at a time when barter was crucial, although North Korea did manage to survive. With the breakup of the bloc, the Soviet Union and then its successor, Russia, demanded payment for the oil at prevailing market rates and in hard currency.[21]

Investment through trade with the Soviet bloc had already been on the decline; before the collapse, replacements to modernize industrial plants, machinery, infrastructure, and vehicles were long overdue.[22] Keep in mind that although North Korea benefited from investments from the USSR and China in the 1950s, along with huge investments of European machinery in 1973 and 1974 (which was never paid for), by the 1990s North Korea was still using this same outdated equipment with no spare parts, and was still relying on these same—now inadequate—investments.

The northeastern part of North Korea took the brunt of the loss of Soviet export markets. Given the resulting squeeze on the economy, the population was forced into precarious dependence on the limited, marginal land available. In mountainous provinces such as Ryanggang, North Hamgyong, and South Hamgyong, this proved a major challenge.[23] These regions had been the main source of the country's industrial base in steel, chemicals, and fertilizers. Foreign import collapse created devastation in these regions, which were also completely dependent on the now increasingly defunct Public Distribution System (PDS).[24]

According to North Korean defectors, in the past farmers in certain areas were ordered to grow opium poppies.[25] North Koreans I interviewed reported that there were opium and tobacco plantations in the northern regions during the 1990s famine. North Korea cultivates approximately 4,000 to 7,000 hectares of opium poppy, which equates to a production of about 30 to 44 metric tons of opium gum annually.[26] More recent studies show that lack of currency is driving the export of drugs, that drugs are being used to dull hunger pains, and that drug use among military officials is widespread.[27]

Food substitution is still seen in North Korea even during contemporary times: the BBC reported that North Korea has developed a "special noodle" which keeps one feeling full longer.[28] Ersatz food has appeared in socialism systems before.[29] This is a feature of the shortage phenomena of classical socialist systems.[30] Postponement is another characteristic, the belief that particular services, such as the delivery of food or health care, will come about later.[31]

In North Korea the procurement of grain rests on an exchange between the government and farmers. Farmers surrender grain at prices well below what they could command in the market, and they receive food and other consumer items in return. The North Korean government at the time of the famine was severely impaired in its ability to uphold its end of the bargain because of declines in the economy.[32] At the same time, promises to increase wages were also unfulfilled.[33] The government could not provide fertilizer and other agricultural supplies, so the exchange with farmers became more and more onesided. According to Haggard and Noland, "the surrender of grain to the government no doubt looked more and more like a one-sided deal or confiscatory tax."[34] The farmers naturally had a strong incentive to protect themselves. In the summer of 1996 many farmers secretly harvested crops before they could be taken by the central government.[35]

The North Korean famine of the 1990s has its roots in the economic and political systems of the country, which has led some scholars to believe that regime change is necessary for current shortages to be resolved.[36] In the past, experts considered the main causes of the agricultural crisis in North Korea to be floods, low incentive to work, little investment, Juche farming methods, and ineffective use of fertilizer.[37] Taken in combination, the agricultural crisis, the economic decline of North Korea, the PDS, and vulnerability in terms of entitlement relations with the state all help to explain how the famine arose and continues to plague the country. In 2004 the Good Friends nongovernmental organization (NGO) asked defectors which reforms they felt were most needed in North Korea; the majority answered that the cooperative farms, the PDS, and the regulation of the market needed to be abolished.

As the food crisis worsened, the political and administrative system, while appearing centralized and hierarchical, decentralized to some extent. As a consequence, local authorities at provincial levels had to coordinate supply with the demand for food, and this led to an increase in local officials' influence in the distribution of food in their areas.[38] People's committees controlled county-level warehouses and played important roles in the collection of food, transmitting targets, supervising grain collection in jurisdictions, and allocating food to retail sites (public distribution centers).

The official means by which food has been and is still today distributed inside North Korea is the PDS. The PDS is said to have subsidized food rations to approximately 13.5 million North Koreas, roughly 62 percent of the population.[39] Access to food depends principally upon access to distributions from the state; however, people have increasingly learned to diversify their sources of food acquisition. Limited access to food through legal or illegal means, rather than aggregates of food production alone, creates greater vulnerability. Thus, legal and affordable access to food beyond the state distribution system would secure livelihoods. In North Korea more than 60 percent of the population depends entirely on the PDS, and the majority of those people live in urban areas, where alternative methods of accessing food such as foraging, market-selling, trading, and so on, are limited. This would indicate that those in urban areas have experienced higher levels of vulnerability.

Entitlement to the PDS is based on factors other than need. Even if one has access to the PDS, the amount is often distributed unequally.[40] As Sue Lautze has argued, access to state-supplied food in the form of domestic produce, imports, or aid is "strictly determined by one's status, with key military units, government officials and urban residents always outranking peasant farmers. In sum, the more important an individual is to the state, the better treated his family will be."[41] Since the late 1990s, access to food is increasingly made through markets, though people who lack sufficient funds cannot get adequate food through these routes.

According to research conducted by the then Korean Buddhist Sharing Movement (also known as Good Friends), when they asked former North Koreans about the approximate date when food distribution stopped, answers varied widely: 13 percent of respondents answered it was 1992 or before while the greatest numbers, 32.3 percent and 28.2 percent, reported the PDS stopped in 1994 and 1995, respectively; only 5.4 percent reported the PDS stopped in 1996 or after.[42] Reports about the continuance or failure of the PDS appear in defector accounts throughout the 2000s and continue to vary at present writing. Aid programs such as the World Food Program and other agencies are required to deliver food through the PDS to local communities. The existence of the system is not in doubt, nor is its capacity to sufficiently supply the country; however, the continuance of the PDS into the future is in question.

The famine in North Korea provides clear evidence that inequality is a preexisting norm within the society. The allocation of rations followed complex systems of occupation and age-related stratification, delivered by the PDS, which had its initial break down, but not official collapse, in the 1990s.[43] Entitlements to food, access to education, type of employment, and residence were all determined by the "perceived political reliability" of individuals, and these differences in entitlement have influenced mortality rates.[44] Since the purges of the 1950s, the Korean Workers' Party has undertaken a succession of efforts to investigate the class background of the population and to classify individuals in terms of their political reliability. As a result, members of the so-called hostile classes were relocated to remote parts of the country—parts of the country that have been off-limits to external monitoring by relief organizations.[45] These membership categories are said to have had powerful indirect effects on access to food, and class positions had important implications for residence location. The top ranks of the political class were also centrally rather than generally supplied, receiving their rations through the Party or special supplies within the government.[46] So this class might be less aware of what was going on in famine areas. The distribution of food reflected quite openly the basic principles of stratification in the socialist system. At the top of the hierarchy of entitlements were the military and special security forces and high-ranking government officials.[47] Two groups fell outside the scope of the PDS—namely, workers on state farms who relied on PDS for only six months of a year and those on cooperative farms; both of these groups could keep some of the grain they harvested.[48]

With rationing coupons, North Koreans "purchase" items from within the PDS. Black markets (jangmadang) offer the chance to purchase items with cash, but at hugely inflated prices. Because access to food and other ration items are officially acquired through the PDS, it is one of the primary means of controlling and monitoring the population. The top ranks of the political class were centrally supplied, receiving their rations through the Party or special supplies reserved for the government. The military maintained its own distribution system, the provisions bureau, under the general services bureau of the ministry of the people's armed forces supplied rations to military units, managing the military's energy war stockpiles of food and fuel.[49] In 1996, in a talk he gave at Kim Il-Sung University, Kim Jong-Il stated that the military was not immune to food shortages and hunger. He urged farmers to avoid stealing from farms and urged the public to be conservative in its consumption so that the military would have enough.[50] There was of course the need for food to be transferred more fairly, but the reason why it was not done so was because of unequal relations of power.[51] The distribution of international relief supplies is said to be contingent on political loyalty or economic utility rather than need.[52] In order to limit the threat of influence posed by the international community, constraints were put on international humanitarian workers. While these constraints went so far as to contravene operational considerations of some of the humanitarian organizations themselves, the main goal was to ensure control of the flow of information, people, and objects within the country. For example, aid workers were denied access to about 25 percent of the country, representing about 15 percent of the population. "There was no way of assessing the needs—if any—of the people in these areas, although the general consensus was that conditions were unlikely to be any better than those in accessible areas." Areas that were once accessible became inaccessible, and vice versa, for "no clear reason."[53] Additionally, because access to official information and data was difficult, and if available at all it was of questionable reliability, it was virtually impossible to determine if the aid was having any positive impact. Morton writes:

> Agencies were not permitted to conduct random monitoring of programmes or spot checks, which are the normal means to determine that aid is properly used. National security overrides every other consideration in the DPRK. If there was a choice between external aid and national security, there was no contest: national security would automatically prevail. This was why certain parts of the country were off-limits. This was why information was restricted. Even giving us a list of beneficiary institutions was perceived to have national security implications.[54]

Communications were also strictly controlled for reasons of national security: long-distance radio communications or satellite phones as well as normal communication operating equipment for UN agencies and NGOs were not permitted. In addition, the use of an emergency international air ambulance service to provide emergency medical evacuation was not guaranteed permission to land in Pyongyang.[55] NGO and UN staff was monitored all the time by a minder provided by the government. The application of this type of control is not particular to foreigners; this degree of control is also applied to North Koreans themselves, or to other visitors to the country, including academics. However, this type of control severely limited the access to information, thus complicating assessment of need in those places where permission to work was granted and, worse, sometimes totally eliminating the possibility for assessment.

It is perhaps unfair to doubt the extent of difficulty involved in trying to establish and maintain humanitarian work in North Korea, both for the foreign agencies and for the government itself, which views foreign agencies as a threat to its national sovereignty. There are problems with roads, energy supplies, and basic resources for the delivery of aid, so it is not a surprise that there would be delays and added confusion with language and translation—particularly as it would all be on the North Korean side. Korean-speaking foreign aid workers were not permitted in North Korea during the 1990s famine.[56] This stipulation seems to have relaxed since then. In the past the linguistic helplessness of aid workers in North Korea contributed to the isolation of the people. The largely monolingual society has no means of interacting with the international community on a direct level—and any interaction is mediated through interpreters and strictly supervised. The linguistic powerlessness of aid workers in North Korea is part of an obvious, deliberate, and sustained effort at control.

The North Korean government acted as the final arbitrator on the needs of its citizens, often using food toward its self-determined ends. The fact that North Korea put political loyalty over humanitarian need in determining who did and did not receive aid resulted in the cessation of operations by NGOs such as Care International, Oxfam, Action against Hunger, Doctors without Borders, and Doctors of the World. However, after speaking with a doctor who worked in North Korea with Doctors without Borders, it seems that individual morals were compromised and this also became untenable. The bystander anxiety that Hugo Slim writes about may not have been uncommon given such conditions—compassion for North Koreans amid powerlessness to take necessary action, frustration, anger, and fear caused many humanitarian workers and NGOs to withdraw from North Korea.[57]

Grain shipments were triaged so that stocks were sent out to some areas but not others. The east coast was particularly limited in terms of food distribution, especially late in 1995. From the start of the relief effort, the government focused relief and monitoring on the west coast, insisting that food be delivered through the main west coast port of Namp'o despite the fact that the transportation system linking the west and east had broken down.

Contributions in the form of fertilizers, improved irrigation systems, reliable electricity, and expanded use of agricultural facilities and equipment have helped to bolster agricultural output. Among international donors, South Korea still gives massive amounts of food aid to North Korea. However, during the mid-1990s the North Korean government stipulated that aid from South Korea would only be accepted if it came in unmarked bags, ensuring that international aid would not bring with it an awareness of the international community for North Korean citizens. Between 1995 and 2012 the South Korea government provided $1.36 billion in aid to North Korea. Private aid to North Korea from the South was nearly another $800 million. Aid contributions from the United States in the form of energy assistance, food aid, and medicine have exceeded $1.3 billion since the United States started providing aid in 1995.[58]

In 1998 eighteen nutritionists from UNICEF, WFP, and the European Commission for Humanitarian Aid and Civil Protection (ECHO), in collaboration with the North Korean government, measured the height and weight of more than 1,500 children aged six months to seven years. The report indicated that 62 percent of the children suffered from chronic malnutrition (based on height for age) and 16 percent were acutely malnourished (based on weight for height). In a joint press release, the agencies underlined that "this puts North Korea among the top 10 countries with the highest malnutrition rates in the world."[59] This suggests that the problems had been long in the making, as assessments on stunting retroactively assess conditions of famine. Military grain stockpiles ranged from 400,000 metric tons to as high as 1.5 million metric tons. That is said to be 5 percent to 20 percent of normal annual demand.[60] The government could have drawn on these, but those I interviewed said that they did not, which suggests that shortages were a function of distribution more than aggregate supply.[61]

Nearly a decade after the famine began to take shape, aid agencies were still not given full and independent access to the population, and there is little systematic information about the famine.[62] For instance, the World Food Programme in 2008 and 2009 still only had access to 131 counties. There are still entire areas about which aid agencies have no knowledge whatsoever. The information that they do have, and their means of distribution, are morally questionable. As Scott Snyder and Gordon Flake explain, the "amount of food distributed through the PDS is no longer an indicator of imminent distress within the North Korean system, yet it has remained the WFP's primary indicator of distress."[63] Fiona Terry, a researcher for Doctors Without Borders, wrote in the *Guardian* that by distributing food through the PDS, their relief operations have become part of the system of oppression.[64]

A decline in international food availability, combined with a supply of external sources, can be identified as a new kind of entitlement problem.[65] Commercial imports of food fell as humanitarian assistance arrived, and the savings created by this were allocated to other resources. Therefore, the 1995 food problem cannot be attributed to decline in domestic food availability alone; rather, the famine developed and worsened as a result of a failure to adjust imports and military expenditures according to the needs of the population. This failure provides clear evidence to evaluate the government's reaction to consequent suffering and deaths during the famine. The regime faced two basic options: the country could either reduce domestic consumption to bring it into line with shrinking domestic supplies, or it could relieve the domestic supply constraints by importing food from abroad. The latter strategy could be achieved through three non-mutually exclusive means: increasing exports to pay for needed imports, sustaining the ability to borrow on commercial terms, or seeking foreign aid.[66]

Every step of the way, the WFP and other aid agencies had to negotiate with the North Korean government about every aspect of aid distribution within the country. At the time of the 1990s famine, the humanitarian effort sought to target its assistance to vulnerable groups inside North Korea, such as children, pregnant and nursing women, and the elderly; these priority groups were to be monitored closely. The North Korean government placed roadblocks in the way of donor activities, making them unable to achieve certain objectives. Because donors were unable to track food donations from port to final consumer, the true benefit of these activities cannot be assessed.[67] The socialist system, in order to maintain power, requires a high threshold of control over the interaction between the population and the international community. However, in this instance it seems that the primary objective of control was the politically unreliable portions of the population that had already been relocated to inhospitable areas of the country, and to the most difficult jobs, or to the most arduous prison camps, in the decades leading up to the famine.

The limitations placed on the international community in North Korea were not only influenced by the run-down infrastructure of the country, which could hardly manage to distribute the foreign aid, but were also ideological. The aid workers were restricted in the locations where they delivered aid and the routes they took to deliver it. They were also linguistically isolated from the North Korean staff with which they worked and the population to whom they delivered the aid. While this has changed in recent years, it is still not possible for aid workers to speak openly and freely with aid recipients.

As Johan Pottier has shown in Kigali, regimes know how to make use of the empathy and guilt that exists in the international aid community. International aid organizations' preferences for authorities' "easy reading" of complex situations have led them to operate according to the authorities' "seal of approval."[68] Many UN officials misread the signals and expressed doubts about the credibility of refugee accounts of the famine. The same misreading occurred elsewhere. "Pentagon analysts looked at satellite photographs and saw none of the signs familiar from African famines, mass graves and hordes of refugees."[69] Migration is one of the most natural responses to famine when other means of survival are proving insufficient. The lack of large-scale migration from North Korea might have been misinterpreted as a sign that the famine was not severe, that the relief efforts within the country were sufficient, or that other coping strategies were working, rather than that the government was controlling migration on a physical as well as an ideological level.

The severity of famine is an issue of numbers for some in the international community. With access to many areas impossible, analysts have few options but to resort to what is known of other famines, but it is a fallacy to expect that famine will manifest in the same ways in different places, particularly when we recognize that famine can come about through different causal factors, can be met with different responses, and can be contained in different ways by the country in which it emerges. Where assessments of famine have been made using satellite images, as in North Korea, the reliability of such images needs to be addressed. Reliance on satellite photos to diagnose famine—in terms of refugee flows and mass graves—is a highly unreliable technique. Reliance on satellite photos to disprove famine is almost immoral.

In the best of cases, photos can only be used as a complementary tool to substantiate allegations of atrocities. As one expert on international conflicts and remote sensing explained, you need to know where and when to look.[70] In addition, satellite imagery can only pick up on relatively large groups, not individuals. Where refugees are concerned, most of the information is gathered from what is left behind in the wake of refugee flows, such as tents, paths, cars, and campfires—in other words, circumstantial evidence. For this evidence to be picked up on satellite, the background must have an exceptionally contrasting effect. In the case of North Korea, we do not have large convoys of refugees heading toward the Chinese border. Pitching a tent or lighting a campfire is out of the question if successful defection is the objective. Border crossers leave no sign of their passage that could attract the attention of soldiers or border guards. Sometimes mass graves can indicate the extent of famine, or prison camps, for example, but trying to disprove the existence of these through satellite images cannot be done with certainty. In order to determine the possibility of mass graves, areas need to be forest- and mountain-free so analysts of satellite images can look at various images of an identical location—before and after the event—and determine whether soil has been turned.

Numerous national disasters contributed to the famine.[71] With arable land in short supply, insistence on self-sufficiency proved lethal. This is nothing unexpected because "socialist governments that pursue policies of self-sufficiency limit their capacity to purchase food and frequently fail to avail themselves of international assistance as well. As a result, they effectively deny their citizens entitlements just as clearly as more localized entitlements or political contract failures do."[72] Some agriculture techniques increased North Korea's vulnerability to natural disasters.

The 1990s started with general declines in agricultural production and the economy. Given the unpromising objective conditions in the agricultural sector, such as the hilly terrain, the northerly latitude, a high ratio of population to arable land, and the short growing seasons, the achievement of production goals required maximization of yields through the heavy application of chemical fertilizers and other agricultural chemicals as well as a reliance on electrically powered irrigation systems. Continuous cropping led to soil depletion and the overuse of ammonium sulfate as a nitrogen fertilizer contributed to acidification of the soil and, eventually, a reduction in yields. As yields declined, hillsides were denuded, which brought more and more marginal land into production. This contributed to soil erosion, river silting, and, ultimately, catastrophic flooding. Isolation from the outside world has also meant that the genetic diversity of North Korean seeds have declined, making plants more vulnerable to disease.[73]

A severe cold front hit in 1993, and when it hit Northeast Asia, it caused 10–30 percent yield damage in northeast China and South Korea. It clearly also adversely affected North Korean crops (although we do not know to what extent). Meanwhile, North Korea had already been experiencing food shortages for several years. The floods helped to speed the crisis—already well under way—to its nadir. The floods also provided an alibi for the North Korean government to save face while requesting outside help. It is generally accepted that North Korea would have experienced a famine with or without the floods that came in 1995 and 1996. Deforestation meant that land was swept away when the floods came in 1995 and 1996. After the floods, "15% of arable land was destroyed, with the incidence of flooding being higher on high-quality land (28%) than on medium- and low-quality land (13%)."[74] The international community was alerted to the humanitarian crisis in the mid-1990s. At that time, the floods offered a convenient decoy to the myriad causes for the famine. According to North Korea, 5.4 million people were displaced, 330,000 hectares of agricultural land washed away, 1.9 million tons of grain lost, and the total cost of flood damages reached $15 billion.

Despite the tight restrictions placed on relief activities, the evidence for chronic malnutrition and a slow-moving famine were discernible to aid agencies on the ground. This might also suggest that the impact of malnutrition had become so pervasive and ordinary in North Korea that these signs had become largely invisible. In terms of infrastructure and economic development, North Koreans fared better than their brethren in the South for about two decades after the division of the Korean Peninsula. However, recent research shows that there is evidence that North Koreans were poorly off in nutrition even in those early decades. Studies with refugees reveal significant discrepancies in height, with those born after 1948 significantly shorter than those born prior to the division, and this discrepancy became greater over time, peeking in the 1980s.[75] Although North Korea did have a more advanced health care system in the 1960s and 1970s, this is not reflected in increased height of North Koreans because their diet was low in quality and quantity. The food shortages and eventual famine were so gradual that adjusting to these difficulties took place over generations, resulting in both demographic and cultural changes.

Kim Jong-Il formulated a connection between subsistence rights of the collective and the right to national self-determination stating: "National self-determination and independence from foreign rule is a fundamental pre-condition to the realization of the nation's subsistence rights and development."[76] North Korea continues to suffer with food shortages and it continues to prioritize national well-being over the welfare of its population.[77]

NOTES

Introduction

1. Amartya Sen and Jean Drèze, *The Amartya Sen & Jean Drèze Omnibus: (comprising) Poverty and Famines; Hunger and Public Action; and India: Economic Development and Social Opportunity* (Oxford: Oxford University Press, 1999), 68.

2. Juche, often translated as "self-reliance," is the central institution or guiding philosophy of North Korean society, paraphrased as doing things "our own way," and being "master of one's own fate." Juche is a product of North Koreans' experiences with colonialism, the Korean War, and economic developments. It frames the proper North Korean ways of being and interpreting the world. All of North Korea's official political, social, and economic activities are organized around the ideology of Juche. Jae-Jung Suh, "Making Sense of North Korea: Juche as an Institution," in *Origins of North Korea's Juche: Colonialism, War and Development*, ed. Jae Jung Suh, 1–32 (Plymouth, UK: Lexington Books, 2013), 2, 8.

3. Stephen Devereux, ed., *The New Famines: Why Famines Persist in an Era of Globalization*, Routledge Studies in Development Economics (New York: Routledge, 2007), 3, 7; and Stephen Devereux, *Theories of Famine: From Malthus to Sen* (Hemel Hempstead, UK: Harvester Wheatsheaf Publishers, 1993), 35.

4. Devereux, *The New Famines*, 7.

5. Devereux, *Theories of Famine*, 137.

6. Andrew Natsios identifies "profound political implications" that resulted from the 1990s famine, particularly in the area of public support for the DPRK government. The North Korean state took measures during the famine years, and subsequent years of ongoing difficulty. These measures can be seen across the period from the famine to the present in what Natsios refers to as the "three shocks." The first shock was at the peak of the famine in 1996; the second occurred after the July 2002 economic reforms in agricultural, food, and industrial sectors; and the third shock occurred in November of 2009 with the currency reforms and ongoing food insecurity in the country. An excellent analysis of these shocks can be read in Andrew S. Natsios, "North Korea's Chronic Food Problem," in *Troubled Transition: North Korea's Politics, Economy, and External Relations*, ed. Choe Sang-Hun, Gi-Wook Shin, and David Straub. (Stanford, CA: Walter H. Shorenstein Asia-Pacific Research Center, Shorenstein APARC, Stanford University, 2013), 120–30.

7. Mamadou Baro and Tara F. Deubel, "Persistent Hunger: Perspectives on Vulnerability, Famine, and Food Security in Sub-Saharan Africa," *Annual Review of Anthropology* 35 (2006): 521–38.

8. Susan George, *How the Other Half Dies: The Real Reasons for World Hunger* (Harmondworth, Middlesex, UK: Penguin, 1976).

9. The term *Konanŭi haenggun* can also be translated as the Arduous March.

10. Alex de Waal, *Famine That Kills: Darfur, Sudan, 1984–1985* (Oxford: Clarendon Press, 1989).

11. Frank Dikötter, *Mao's Great Famine: The History of China's Most Devastating Catastrophe, 1958–62* (London: Bloomsbury, 2010).

12. Jean-Luc Nancy, *Listening*, trans. Charlotte Mandell (New York: Fordham University Press, 2007), 10.

1. The Busy Years

1. Andrew S. Natsios, "North Korea's Chronic Food Problem," in *Troubled Transition: North Korea's Politics, Economy and External Relations*, ed. Choe Sang-Hun, Gi-Wook Shin, and David Straub, 117–38 (Stanford, CA: Walter H. Shorenstein Asia-Pacific Research Center, Stanford University), 118.

2. Ibid., 118–19.

3. Daniel Schwekendiek, "Regional Variations in Living Conditions During the North Korean Food Crisis of the 1990s," *Asia Pacific Journal of Public Health*, May 25, 2009.

4. Daniel Schwekendiek, "A Meta-Analysis of North Koreans Migrating to China and South Korea," in *Korea: Politics, Economy, Society*, ed. R. Frank, J. Hoare, P. Koellner, S. Pares, 247–70 (Leiden: Brill, 2011).

5. The following chronology is excellently illustrated in table form in Schwekendiek, "Regional Variations," 3.

6. In descriptions of class distinctions, the term "hostile class" is often used in human rights reports. Kay Seok, "North Korea's Transformation: Famine, Aid and Markets," in *Review of North Korea Economy*, April 16, 2008, available at Human Rights Watch website, http://www.hrw.org/en/news/2008/04/14/north-korea-s-transformation-famine-aid-and-markets; Human Rights Watch, "Denied Status, Denied Education: Children of North Korean Women in China," Human Rights Watch, April 2008, http://www.hrw.org/en/reports/2008/04/11/denied-status-denied-education; Human Rights Watch, "North Korea: Harsher Policies against Border-Crossers," Human Rights Watch, March 5, 2007, http://www.hrw.org/en/reports/2007/03/05/north-korea-harsher-policies-against-border-crossers; and Human Rights Watch, "The Invisible Exodus: North Koreans in the People's Republic of China," Human Rights Watch, November 19, 2002, http://www.hrw.org/reports/2002/11/19/invisible-exodus-0. See also, Amnesty International, "Democratic People's Republic of Korea: Persecuting the Starving: The Plight of North Koreans Fleeing to China," Amnesty International, December 15, 2000, http://www.amnesty.org/en/library/info/ASA24/003/2000/en; and Amnesty International, "Starved of Rights: Human Rights and the Food Crisis in the Democratic People's Republic of Korea (North Korea)," Amnesty International, January 17, 2004, http://www.amnesty.org/en/library/info/ASA24/003/2004/en. In academic materials, see Kong Dan Oh and Ralph C. Hassig, *Through the Looking Glass* (Washington, DC: Brookings Institution Press, 2000); and Stephen Haggard and Marcus Noland, *Famine in North Korea: Markets, Aid and Reform* (New York: Columbia University Press, 2007). In oral accounts, many North Koreans used expressions like *hwan kyongi an choŭn saramdŭl* (people of bad "environment" or background).

7. Schwekendiek, "Regional Variations."

8. Ibid., 9.

9. Prahar, Peter A., "North Korea: Illicit Activity Funding the Regime." Statement Before the Subcommittee on Federal Financial Management, Government Information, and International Security, Senate Homeland Security and Government Affairs Committee, April 25, 2006, hsgac.senate.gov/public/_files/042506Prahar.pdf, p. 41. For more contemporary research on North Korea's illicit trade, see the 2014 report for Human Rights in North Korea by Sheena Chestnut Greitens, "Illicit: North Korea's Evolving Operations to Earn Hard Currency." Committee for Human Rights in North Korea, 2014, http://www.hrnk.org/uploads/pdfs/SCG-FINAL-FINAL.pdf.

10. Robert Dirks, "Social Responses During Severe Food Shortages and Famine [and Comments and Reply]," *Current Anthropology* 21, no. 1 (February 1980): 27.

11. Quoted in Oh and Hassig, *Through the Looking Glass.*

12. See, for example, the website http://www.uriminzokkiri.com/, which appears in Korean and English, offering extended texts by and about the Kim family and the rescue of the Korean people.

13. Haggard and Noland, *Famine in North Korea*, 51.

14. Seok, "North Korea's Transformation"; and Human Rights Watch, "Denied Status, Denied Education."

15. Oh and Hassig, *Through the Looking Glass*, 32. The term "Red Banner Sprit," or "the Red Flag" (*Pulkŭnki Chaeng Chi'wi Undong*), first appeared in an editorial in the *Rodong Shinmun* on January 9, 1996. Further details are available in Korean at http://www.kcna.co.jp/calendar/2005/11/11-18/2005-1118-004.html, and at https://www.dailynk.com/korean/read.php?cataId=nk00700&num=7828.

16. Good Friends Centre for Peace, Human Rights and Refugees, "Human Rights in North Korea and the Food Crisis: A Comprehensive Report on North Korean Human Rights Issues," March 2000, p. 22, www.goodfriends.or.kr/eng/data/NKHR2004-final.doc.

17. Jasper Becker, *Rogue Regime: Kim Jong Il and the Looming Threat of North Korea* (Oxford: Oxford University Press, 2005), 29.

18. Richard Seaton, *Hunger in Groups: An Arctic Experiment* (Chicago: Quartermaster Food and Container Institute, U.S. Army, 1962), 90, http://oai.dtic.mil/oai/oai?verb=getRecord&metadataPrefix=html&identifier=AD0284922.

19. See Alex Argenti-Pillen, "The Discourse on Trauma in Non-Western Cultural Contexts: Contributions of an Ethnographic Method," in *International Handbook of Human Response to Trauma*, ed. A. Shalev, R. Yehuda, and M. D. McFarlane (New York: Kluwer Academic/Plenum, 2000), 96.

20. Arjun Appadurai, *Fear of Small Numbers: An Essay on the Geography of Anger* (Durham, NC: Duke University Press, 2006); and Vigdis Broch-Due, ed. *Violence and Belonging: The Quest for Identity in Post-Colonial Africa* (New York: Routledge, 2004).

21. Alexander de Waal, *Famine Crimes: Politics and the Disaster Relief Industry in Africa* (Bloomington: Indiana University Press, 1997), 215.

22. David Turton, "Response to Drought: The Mursi of Southwestern Ethiopia," *Disasters* 1, no. 4 (1997): 284. doi:10.1111/j.1467-7717.1977.tb00047.x.

23. Klaus Mühlhahn, "Hunger, Starvation and State Violence in the PRC, 1949–1979," Unpublished paper presented at the Hunger, Nutrition and Systems of Rationing Under State Socialism (1917–2006) conference, Institute for East Asian Studies, Sinology University of Vienna, February 23, 2008.

24. Viktor E. Frankl, *Man's Search for Meaning* (New York: Washington Square Press Pocket Books, 1963), 14.

25. Judith Herman, *Trauma and Recovery: The Aftermath of Violence from Domestic Violence to Political Terror* (New York: Basic Books, 1997), 77.

26. The psychological tendency to align oneself with the oppressor has been noted in various studies on domestic and political violence, of which Judith Herman's 1997 book *Trauma and Recovery* is perhaps the best known.

27. János Kornai, *The Socialist System: The Political Economy of Communism* (Oxford: Oxford University Press, 1992), 56.

28. Andrei Lankov, "The Natural Death of North Korean Stalinism," *Asia Policy*, no. 1 (January 2006): 111.

29. Ibid.

2. Cohesion and Disintegration

1. Suk-young Kim, *Illusive Utopia: Theater, Film, and Everyday Performance in North Korea* (Ann Arbor: University of Michigan Press, 2010).

2. Hy-Sang Lee, "Supply and Demand for Grains in North Korea: A Historical Movement Model for 1966–1993," *Korea and World Affairs* 18, no. 3 (1994): 551; and Marcus Noland, Sherman Robinson, and Tao Wang "Famine in North Korea: Causes and Cures" *Economic Development and Cultural Change* 49, no. 4 (July 2001): 743.

3. Michael Schloms, *North Korea and the Timeless Dilemma of Aid: A Study of Humanitarian Action in Famines* (Berlin: Lit Verlag Münster, 2004), 96.

4. Monique Macias, "In North Korea, China's Tiananmen Square Protests Stirred Hope for Change," *Guardian*, June 4, 2014, http://www.theguardian.com/world/2014/jun/04/north-korea-china-tiananmen-square-protests.

5. Daily NK Special Report Team, "Anti-Regime Activities Inside North Korea Revealed for the First Time," *DailyNK*, January 26, 2005, http://www.dailynk.com/english/read.php?num=17&cataId=nk00100.

6. So Yeol Kim, "Remembering the Coup d'Etat in 1996 [Prospects for North Korean Change] Part 2," *Daily NK*, February 5, 2011, http://www.dailynk.com/english/read.php?cataId=nk02100&num=7321; Macias, "In North Korea"; and Young Jin Kim, "Mass Protest Incident in Hoiryeong," *Daily NK*, November 9, 2006, http://www.dailynk.com/english/read.php?num=1290&cataId=nk01500.

7. Charles Armstrong, "Familism, Socialism and Political Religion in North Korea," *Totalitarian Movements and Political Religions* 6, no. 3 (December 2005): 384.

8. Kim *Illusive Utopia*.

9. Ibid.

10. Kong Dan Oh and Ralph C. Hassig, *Through the Looking Glass* (Washington, DC: Brookings Institution Press, 2000).

11. Stephen Haggard and Marcus Noland, *Famine in North Korea: Markets, Aid and Reform* (New York: Columbia University Press, 2007).

12. Pitirim A. Sorokin, *Hunger as a Factor in Human Affairs*, ed. and trans. Elena P. Sorokin (Gainesville: University Presses of Florida, 1975), 149. Sorokin's study was written during the 1921–22 Povolzhye famine, while Sorokin suffered famine himself. It was prepared for publication in Leningrad in 1922 but was censored and the author banished from the USSR. His wife, Elena P. Sorokin, edited and translated the text, which was published by the University Presses of Florida in 1975.

13. Andrew S. Natsios, "North Korea's Chronic Food Problem," in *Troubled Transition: North Korea's Politics, Economy, and External Relations*, ed. Choe Sang-Hun, Gi-Wook Shin, and David Straub,117–38 (Stanford: Walter H. Shorenstein Asia-Pacific Research Center, Stanford University, 2013), 129.

14. Louis Althusser, *Lenin and Philosophy and Other Essays Part Two.* Trans. from the French by Ben Brewster (New York: Monthly Review Press 1971), 166; emphasis added, 165, 169.

15. Kim, *Illusive Utopia.*

16. Ibid.

17. Tzvetan Todorov, *Hope and Memory: Reflections on the Twentieth Century.* Trans. David Bellos (London: Atlantic Books, 2003).

18. Oh and Hassig, *Through the Looking Glass*, 33.

19. Referenced in ibid.

20. Amartya Sen and Jean Drèze, *The Amartya Sen & Jean Drèze Omnibus: (comprising) Poverty and Famines; Hunger and Public Action; and India: Economic Development and Social Opportunity* (Oxford: Oxford University Press, 1999), 171; and Stephen Devereux, ed., *The New Famines: Why Famines Persist in an Era of Globalization*, Routledge Studies in Development Economics (New York: Routledge, 2007), 3.

21. AsiaPress International, *Rimjin-gang: News by North Korean Journalists from Inside North Korea*, part 3, "The Kim Jong-il Regime and the People" (Osaka, Japan: AsiaPress 2010), 294.

22. Claude Lévi-Strauss, *Tristes Tropiques*, trans. John Weightman and Doreen Weightman (New York: Penguin, 1955).

23. Armstrong, "Familism, Socialism and Political Religion," 388.

24. Hyok Kang, *This Is Paradise!* With Philippe Grangereau. Trans. from the French by Shaun Whiteside (London: Little, Brown, 2005), 89.

25. Ibid., 91.

26. Sorokin, *Hunger as a Factor in Human Affairs*, 232.

27. There have been efforts to link women's mortality advantage with prostitution, but because this coping strategy places women at an increased risk of death from violence and disease, the connections between mortality advantage and this coping strategy are likely to be weak. It is as yet unclear whether more women survived the North Korean famine than men; there are indicators from other famines that

women's greater knowledge of famine foods and cooking responsibilities, which gives them more access to food, results in greater likelihood of survival. The dispersal of information concerning famine foods was universal in North Korea and not given to men or women only. While research from other famines shows that women are more likely to seek help from relief agencies and hospitals, and relief agencies are likely to classify women and children as more vulnerable and thus distribute relief accordingly, in the case of North Korea where engagement with relief agencies was fully regulated, it is not possible to predict if these characteristics were the same. See Kate Macintyre, "Female Mortality Advantage," in *Famine Demography: Perspectives from the Past and Present*, ed. Tim Dyson and Cormac O Gráda, 240–59 (Oxford: Oxford University Press, 2002).

28. Chol-Hwan Kang with Pierre Rigoulot, *The Aquariums of Pyongyang: Ten Years in a North Korean Gulag*, trans. Yair Reiner (New York: Basic Books, 2001), 142.

29. Nancy Scheper-Hughes, *Death Without Weeping: The Violence of Everyday Life in Brazil*. Berkeley: University of California Press, 1993.

30. Václav Havel, "The Power of the Powerless," in *Open Letters: Selected Writings: 1965–1990*, trans. and ed. Paul Wilson (New York: Knopf, 1991), 42.

3. The Life of Words

1. See John L. Austin, *How to Do Things with Words* (Oxford: Clarendon Press, 1962).

2. Information about the Red Banner Sprit or the Red Flag Movement, *pulgŭn ki chaengch'wi undong*, can be found in a *Rodong Shinmun* editorial published on November 18, 1995. Further details are available in Korean at http://www.kcna.co.jp/calendar/2005/11/11-18/2005-1118-004.html, and at https://www.dailynk.com/korean/read.php?cataId=nk00700&num=7828, both last accessed on September 9, 2011.

3. Robert Dirks, "Social Responses During Severe Food Shortages and Famine [and Comments and Reply]," in *Current Anthropology* 21, no. 1 (February 1980): 21–44.

4. Richard Seaton, *Hunger in Groups: An Arctic Experiment* (Chicago: Quartermaster Food and Container Institute, U.S. Army, 1962), 90.

5. See Austin, *How to Do Things with Words*; John Searle, "Speech Acts: An Essay in the Philosophy of Language" (Cambridge: Cambridge University Press, 1969); Judith Butler, *Giving an Account of Oneself* (Assen, Neth.: Royal Van Gorcum, 2003); and Shoshana Felman, *The Literary Speech Act: Don Juan with J. L. Austin, or Seduction in Two Languages*, trans. Catherine Porter (Ithaca, NY: Cornell University Press, 2002), 6.

6. Charles Armstrong, *The Koreas* (New York: Routledge, 2007), 78.

7. V. N. Vološinov, *Marxism and the Philosophy of Language*, trans. Ladislav Matejka and I. R. Titunik (New York: Seminar Press, 1973); and Lev S. Vygotsky, *Thought and Language*, rev. and exp. ed., with a new introduction by Alex Kozulin, ed. and trans. Eugenia Hanfmann, Gertrude Vakar, and Alex Kozulin (Cambridge, MA: MIT Press, 2012).

8. Vološinov was, among other outstanding intellectuals, a victim of the Stalinist purges of the 1930s, at which time he and his work were consigned to oblivion. His own fate remains a mystery. This confluence of his intellectual work and the silencing of both him and the work are not without relation.

9. Hannah Arendt, *The Origins of Totalitarianism* (Boston: Houghton Mifflin Harcourt 1973); Tzvetan Todorov, *Voices from the Gulag: Life and Death in Communist Bulgaria*, trans. Robert Zaretsky (University Park: Penn State University Press, 1999); and Tzvetan Todorov, *Hope and Memory: Reflections on the Twentieth Century*, trans. David Bellos (London: Atlantic Books, 2003).

10. Elinor Ochs, "Narrative Lessons," in *A Companion to Linguistic Anthropology*, ed. A. Duranti, 269–89 (Oxford: Blackwell, 2004), 271.

11. Alex de Waal, *Famine That Kills: Darfur, Sudan, 1984–1985* (Oxford: Clarendon Press, 1989).

12. James Scott, *Seeing Like a State: How Certain Schemes to Improve the Human Condition Have Failed* (New Haven, CT: Yale University Press, 1998).

13. Caroline Humphrey, "Remembering an 'Enemy': The Boyd Khan in Twentieth-Century Mongolia," in *Memory, History and Opposition Under State Socialism*, ed. Rubie S. Watson, 24–27 (Santa Fe, NM: School of American Research Press, 1994).

14. Robert Desjarlais, Leon Eisenberg, Byron Good, and Arthur Kleinman, *World Mental Health: Problems and Priorities in Low-Income Countries* (New York: Oxford University Press, 1995), 175; and J. H. Jenkins, "The Medical Anthropology of Political Violence: A Cultural and

Feminist Agenda," *Medical Anthropology Quarterly* 12, no. 1 (1998): 122–31, doi:10.1525/maq.1998.12.1.122.

15. Mary Douglas, *Natural Symbols: Explorations in Cosmology* (New York: Pantheon Books, 1982); and Mary Douglas, *Purity and Danger: An Analysis of the Concepts of Pollution and Taboo* (Boston: Ark Paperbacks, 1985).

16. Sigmund Freud, *Jokes and Their Relation to the Unconscious*, trans. and ed. James Strachey, with a biographical introduction by Peter Gay (New York: Norton, 1960), 11, 49, 156, 208.

17. Alex Argenti-Pillen, "The Global Flow of Knowledge on War Trauma: The Role of the 'Cinnamon Garden Culture' in Sri Lanka," in *Negotiating Local Knowledge: Power and Identity in Development*, ed. Johan Pottier, Alan Bicker, and Paul Stillitoe, 189–214 (London: Pluto Press, 2003); and Alex Argenti-Pillen, *Masking Terror: How Women Contain Violence in Southern Sri Lanka* (Philadelphia: University of Pennsylvania Press, 2003).

18. Douglas, *Purity and Danger*.

19. Marcelo M. Suarez-Orozco, "Speaking of the Unspeakable: Toward a Psychosocial Understanding of Responses to Terror," *Ethos* 18, no. 3 (September 1990): 353–83.

20. Václav Havel, "The Power of the Powerless," in *Open Letters: Selected Writings: 1965–1990*, trans. and ed. Paul Wilson (New York: Knopf, 1991), 25–26.

21. Ibid., 31.

22. Shin-Wha Lee, "International Engagement in North Korea's Humanitarian Crisis: The Role of State and Non-State Actors," *East Asia: An International Quarterly* 20, no. 2 (Summer 2003): 82.

23. Todorov, *Hope and Memory*; and Havel, *Power of the Powerless*.

24. Kong Dan Oh and Ralph C. Hassig, *Through the Looking Glass* (Washington, DC: Brookings Institution Press, 2000).

25. Suarez-Orozco, "Speaking of the Unspeakable," 367.

26. Juan Carlos Kusnetzoff, quoted in ibid.

27. See, for instance, how this is explained in the North Korean encyclopedia *Chosŏn Ensik'lip'edia* (Pyongyang, DPRK: Paekhwasachŏn Publishing House, 1995), 179–81.

28. See, for example, de Waal, *Famine That Kills*; Amartya Sen and Jean Drèze, *The Amartya Sen & Jean Drèze Omnibus: (comprising) Poverty and Famines; Hunger and Public Action; and India: Economic Development and Social Opportunity* (Oxford: Oxford University Press, 1999; Margaret Kelleher, *The Feminization of Famine: Expressions of the Inexpressible?* (Durham, NC: Duke

University Press, 1997); and Rae Yang, *Spider Eaters: A Memoir* (Berkeley: University of California Press, 1997).

29. Alex Argenti-Pillen, "The Discourse on Trauma in Non-Western Cultural Contexts: Contributions of an Ethnographic Method," in *International Handbook of Human Response to Trauma*, ed. A. Shalev, R. Yehuda, and M. D. McFarlane, 87–102 (New York: Kluwer Academic/Plenum, 2000), 88–89, 92, 93.

30. Todorov, *Hope and Memory*, 115.

31. Yang, *Spider Eaters*, 59.

32. Oh and Hassig, *Through the Looking Glass*, 32.

33. Personal interview with Dr. Vollertsen, Seoul, South Korea, August 2006.

34. Nancy Scheper-Hughes, *Death Without Weeping: Violence of Everyday Life in Brazil* (Berkeley: University of California Press, 1992), 174.

4. Life Leaves Death Behind

1. After Todorov: "But facts don't come with their meaning attached, and it is the meaning that interests me." Tzvetan Todorov, *Hope and Memory: Reflections on the Twentieth Century*, trans. David Bellos (London: Atlantic Books, 2003), 1.

2. See Elinor Ochs, "Narrative Lessons," in *A Companion to Linguistic Anthropology*, ed. A. Duranti, 269–89 (Oxford: Blackwell, 2004).

3. Rubie S. Watson, ed. *Memory, History and Opposition Under State Socialism* (Santa Fe, NM: School of American Research, 1994).

4. For further discussion on socialism's relationship to science, see Todorov, *Hope and Memory*, 32–33.

5. Ibid., 44; and Watson, *Memory, History and Opposition*.

6. Shin-Wha Lee, "International Engagement in North Korea's Humanitarian Crisis: The Role of State and Non-State Actors," *East Asia: An International Quarterly* 20, no. 2 (Summer 2003): 74–93.

7. Don Oberdorfer, *The Two Koreas* (Reading, MA: Addison-Wesley, 1997), 20.

8. Alessandro Triulzi, "The Past as Contested Terrain: Commemorating Newsites of Memory in War Torn Ethiopia," in *Violence, Political Culture and Development in Africa*, ed. Preben Kaarsholm, 122–138 (London: James Currey, 2006), 123.

9. Jerome Bruner, "Life as a Narrative," *Social Research* 54, no. 1 (1987): 15.

10. X. Zhang, *Grass Soup*, trans. Martha Avery (London: Secker & Warburg, 1994).

11. "N Korea 'Develops Special Noodle,'" *BBC News*, August 23, 2008, http://news.bbc.co.uk/2/hi/asia-pacific/7578231.stm.

12. James Burnham, *The Managerial Revolution* (Bloomington: Indiana University Press, 1960), 222–26.

13. János Kornai, *The Socialist System: The Political Economy of Communism* (Oxford: Oxford University Press, 1992), 231.

14. Korea Institute for National Unification (KINU), White Paper on Human Rights in North Korea, September 25, 2008, http://www.kinu.or.kr/eng/pub/pub_04_01.jsp?bid=DATA04&page=1&num=26&mode=view&category=2672; and KINU, White Paper on Human Rights in North Korea, December 31, 2006, http://www.kinu.or.kr/eng/pub/pub_04_01.jsp?bid=DATA04&page=1&num=22&mode=view&category=2672.

15. Stephen Haggard and Marcus Noland, "Hunger and Human Rights: the Politics of Famine in North Korea" (Washington, DC: U.S. Committee for Human Rights in North Korea, 2005), http://hrnk.org/uploads/pdfs/Hunger_and_Human_Rights.pdf.

16. Vigdis Broch-Due, ed. *Violence and Belonging: The Quest for Identity in Post-Colonial Africa* (New York: Routledge, 2004), 24.

17. Ibid., 17.

18. Edward Peters, *Torture* (Oxford: Basil Blackwell, 1986), 171.

19. Maria B. Olujic, "Embodiment of Terror: Gendered Violence in Peacetime and Wartime in Croatia and Bosnia- Herzegovina," *Medical Anthropology Quarterly* 12, no. 1 (March 1998): 46.

20. Robert Desjarlais, Leon Eisenberg, Byron Good, and Arthur Kleinman, *World Mental Health: Problems and Priorities in Low-Income Countries* (New York: Oxford University Press, 1995); Nancy Scheper-Hughes, *Death Without Weeping: Violence of Everyday Life in Brazil* (Berkeley: University of California Press, 1992); and Marcelo M. Suarez-Orozco, "Speaking of the Unspeakable: Toward a Psychosocial Understanding of Responses to Terror," *Ethos* 18, no. 3 (September 1990): 353–83.

21. Olujic, "Embodiment of Terror," 31.

22. Alex de Waal, "Whose Emergency Is It Anyway? Dreams, Tragedies and Traumas in the Humanitarian Encounter," *Centre for Research Architecture*, December 2008, http://roundtable.kein.org/node/1078.

23. Nancy Scheper-Hughes and Philippe Bourgois, eds., *Violence in War and Peace: An Anthology* (Malden, MA: Blackwell, 2004); Michel Foucault, *Power: Essential Works of Foucault 1954–1984*, vol. 3, ed. James E. Faubion, trans. Robert Hurley and others. (London: Penguin, 1994), 385.

24. Broch-Due, *Violence and Belonging*, 24; and Foucault, *Power*, 402–3, 330.

25. Caroline Nordstrom and JoAnn Martin, *The Paths to Domination, Resistance and Terror* (Berkeley: University of California Press, 1992), 8.

26. Carole Nagengast, "Violence, Terror, and the Crisis of the State," in *Annual Review of Anthropology* 23 (1994): 111.

5. Breaking Points

1. Republic of Korea Ministry of Unification, Data & Statistics, "Major Statistics in Inter-Korean Relations," http://eng.unikorea.go.kr/index.do?menuCd=DOM_000000204003000000.

2. Even if we take the highest estimates of North Korean defectors in China as 300,000 and defectors in South Korea, Japan, and abroad as about 35,000, the percentage of North Koreans who leave home is still very tiny compared to the number who have stayed.

3. For details concerning defection and punishment, see "Report on the Detailed Findings of the Commission of Inquiry on Human Rights in the Democratic People's Republic of Korea" Human Rights Council, Twenty-fifth session, Agenda item 4, "Human Rights Situations that Require the Council's Attention," February 7, 2014, p. 107, para. 381–84, http://www.ohchr.org/EN/HRBodies/HRC/CoIDPRK/Pages/Reportof theCommissionofInquiryDPRK.aspx; for information on shoot to kill policy, see ibid., p. 112, para. 402.

4. The Sino-DPRK border is guarded by the Korean People's Army and the State Security Department on the DPRK side, and by the Ministry of People's Security on the Chinese side.

5. Kong Dan Oh and Ralph C. Hassig, *Through the Looking Glass* (Washington, DC: Brookings Institution Press, 2000), 37.

6. Stephen Jones, "Old Ghosts and New Chains: Ethnicity and Memory in the Georgian Republic," in *Memory, History and Opposition Under State Socialism*, ed. Rubie S. Watson, 149–65 (Santa Fe, NM: School of American Research Press, 1994), 153–56.

7. Michel Foucault, *Power: Essential Works of Foucault 1954–1984*, vol. 3, ed. James E. Faubion, trans. Robert Hurley and others (London: Penguin, 1994), 449.

8. Tessa Morris-Suzuki, *Exodus to North Korea: Shadows from Japan's Cold War* (Lanham, MD: Rowman and Littlefield, 2007).

9. As observed in Sri Lanka by Argenti-Pillen. See Alex Argenti-Pillen, "The Discourse on Trauma in Non-Western Cultural Contexts: Contributions of an Ethnographic Method," in *International Handbook of Human Response to Trauma*, ed. A. Shalev, R. Yehuda, M. D. McFarlane, 87–102 (New York: Kluwer Academic/Plenum, 2000), 92.

10. S. H. Bak and C. S. Bak, *Kulmchulimpota musŏun kŏsŭn hŭimangŭl ilhŏpŏlinŭn ilipnita* [More frightening than starvation is the loss of hope] (Seoul: Sidae chŏngsin, 2000).

11. Ibid., 29–30.

12. Ibid., 32–33.

13. Ibid., 34–35.

14. See, for example, Viktor E. Frankl, *Man's Search for Meaning* (New York: Washington Square Press Pocket Books, 1963).

15. Bak and Bak, *More Frightening than Starvation*, 38.

16. Ibid., 141.

6. The New Division

1. Good Friends Centre for Peace, Human Rights and Refugees, "Human Rights in North Korea and the Food Crisis: A Comprehensive Report on North Korean Human Rights Issues," March 2004, 23, http://reliefweb.int/report/democratic-peoples-republic-korea/human-rights-north-korea-and-food-crisis-comprehensive. See also Good Friends: Centre for Peace, Human Rights and Refugees *Choŭn Pŏttŭl*, http://goodfriends.co.kr/ (Korean Site), or http://goodfriends.or.kr/eng/ (English site).

2. Tessa Morris-Suzuki, *Exodus to North Korea: Shadows from Japan's Cold War* (Lanham, MD: Rowman and Littlefield, 2007), 231.

3. Ibid.

4. Fifty *pyeong* is equal to approximately 165 square meters.

5. Defected North Koreans in China, South Korea, and elsewhere sometimes opt to purchase Chinese mobile phones and arrange for these to be smuggled to family in border hometowns. These phones can then

be used to contact family inside North Korea using Chinese mobile telecommunications that leak over the Sino-DPRK border.

6. James Foley, *Korea's Divided Families: Fifty Years of Separation* (London: Routledge Curzon, 2003).

7. The Korean War Armistice was signed by the United Nations Command represented by U.S. army lieutenant general William Harrison Jr., the North Korean People's Army represented by North Korean general Nam-Il, and the Chinese People's Volunteer Army. The Republic of Korea has not signed the armistice.

8. Women and children are given medical, psychiatric, and education support at Hanawon Resettlement Center in Anseong, Gyeonggi Province, while North Korean men receive the same support through the Hwachon-gun, Gangwon Province resettlement center.

9. The Constitution of the Republic of Korea states in chapter 1, article 3 that the territory of the ROK is the Korean peninsula and its adjacent islands, http://korea.assembly.go.kr/res/low_01_read.jsp.

10. Although, for example, the South Korean National Security Act, article 8, identifies correspondence with antistate groups or those under their control a crime punishable up to ten years in prison, defectors in South Korea maintain reasonably regular contact with family by calling them on Chinese mobile phones smuggled into the North. Mobile reception in the North leaks across the Sino-Korean border, making these calls dangerous but possible.

11. Kum-Sok No with J. Roger Osterholm, *A MiG-15 to Freedom: Memoir of the Wartime North Korean Defector Who First Delivered the Secret Fighter Jet to the Americans in 1953* (Jefferson, NC: McFarland & Company, 1996).

12. Hyun Hee Kim, *The Tears of My Soul: The True Story of a North Korean Spy* (New York: William Morrow, 1993).

13. In 1962 the South Korean government introduced the "Special law on the protection of defectors from the North." For more details, see Andrei Lankov, *North of the DMZ: Everyday Life in North Korea* (Jefferson, NC: McFarland & Company, 2007), 292.

14. J. J. Suh, "North Korean Defectors: Their Adaptation and Resettlement," in *East Asian Review* 14, no. 3 (2002): 67–86; and Crisis International, "Strangers at Home," *Asia Report* no. 208 (July 14, 2011), http://www.crisisgroup.org/en/regions/asia/north-east-asia/north -korea/208-strangers-at-home-north-koreans-in-the-south.aspx.

15. In the last decade an increasing number of memoirs by North Koreans have been published in South Korea and abroad. A large number of these are by prison camp escapees. Consider the following: An Myŏng-Chol, *Wanchŏn t'ongche kuyŏk* [Complete control zone] (Shidae Chongshin: South Korea, Seoul, 2007); Chul-Hwan Kang and Kim Yongsam, *A! Yotŏkk: Pukhan Auspich chŏng ch'i su suyungso kŭ chiok eso salana onn saram tŭl ŭi chŭng on* [Ah! *Yodok: The Testimony of North Korea's Auschwitz Survivors*] (Chosun Chulpan Marketing, 2006); Chol-Hwan Kang with Pieire Rigoulot, *The Aquariums of Pyongyang: Ten Years in a North Korean Gulag*, trans. Yair Reiner (New York: Basic Books, 2001); Kim Yong with Kim Suk-Young, *The Long Road Home: Testimony of a North Korean Camp Survivor* (New York: Columbia University Press, 2009); Kim Young Sun, *Nanŭn Sŏng Hye Rim ŭi ch'ingu yŏtta* [I was a friend of Song Hye Rim] (Seoul: Tongshin, 2008); and Dong-Hyuck Shin, *Chŏngchi̇̆ pŏp suyongso wanchŏn t'ongche kuyŏk sesange pakŭlo naoda* [Complete control political prison camp: Out into the world] (Seoul: Pukhan inkwonchongbŏ senttŏ, 2007).

16. Crisis International, "Strangers at Home."

17. Stephen Haggard and Marcus Noland, *Famine in North Korea: Markets, Aid and Reform* (New York: Columbia University Press, 2007).

18. North Koreans who defect to South Korea are increasingly moving on to other countries for permanent settlement, such as Japan, the United Kingdom, Canada, and the United States. See Stephen Haggard and Marcus Noland, "The Winter of Their Discontent: Pyongyang Attacks the Market," Policy Briefs PB10-1, Peterson Institute for International Economics (2010); and Marcus Noland, and Stephen Haggard, "Political Attitudes Under Repression: Evidence from North Korean Refugees," MPRA Paper 21713, University Library of Munich, Germany (2010).

Conclusion

1. Woo Taek Jeon, Chang Hyung Hong, Chang Ho Lee, Dong Kee Kim, Mooyoung Han, and Sung Kil Min, "Correlation Between Traumatic Events and Posttraumatic Stress Disorder Among North Korean Defectors in South Korea," *Journal of Traumatic Stress* 18, no. 2 (2005): 151.

2. Cathy Caruth, *Unclaimed Experience: Trauma, Narrative, and History* (Baltimore: Johns Hopkins University Press, 1996); Margaret Kelleher,

The Feminization of Famine: Expressions of the Inexpressible? (Durham, NC: Duke University Press, 1997); Dominic LaCapra, *Writing History, Writing Trauma* (Baltimore: Johns Hopkins University Press, 2001); and Shoshana Felman and Dori Laub, MD. *Testimony: Crises of Witnessing in Literature, Psychoanalysis, and History* (New York: Routledge, 1992).

3. Robert Desjarlais, Leon Eisenberg, Byron Good, and Arthur Kleinman, *World Mental Health: Problems and Priorities in Low-Income Countries* (New York: Oxford University Press, 1995), 175; and J. H. Jenkins, "The Medical Anthropology of Political Violence: A Cultural and Feminist Agenda," *Medical Anthropology Quarterly* 12, no. 1 (1998): 187.

4. Judith Butler, *Giving an Account of Oneself* (Assen, Neth.: Royal Van Gorcum 2003), 12, 38.

5. Adriana Cavarero, quoted in ibid., 26.

6. See Jean-Luc Nancy, *Listening*, trans. Charlotte Mandell (New York: Fordham University Press, 2007), 10.

7. Gillian Whitlock, *Soft Weapons: Autobiography in Transit* (Chicago: University of Chicago Press, 2007).

8. Michel Foucault, *The Archaeology of Knowledge: And the Discourse on Language* (New York: Pantheon, 1972), 216.

9. Just as torture does, language too can make and unmake the world. See Elaine Scarry, *The Body in Pain: The Making and Unmaking of the World* (New York: Oxford University Press, 1985).

10. Foucault, *The Archaeology of Knowledge*, 216.

11. Suk-young Kim, *Illusive Utopia Theater, Film, and Everyday Performance in North Korea* (Ann Arbor: University of Michigan Press, 2010); Kong Dan Oh and Ralph C. Hassig, *Through the Looking Glass* (Washington, DC: Brookings Institution Press, 2000); and Sonia Ryang, *Reading North Korea: An Ethnological Inquiry* (Cambridge, MA: Harvard University Press, 2012).

12. Felman Shoshana, *The Literary Speech Act: Don Juan with J. L. Austin, or Seduction in Two Languages*, trans. Catherine Porter (Ithaca, NY: Cornell University Press, 2002), 85.

13. Ibid.

14. Václav Havel, "Power of the Powerless Havel," in *Open Letters: Selected Writings: 1965–1990*, trans. and ed. Paul Wilson (New York: Knopf, 1991).

15. Bruner Jerome, "Life as a Narrative," *Social Research* 54, no. 1 (1987): 15.

16. Judith Herman, *Trauma and Recovery: The Aftermath of Violence from Domestic Violence to Political Terror* (New York: Basic Books, 1997).

17. V. N. Vološinov, *Marxism and the Philosophy of Language*, trans. Ladislav Matejka and I. R. Titunik (New York: Seminar Press, 1973).

18. Sue Lautze, "The Famine in North Korea: Humanitarian Responses in Communist Nations," Feinstein International Famine Center Working Paper, School of Nutrition Science and Policy (Medford, MA: Tufts University, June 1997), 6, http://repository.forcedmigration.org/show_metadata.jsp?pid=fmo:1744.

19. Jane Mansbridge, "The Making of Oppositional Consciousness," in *Oppositional Consciousness: The Subjective Roots of Social Protest*, ed. Jane Mansbridge and Aldon Morris, 1–19 (Chicago: University of Chicago Press, 2001); see also Herman, *Trauma and Recovery*.

20. János Kornai, *The Socialist System: The Political Economy of Communism* (Oxford: Oxford University Press, 1992), 427.

21. Herman, *Trauma and Recovery*.

22. Nanci Adler, *Keeping Faith with the Party: Communist Believers Return from the Gulag* (Bloomington: Indiana University Press, 2012), 23.

23. For example, see Mark E. Manyin, "Kim Jong-il's Death: Implications for North Korea's Stability and U.S. Policy," *Congressional Research Report*, January 11, 2012, http://www.fas.org/sgp/crs/row/R42126.pdf; and Victor Cha and Ellen Kim, "U.S.–Korea Relations: Death of Kim Jong-Il," *Comparative Connections*, January 2012, http://csis.org/files/publication/1103qus_korea.pdf.

Appendix

1. Stephen Devereux, ed., *The New Famines: Why Famines Persist in an Era of Globalization*, Routledge Studies in Development Economics (New York: Routledge, 2007); and Stephen Devereux, *Theories of Famine: From Malthus to Sen* (Hemel Hempstead, UK: Harvester Wheatsheaf, 1993).

2. Devereux, *Famine Theory*, 137.

3. Devereux, *The New Famines*, 4, 7.

4. Amartya Sen, *Poverty and Famines: An Essay on Entitlements and Deprivation* (Oxford: Clarendon Press, 1981).

5. Victor Cha, "DPRK Briefing Book: North Korea's Economic Reforms and Security Intentions," testimony of Dr. Victor D. Cha for the Sen-

ate Foreign Relations Committee (March 2, 2004), 4, http://nautilus
.org/publications/books/dprkbb/transition/dprk-briefing-book-north
-koreas-economic-reforms-and-security-intentions/#axzz32Y2vr5vX.

6. See Devereux, *Famine Theory*.

7. Marcus Noland, Sherman Robinson, and Tao Wang, "Famine in North Korea: Causes and Cures," *Economic Development and Cultural Change* 49, no. 4 (July 2001): 741–67.

8. Stephen Haggard and Markus Noland, *Famine in North Korea: Markets, Aid, and Reform* (New York: Columbia University Press, 2007), 73–76.

9. For a discussion of entitlements, see Sen, *Poverty and Famines*; for relations of power, see Susan George, *How the Other Half Dies: The Real Reasons for World Hunger* (Harmondworth, Middlesex, UK: Penguin, 1976).

10. James Scott, *Seeing Like a State: How Certain Schemes to Improve the Human Condition Have Failed* (New Haven, CT: Yale University Press, 1998), 5.

11. Hy-Sang Lee, "Supply and Demand for Grains in North Korea: A Historical Movement Model for 1966–1993," *Korea and World Affairs* 18, no. 3 (1994): 551.

12. Grace Lee, "The Political Philosophy of Juche," *Stanford Journal of East Asian Affairs* 3, no. 1 (2003): 108.

13. Don Oberdorfer, *The Two Koreas* (Reading, MA: Addison-Wesley, 1997), 20.

14. Haggard and Noland, *Famine in North Korea*; and Kong Dan Oh and Ralph C. Hassig, *Through the Looking Glass* (Washington, DC: Brookings Institution Press, 2000), 52.

15. Peter Gey, "North Korea: Soviet-Style Reform and the Erosion of the State Economy" Friedrich Ebert Stiftung Information Series, Seoul in Dialogue + Cooperation (2004), 34, http://library.fes.de/pdf-files/bueros/singapur/04601/d+c2004-1.pdf.

16. For more information on wages and pricing in North Korea, see Andrei Lankov, "How Much Money Do North Koreans Make? Thanks to Black Market, Official Salaries Provide Very Poor Barometer," March 25, 2014, *NK News.org*, http://www.nknews.org/2014/03/how -much-money-do-north-koreans-make/.

17. Gey, "North Korea: Soviet-Style Reform," 34.

18. Michael Schloms, *North Korea and the Timeless Dilemma of Aid: A Study of Humanitarian Action in Famines* (Berlin: Lit Verlag Münster, 2004), 95.

19. Nicholas Eberstadt, "The Shakedown State," *American Enterprise Institute*, October 31, 2003, http://nautilus.org/publications/books/dprkbb/economy/dprk-briefing-book-policy-area-economy/#axzz32Y2vr5vX.

20. Kimberley Ann Elliot, "The Role of Economic Leverage in Negotiations with North Korea," *Institute for International Economics, Nautilus Institute*, April 1, 2003, http://nautilus.org/publications/books/dprkbb/sanctions/dprk-briefing-book-the-role-of-economic-leverage-in-negotiations-with-north-korea/#axzz32Y2vr5vX.

21. Schloms, *North Korea and the Timeless Dilemma of Aid*, 98.

22. Gey, "North Korea: Soviet-Style Reform," 33.

23. Schloms, *North Korea and the Timeless Dilemma of Aid*, 106.

24. Haggard and Noland, *Famine in North Korea*, 63.

25. Liana Sun Wyler, and Dick K. Nanto, "North Korean Crime-for-Profit Activities," CRS Report for Congress, August 25, 2008, 7, http://fpc.state.gov/documents/organization/110378.pdf.

26. Peter Prahar, "North Korea: Illicit Activity Funding the Regime," statement before the Subcommittee on Federal Financial Management, Government Information, and International Security, Senate Homeland Security and Government Affairs Committee, April 25, 2006, hsgac.senate.gov/public/_files/042506Prahar.pdf.

27. Wyler and Nanto, "North Korean Crime-for-Profit Activities," 7.

28. "N Korea 'Develops Special Noodle,'" *BBC News*, August 23, 2008, http://news.bbc.co.uk/2/hi/asia-pacific/7578231.stm.

29. James Burnham, *The Managerial Revolution* (Bloomington: Indiana University Press, 1960), 222–26.

30. János Kornai, *The Socialist System: The Political Economy of Communism* (Oxford: Oxford University Press, 1992), 231.

31. Ibid., 237.

32. Haggard and Noland, *Famine in North Korea*, 57.

33. Cha, "North Korea's Economic Reforms and Security Intentions."

34. Haggard and Noland, *Famine in North Korea*, 57.

35. Andrew S. Natsios, "North Korea's Chronic Food Problem," in *Troubled Transition: North Korea's Politics, Economy, and External Relations*, ed. Choe Sang-Hun, Gi-Wook Shin, and David Straub (Stanford, CA: Walter H. Shorenstein Asia-Pacific Research Center, Shorenstein APARC, Stanford University, 2013), 122.

36. Haggard and Noland, *Famine in North Korea*, 3.

37. Dong-eon Hwang, "Agricultural Reforms in North Korea, and Inter-Korean Cooperation," *East Asian Review* 4, no. 3 (August 1997): 75.

38. Haggard and Noland, *Famine in North Korea*, 52, 53.

39. Noland, Robinson, and Wang "Famine in North Korea," 754, 747.

40. Gey, "North Korea: Soviet-Style Reform," 34.

41. Sue Lautze, "The Famine in North Korea: Humanitarian Responses in Communist Nations," Feinstein International Famine Center, Working Paper, School of Nutrition Science and Policy (Medford, MA: Tufts University, June 1997), dl.tufts.edu/file_assets/tufts:UA197.019.019.00002, p. 10.

42. Haggard and Noland, *Famine in North Korea*, 59.

43. Ibid., 53.

44. Ibid., 51–52.

45. Ibid., 55.

46. Shin-Wha Lee, "International Engagement in North Korea's Humanitarian Crisis: The Role of State and Non-State Actors," *East Asia: An International Quarterly* 20, no. 2 (Summer 2003): 76.

47. Haggard and Noland, *Famine in North Korea*, 53.

48. Ibid.

49. Ibid., 56.

50. Quoted in ibid.

51. George, *How the Other Half Dies*, 206–13.

52. Lee, "International Engagement in North Korea's Humanitarian Crisis," 76.

53. Schloms, *North Korea and the Timeless Dilemma of Aid*, 104n21.

54. David Morton, "Steep Learning Curves in the DPRK," in *Humanitarian Diplomacy: Practitioners and Their Craft*, ed. L. Minearl and H. Smith, 194–214 (Tokyo: United Nations University Press, 2007), 200.

55. Jon Bennett, "North Korea: The Politics of Food Aid," Network paper no. 28, Overseas Development Institute, Relief and Rehabilitation Network, http://repository.forcedmigration.org/show_metadata.jsp?pid=fmo:3445.

56. Haggard and Noland, *Famine in North Korea*, 206.

57. Hugo Slim, "Positioning Humanitarianism in War: Principles of Neutrality, Impartiality and Solidarity," Centre for Development and Emergency Planning, Oxford Brookes University (Paper presented to the Aspects of Peacekeeping Conference Royal Military Academy, Sandhurst,

UK, January 22–24, 1997), http://repository.forcedmigration.org/show_metadata.jsp?pid=fmo:2232.

58. NK Briefs, "Lee Myung-bak Administration Sets the Lowest Record for Assistance to North Korea," Institute for Far Eastern Studies, January 31, 2013, http://ifes.kyungnam.ac.kr/eng/FRM/FRM_0101V.aspx?code=FRM130131_0001; and Mark E. Manyin and Mary Beth D. Nikitin, "Foreign Assistance to North Korea" Congressional Research Service, R40095, 7-5700, April 2, 2014, fas.org/sgp/crs/row/R40095.pdf.

59. WFP/UNICEF/ECHO reports quoted in Schloms, *North Korea and the Timeless Dilemma of Aid*, 112.

60. Lautze, "Famine in North Korea"; and Marcus Noland, *Avoiding the Apocalypse: The Future of the Two Koreas* (Washington, DC: Institute for International Economics, 2000).

61. Amnesty International, "Starved of Rights: Human Rights and the Food Crisis in the Democratic People's Republic of Korea (North Korea)," Amnesty International, January 17, 2004, http://www.amnesty.org/en/library/info/ASA24/003/2004/en; and Gordon L. Flake and Scott Snyder, eds. *Paved with Good Intentions: The NGO Experience in North Korea*. Mansfield Centre for Pacific Affairs (Westport, CT: Praeger, 2003).

62. Flake and Snyder, *Paved with Good Intentions*.

63. Ibid.

64. Fiona Terry, "Feeding the Dictator," Special Report, *Guardian*, August 6, 2001, http://www.theguardian.com/world/2001/aug/06/famine.comment.

65. Haggard and Noland, *Famine in North Korea*, 10.

66. Ibid., 13.

67. Meredith Woo-Cumings, "The Political Ecology of Famine: The North Korean Catastrophe and Its Lessons" (Asian Development Bank Institute, Research Paper 31, January 1, 2002), 27–29, http://www.adbi.org/research%20paper/2002/01/01/115.political.ecology/.

68. Johan Pottier, *Re-Imagining Rwanda: Conflict, Survival and Disinformation in the Late Twentieth Century* (Cambridge: Cambridge University Press, 2002).

69. Bjørn Willum, "Eyes in the Sky: In Service of Humanity?" *Imaging Notes USA*, September/October 2000, www.willum.com/articles/imaging sept2000.

70. Ibid.

71. Noland, *Avoiding the Apocalypse*, 171–72; see also Woon-Keun Kim, "Recent Changes in North Korean Agricultural Policies and Projected Impacts on the Food Shortage," *East Asian Review* 2, no. 3 (Autumn 1999): 93–110; and Woon-Keun Kim, "The Agricultural Situation of North Korea," Food & Fertilizer Technology Center, September 1, 1999, http://www.agnet.org/library.php?func=view&id=20110726131553.

72. Noland, Robinson, and Wang, "Famine in North Korea," 754.

73. Schloms, *North Korea and the Timeless Dilemma of Aid*, 127.

74. Ibid., 113.

75. Daniel Schwekendiek, "Height and Weight Differences Between North and South Korea," *Journal of Biosocial Science* 41, no. 1 (2009): 51.

76. Kim Jong-Il, quoted in Robert Weatherly and Jiyoung Song, "The Evolution of Human Rights Thinking in North Korea," *Journal of Communist Studies and Transition Politics* 24, no. 2: 272–96, 289–90.

77. New Focus International, "North Korea Orders All Privately Cultivated Crops to Be Cut Down" June 17, 2014, http://newfocusintl.com/north-korea-orders-privately-cultivated-crops-cut/; and New Focus International, "Exclusive: Now Even Party Cadres Must Take Part in the 'Arduous March'," April 27, 2014, http://newfocusintl.com/exclusive-party-cadres-arduous-march/.

BIBLIOGRAPHY

Adler, Nanci. *Keeping Faith with the Party: Communist Believers Return from the Gulag.* Bloomington: Indiana University Press, 2012.

Althusser Louis, *Lenin and Philosophy and Other Essays Part Two.* Trans. from the French by Ben Brewster. New York: Monthly Review Press, 1971.

Amnesty International. "Democratic People's Republic of Korea: Persecuting the Starving: The Plight of North Koreans Fleeing to China." Amnesty International, December 15, 2000. http://www.amnesty.org/en/library/info/ASA24/003/2000/en.

——. "Starved of Rights: Human Rights and the Food Crisis in the Democratic People's Republic of Korea (North Korea)." Amnesty International, January 17, 2004. http://www.amnesty.org/en/library/info/ASA24/003/2004/en.

Appadurai, Arjun. *Fear of Small Numbers: An Essay on the Geography of Anger.* Durham, NC: Duke University Press, 2006.

Arendt, Hannah, *Origins of Totalitarianism.* Boston: Houghton Mifflin Harcourt, 1973.

Argenti-Pillen, Alex. "The Discourse on Trauma in Non-Western Cultural Contexts: Contributions of an Ethnographic Method." In *International Handbook of Human Response to Trauma,* ed. A. Shalev, R. Yehuda, M. D. Mc-Farlane, 87–102 (New York: Kluwer Academic/Plenum, 2000).

——. "The Global Flow of Knowledge on War Trauma: The Role of the 'Cinnamon Garden Culture' in Sri Lanka." In *Negotiating Local Knowledge: Power and Identity in Development,* ed. Johan Pottier, Alan Bicker, and Paul Stillitoe, 189–214. London: Pluto Press, 2003.

———. *Masking Terror: How Women Contain Violence in Southern Sri Lanka*. Philadelphia: University of Pennsylvania Press, 2003.

Armstrong Charles. "Familism, Socialism and Political Religion in North Korea," *Totalitarian Movements and Political Religions* 6, no. 3 (December 2005): 383–94.

———. *The Koreas*. New York: Routledge, 2007.

AsiaPress International. *Rimjin-gang: News by North Korean Journalists from Inside North Korea*. Part 3, "The Kim Jong-il Regime and the People." Osaka, Japan: AsiaPress, 2010.

Austin, John L., *How to Do Things with Words*. Oxford: Clarendon Press, 1962.

Bak, S. H., and C. S. Bak. *Kulmchulimpota musŏun kŏsŭn hŭimangŭl ilhŏpŏlinŭn ilipnita* [More frightening than starvation is the loss of hope]. Seoul: Sidae chŏngsin, 2000.

Baro, Mamadou, and Tara F. Deubel. "Persistent Hunger: Perspectives on Vulnerability, Famine, and Food Security in Sub-Saharan Africa." *Annual Review of Anthropology* 35 (2006): 521–38.

Becker, Jasper. *Rogue Regime: Kim Jong Il and the Looming Threat of North Korea*. Oxford: Oxford University Press 2005.

Bennett Jon. "North Korea: The Politics of Food Aid," Network Paper no. 28, Overseas Development Institute, Relief and Rehabilitation Network. http://repository.forcedmigration.org/show_metadata.jsp?pid=fmo:3445.

Broch-Due, Vigdis, ed. *Violence and Belonging: The Quest for Identity in Post-Colonial Africa*. New York: Routledge, 2004.

Bruner, Jerome. "Life as a Narrative." *Social Research* 54, no. 1 (1987): 11–32.

Burnham, James. *The Managerial Revolution*. Bloomington: Indiana University Press, 1960.

Butler Judith. *Giving an Account of Oneself*. Assen, Netherlands: Royal Van Gorcum, 2003.

Caruth, Cathy. *Unclaimed Experience: Trauma, Narrative, and History*. Baltimore: Johns Hopkins University Press, 1996.

Cha, Victor. "DPRK Briefing Book: North Korea's Economic Reforms and Security Intentions." Testimony of Dr. Victor D. Cha for Senate Foreign Relations Committee, March 2, 2004, 4. http://nautilus.org/publications/books/dprkbb/transition/dprk-briefing-book-north-koreas-economic-reforms-and-security-intentions/#axzz32Y2vr5vX.

Cha, Victor, and Ellen Kim. "U.S.–Korea Relations: Death of Kim Jong-Il." *Comparative Connections*, January 2012. http://csis.org/files/publication/1103qus_korea.pdf.

Crisis International. "Strangers at Home." *Asia Report*, no. 208 (July 14, 2011). http://www.crisisgroup.org/en/regions/asia/north-east-asia/north-korea/208-strangers-at-home-north-koreans-in-the-south.aspx.

Daily NK Special Report Team. "Anti-Regime Activities Inside North Korea Revealed for the First Time." *DailyNK*, January 26, 2005. http://www.dailynk.com/english/read.php?num=17&cataId=nk00100.

Desjarlais, Robert, Leon Eisenberg, Byron Good, and Arthur Kleinman. *World Mental Health: Problems and Priorities in Low-Income Countries.* New York: Oxford University Press, 1995.

Devereux, Stephen, ed. *The New Famines: Why Famines Persist in an Era of Globalization.* Routledge Studies in Development Economics. New York: Routledge, 2007.

——. *Theories of Famine: From Malthus to Sen.* Hemel Hempstead, UK: Harvester Wheatsheaf, 1993.

de Waal, Alex. *Famine Crimes: Politics and the Disaster Relief Industry in Africa.* Bloomington: Indiana University Press, 1997.

——. *Famine That Kills: Darfur, Sudan, 1984–1985.* Oxford: Clarendon Press, 1989.

——. "Whose Emergency Is It Anyway? Dreams, Tragedies and Traumas in the Humanitarian Encounter." *Centre for Research Architecture*, 2008. http://roundtable.kein.org/node/1078.

Dikötter, Frank. *Mao's Great Famine: The History of China's Most Devastating Catastrophe, 1958–62.* London: Bloomsbury, 2010.

Dirks, Robert. "Social Responses During Severe Food Shortages and Famine [and Comments and Reply]." *Current Anthropology* 21, no. 1 (February 1980): 21–44.

Douglas, Mary *Natural Symbols: Explorations in Cosmology.* New York: Pantheon Books, 1982.

——. *Purity and Danger: An Analysis of the Concepts of Pollution and Taboo.* Boston: Ark Paperbacks, 1985.

Dyson, Tim, and Cormac O Gráda, eds. *Famine Demography: Perspectives from the Past and Present.* Oxford: Oxford University Press, 2002.

Eberstadt, Nicholas. "The Shakedown State." *American Enterprise Institute*, October 31, 2003. http://nautilus.org/publications/books/dprkbb/economy/dprk-briefing-book-policy-area-economy/#axzz32Y2vr5vX.

Elliot, Kimberley Ann. "The Role of Economic Leverage in Negotiations with North Korea." *Institute for International Economics, Nautilus Institute,* April 1, 2003. http://nautilus.org/publications/books/dprkbb/sanctions/dprk-briefing-book-the-role-of-economic-leverage-in-negotiations-with-north-korea/#axzz32Y2vr5vX.

Felman Shoshana, *The Literary Speech Act: Don Juan with J. L. Austin, or Seduction in Two Languages.* Trans. Catherine Porter. Ithaca, NY: Cornell University Press, 2002.

Felman, Shoshana, and Dori Laub, MD. *Testimony: Crises of Witnessing in Literature, Psychoanalysis, and History.* New York: Routledge, 1992.

Flake, Gordon L., and Scott Snyder, eds. *Paved with Good Intentions: The NGO Experience in North Korea.* Mansfield Centre for Pacific Affairs. Westport, CT: Praeger, 2003.

Foley, James. *Korea's Divided Families: Fifty Years of Separation.* London: Routledge Curzon, 2003.

Foucault, Michel. *The Archaeology of Knowledge: And the Discourse on Language.* New York: Pantheon Books, 1972.

——. *Power: Essential Works of Foucault 1954–1984,* vol. 3. Ed. James E. Faubion, trans. Robert Hurley et al. London: Penguin, 1994.

Frankl, Viktor E. *Man's Search for Meaning.* New York: Washington Square Press Pocket Books, 1963.

Freud, Sigmund. *Jokes and Their Relation to the Unconscious.* Trans. and ed. James Strachey, with a biographical introduction by Peter Gay. New York: Norton, 1960.

George, Susan. *How the Other Half Dies: The Real Reasons for World Hunger.* Harmondworth, Middlesex, UK: Penguin, 1976.

Gey, Peter. "North Korea: Soviet-Style Reform and the Erosion of the State Economy." Friedrich Ebert Stiftung Information Series, Seoul in Dialogue + Cooperation (2004). http://library.fes.de/pdf-files/bueros/singapur/04601/d+c2004-1.pdf.

Good Friends Centre for Peace, Human Rights and Refugees. "Human Rights in North Korea and the Food Crisis: A Comprehensive Report on North Korean Human Rights Issues." March 2004. www.goodfriends.or.kr/eng/data/NKHR2004-final.doc.

Greitens, Sheena Chestnut. "Illicit: North Korea's Evolving Operations to Earn Hard Currency." Committee for Human Rights in North Korea, 2014. http://www.hrnk.org/uploads/pdfs/SCG-FINAL-FINAL.pdf.

Haggard, Stephen, and Marcus Noland. *Famine in North Korea: Markets, Aid and Reform*. New York: Columbia University Press, 2007.

——. "Hunger and Human Rights: The Politics of Famine in North Korea." Washington, DC: U.S. Committee for Human Rights in North Korea, 2005. http://hrnk.org/uploads/pdfs/Hunger_and_Human_Rights.pdf.

——. "The Winter of Their Discontent: Pyongyang Attacks the Market," Policy Briefs PB10-1, Peterson Institute for International Economics. 2010.

Havel, Václav. "The Power of the Powerless." In *Open Letters: Selected Writings: 1965–1990*. Trans. and ed. Paul Wilson. New York: Knopf, 1991.

Herman, Judith. *Trauma and Recovery: The Aftermath of Violence from Domestic Violence to Political Terror*. New York: Basic Books, 1997.

Human Rights Watch. "Denied Status, Denied Education: Children of North Korean Women in China." Human Rights Watch, April 2008. http://www.hrw.org/en/reports/2008/04/11/denied-status-denied-education.

——. "The Invisible Exodus: North Koreans in the People's Republic of China." Human Rights Watch, November 19, 2002. http://www.hrw.org/reports/2002/11/19/invisible-exodus-0.

——. "North Korea: Harsher Policies against Border-Crossers." Human Rights Watch, March 5, 2007. http://www.hrw.org/en/reports/2007/03/05/north-korea-harsher-policies-against-border-crossers.

Humphrey, Caroline. "Remembering an 'Enemy': The Boyd Khan in Twentieth-Century Mongolia." In *Memory, History and Opposition Under State Socialism*, ed. Rubie S. Watson, 23–27. Santa Fe, NM: School of American Research Press, 1994.

Hwang, Dong-eon. "Agricultural Reforms in North Korea, and Inter-Korean Cooperation." *East Asian Review* 43, no. 3 (August 1997): 57–75.

Jang, Jin-sung. *Dear Leader: Poet, Spy, Escapee—A Look Inside North Korea*. New York: Atria/37 Ink, 2014.

Jenkins, J. H. "The Medical Anthropology of Political Violence: A Cultural and Feminist Agenda." *Medical Anthropology Quarterly*, 12, no. 1 (1998): 122–31. doi:10.1525/maq.1998.12.1.122.

Jeon, Woo Taek, Chang Hyung Hong, Chang Ho Lee, Dong Kee Kim, Mooyoung Han, and Sung Kil Min, "Correlation Between Traumatic Events and Posttraumatic Stress Disorder Among North Korean Defectors in South Korea." *Journal of Traumatic Stress* 18, no. 2 (2005): 147–54.

Jones, Stephen. "Old Ghosts and New Chains: Ethnicity and Memory in the Georgian Republic." In *Memory, History and Opposition under State Social-*

ism, ed. Rubie S. Watson, 149–65. Santa Fe, NM: School of American Research Press, 1994.

Kang, Chol-Hwan, with Pieire Rigoulot. *The Aquariums of Pyongyang: Ten Years in a North Korean Gulag.* Trans. Yair Reiner. New York: Basic Books, 2001.

Kang, Hyuk, *This Is Paradise!* With Philippe Grangereau. Trans. from the French by Shaun Whiteside. London: Little, Brown, 2005.

Kelleher, Margaret. *The Feminization of Famine: Expressions of the Inexpressible?* Durham, NC: Duke University Press, 1997.

Kim, Hyun Hee. *The Tears of My Soul: The True Story of a North Korean Spy.* New York: William Morrow, 1993.

Kim, So Yeol. "Remembering the Coup d'Etat in 1996 [Prospects for North Korean Change] Part 2." *Daily NK*, February 5, 2011. http://www.dailynk .com/english/read.php?cataId=nk02100&num=7321.

Kim, Suk-young, *Illusive Utopia: Theater, Film, and Everyday Performance in North Korea.* Ann Arbor: University of Michigan Press, 2010.

Kim, Woon-Keun, "The Agricultural Situation of North Korea." Food & Fertilizer Technology Center, September 1, 1999. http://www.agnet.org/ library.php?func=view&id=20110726131553.

——.. "Recent Changes in North Korean Agricultural Policies and Projected Impacts on the Food Shortage." *East Asian Review* 2, no. 3 (Autumn 1999): 93–110.

Kornai, János. *The Socialist System: The Political Economy of Communism.* Oxford: Oxford University Press, 1992.

LaCapra, Dominic. *Writing History, Writing Trauma.* Baltimore: Johns Hopkins University Press, 2001.

Lankov, Andrei. "How Much Money Do North Koreans Make? Thanks to Black Market, Official Salaries Provide Very Poor Barometer." March 25, 2014, *NK News.org.* http://www.nknews.org/2014/03/how-much-money -do-north-koreans-make/.

——. "The Natural Death of North Korean Stalinism." *Asia Policy*, no. 1 (January 2006): 95–121.

——. *North of the DMZ: Everyday Life in North Korea.* Jefferson, NC: McFarland & Company, 2007.

Lautze, Sue. "The Famine in North Korea: Humanitarian Responses in Communist Nations." Feinstein International Famine Center, Working Paper, School of Nutrition Science and Policy. Medford, MA: Tufts University, June 1997), dl.tufts.edu/file_assets/tufts:UA197.019.019.00002.

Lee Grace. "The Political Philosophy of Juche," *Stanford Journal of East Asian Affairs* 3, no 1. (2003): 105–11.

Lee, Hy-Sang, "Supply and Demand for Grains in North Korea: A Historical Movement Model for 1966–1993." *Korea and World Affairs* 18, no. 3 (1994): 509–54.

Lee, Shin-Wha. "International Engagement in North Korea's Humanitarian Crisis: The Role of State and Non-State Actors." *East Asia: An International Quarterly* 20, no. 2 (Summer 2003): 74–93.

Levi-Strauss, Claude. *Tristes Tropiques.* Trans. John Weightman and Doreen Weightman. New York: Penguin, 1955.

Macias, Monique. "In North Korea, China's Tiananmen Square Protests Stirred Hope for Change." *Guardian*, June 4, 2014. http://www.theguardian.com/world/2014/jun/04/north-korea-china-tiananmen-square-protests.

Macintyre, Kate, "Female Mortality Advantage." In *Famine Demography: Perspectives from the Past and Present*, ed. Tim Dyson and Cormac O Gráda, 240–59. Oxford: Oxford University Press, 2002.

Mansbridge Jane, "The Making of Oppositional Consciousness." In *Oppositional Consciousness: The Subjective Roots of Social Protest*, ed. Jane Mansbridge and Aldon Morris, 1–19. Chicago: University of Chicago Press, 2001.

Manyin, Mark E. "Kim Jong-il's Death: Implications for North Korea's Stability and U.S. Policy." *Congressional Research Report*, January 11, 2012. http://www.fas.org/sgp/crs/row/R42126.pdf.

Manyin, Mark E., and Mary Beth D. Nikitin. "Foreign Assistance to North Korea." Congressional Research Service, R40095, 7-5700, April 2, 2014. fas.org/sgp/crs/row/R40095.pdf.

Morris-Suzuki, Tessa. *Exodus to North Korea: Shadows from Japan's Cold War.* Lanham, MD: Rowman and Littlefield, 2007.

Morton David, "Steep Learning Curves in the DPRK." In *Humanitarian Diplomacy: Practitioners and Their Craft*, ed. L. Minearl and H. Smith, 194–214. Tokyo: United Nations University Press, 2007.

Mühlhahn, Klaus. "Hunger, Starvation and State Violence in the PRC, 1949–1979." Unpublished paper presented at the Hunger, Nutrition and Systems of Rationing under State Socialism (1917–2006) conference, Institute for East Asian Studies, Sinology University of Vienna, February 23, 2008.

Nagengast, Carole "Violence, Terror, and the Crisis of the State." *Annual Review of Anthropology* 23 (1994): 109–26.

Nancy, Jean-Luc. *Listening.* Trans. Charlotte Mandell. New York: Fordham University Press. 2007.

Natsios, Andrew S. "North Korea's Chronic Food Problem." In *Troubled Transition: North Korea's Politics, Economy, and External Relations*, ed. Choe Sang-Hun, Gi-Wook Shin, and David Straub. Stanford, CA: Walter H. Shorenstein Asia-Pacific Research Center, Shorenstein APARC, Stanford University, 2013.

NK Briefs. "Lee Myung-bak Administration Sets the Lowest Record for Assistance to North Korea." Institute for Far Eastern Studies, January 31, 2013. http://ifes.kyungnam.ac.kr/eng/FRM/FRM_0101V.aspx?code=FRM130131_0001.

New Focus International. "Exclusive: Now Even Party Cadres Must Take Part in the 'Arduous March'." *New Focus International*, April 27, 2014. http://newfocusintl.com/exclusive-party-cadres-arduous-march/.

——. "North Korea Orders All Privately Cultivated Crops to Be Cut Down." *New Focus International*, June 17, 2014. http://newfocusintl.com/north-korea-orders-privately-cultivated-crops-cut/.

No, Kum-Sok, with J. Roger Osterholm, *A MiG-15 to Freedom: Memoir of the Wartime North Korean Defector Who First Delivered the Secret Fighter Jet to the Americans in 1953*. Jefferson, NC: McFarland & Company, 1996.

Noland, Marcus. *Avoiding the Apocalypse: The Future of the Two Koreas*. Washington, DC: Institute for International Economics, 2000.

Noland, Marcus, and Stephen Haggard. "Political Attitudes Under Repression: Evidence from North Korean Refugees," MPRA Paper 21713, University Library of Munich, Germany. 2010.

Noland Marcus, Sherman Robinson, and Tao Wang. "Famine in North Korea: Causes and Cures" *Economic Development and Cultural Change* 49, no. 4 (July 2001): 741–67.

Nordstrom, Caroline, and JoAnn Martin. *The Paths to Domination, Resistance and Terror*. Berkeley: University of California Press, 1992.

Oberdorfer, Don. *The Two Koreas*. Reading, MA: Addison-Wesley, 1997.

Ochs, Elinor. "Narrative Lessons." In *A Companion to Linguistic Anthropology*, ed. A. Duranti, 269–89. Oxford: Blackwell, 2004.

Oh, Kong Dan, and Ralph C. Hassig. *Through the Looking Glass*. Washington, DC: Brookings Institution Press, 2000.

Olujic, Maria B. "Embodiment of Terror: Gendered Violence in Peacetime and Wartime in Croatia and Bosnia- Herzegovina." *Medical Anthropology Quarterly* 12, no. 1 (March 1998): 31–50.

Peters, Edward. *Torture*. Oxford: Basil Blackwell, 1986.

Pottier, Johan. *Re-Imagining Rwanda: Conflict, Survival and Disinformation in the Late Twentieth Century.* Cambridge: Cambridge University Press, 2002.

Prahar Peter. "North Korea: Illicit Activity Funding the Regime." Statement Before the Subcommittee on Federal Financial Management, Government Information, and International Security, Senate Homeland Security and Government Affairs Committee, April 25, 2006. hsgac.senate.gov/public/_files/042506Prahar.pdf.

Ryang, Sonia. *Reading North Korea: An Ethnological Inquiry.* Cambridge, MA: Harvard University Press, 2012.

Scarry Elaine, *The Body in Pain: The Making and Unmaking of the World.* New York: Oxford University Press, 1985.

Scheper-Hughes, Nancy. *Death Without Weeping: Violence of Everyday Life in Brazil.* Berkeley: University of California Press, 1993.

Scheper-Hughes, Nancy, and Philippe Bourgois, eds. *Violence in War and Peace: An Anthology.* Malden, MA: Blackwell, 2004.

Schloms Michael, *North Korea and the Timeless Dilemma of Aid: A Study of Humanitarian Action in Famines.* Berlin: Lit Verlag Münster, 2004.

Schwekendiek, Daniel. "Height and Weight Differences Between North and South Korea." *Journal of Biosocial Science* 41, no. 1 (2009): 51.

——. "A Meta-Analysis of North Koreans Migrating to China and South Korea." In *Korea: Politics, Economy, Society.* Ed. R. Frank, J. Hoare, P. Koellner, S. Pares, 247–70. Leiden: Brill, 2011.

——. "Regional Variations in Living Conditions During the North Korean Food Crisis of the 1990s." *Asia Pacific Journal of Public Health*, May 25, 2009.

Scott, James. *Seeing Like a State: How Certain Schemes to Improve the Human Condition Have Failed.* New Haven, CT: Yale University Press, 1998.

Searle John. "Speech Acts: An Essay in the Philosophy of Language." Cambridge: Cambridge University Press, 1969.

Seaton, Richard. *Hunger in Groups: An Arctic Experiment.* Chicago: Quartermaster Food and Container Institute, U.S. Army, 1962. http://oai.dtic.mil/oai/oai?verb=getRecord&metadataPrefix=html&identifier=AD0284922.

Sen, Amartya. *Poverty and Famines: An Essay on Entitlements and Deprivation.* Oxford: Clarendon Press, 1981.

Sen, Amartya, and Jean Drèze. *The Amartya Sen & Jean Drèze Omnibus: (comprising) Poverty and Famines; Hunger and Public Action; and India: Economic Development and Social Opportunity.* Oxford: Oxford University Press, 1999.

Seok, Kay. "North Korea's Transformation: Famine, Aid and Markets." *Review of North Korea Economy*, April 16, 2008. Available at Human Rights Watch website, http://www.hrw.org/en/news/2008/04/14/north-korea-s-transformation-famine-aid-and-markets.

Slim Hugo, "Positioning Humanitarianism in War: Principles of Neutrality, Impartiality and Solidarity." Centre for Development and Emergency Planning, Oxford Brookes University. Paper presented to the Aspects of Peacekeeping Conference Royal Military Academy, Sandhurst UK, January 22–24, 1997. http://repository.forcedmigration.org/show_metadata.jsp?pid=fmo:2232.

Sorokin, Pitirim A., *Hunger as a Factor in Human Affairs*, ed. and trans. Elena P. Sorokin. Gainesville: University Presses of Florida, 1975.

Suarez-Orozco, Marcelo M. "Speaking of the Unspeakable: Toward a Psychosocial Understanding of Responses to Terror." *Ethos* 18, no. 3 (September 1990): 353–83.

Suh, Jae-Jung. "Making Sense of North Korea: *Juche* as an Institution." In *Origins of North Korea's Juche: Colonialism, War and Development*, ed. Jae Jung Suh, 1–32. Plymouth, UK: Lexington Books, 2013.

——. "North Korean Defectors: Their Adaptation and Resettlement." *East Asian Review* 14, no. 3 (2002): 67–86.

Terry, Fiona. "Feeding the Dictator." Special Report, *Guardian*, August 6, 2001. http://www.theguardian.com/world/2001/aug/06/famine.comment.

Todorov, Tzvetan. *Hope and Memory: Reflections on the Twentieth Century*. Trans. David Bellos. London: Atlantic Books, 2003.

——. *Voices from the Gulag: Life and Death in Communist Bulgaria*. Trans. Robert Zaretsky. University Park: Penn State University Press, 1999.

Triulzi, Alessandro. "The Past As Contested Terrain: Commemorating Newsites of Memory in War Torn Ethiopia." In *Violence, Political Culture and Development in Africa*, ed. Preben Kaarsholm, 122–38. London: James Currey, 2006.

Turton, David. "Response to Drought: The Mursi of Southwestern Ethiopia." *Disasters* 1 no. 4 (1997): 275–87. doi:10.1111/j.1467-7717.1977.tb00047.x.

Vološinov, V. N., *Marxism and the Philosophy of Language*. Trans. Ladislav Matejka and I. R. Titunik. New York: Seminar Press, 1973.

Vygotsky, Lev S. *Thought and Language*, rev. and exp. ed., with a new introduction by Alex Kozulin. Ed. and trans. Eugenia Hanfmann, Gertrude Vakar, and Alex Kozulin. Cambridge, MA: MIT Press, 2012.

Watson Rubie S., ed. *Memory, History and Opposition Under State Socialism*. Santa Fe, NM: School of American Research Press, 1994.

Weatherly, Robert, and Jiyoung Song. "The Evolution of Human Rights Thinking in North Korea." *Journal of Communist Studies and Transition Politics* 24, no. 2: 272–96.

Whitlock, Gillian. *Soft Weapons: Autobiography in Transit*. Chicago: University of Chicago Press, 2007.

Willum, Bjørn, "Eyes in the Sky: In Service of Humanity?" *Imaging Notes USA*, September October 2000, www.willum.com/articles/imagingsept2000.

Woo-Cumings, Meredith. "The Political Ecology of Famine: The North Korean Catastrophe and Its Lessons." Asian Development Bank Institute, Research Paper 31, January 1, 2002. http://www.adbi.org/research%20paper/2002/01/01/115.political.ecology/.

Woo, Seongji. "North Korea's Food Crisis." *Korea Focus*, May–June 2004, 63–80.

Wyler, Liana Sun, and Dick K. Nanto. "North Korean Crime-for-Profit Activities." CRS Report for Congress, August 25, 2008, 7. http://fpc.state.gov/documents/organization/110378.pdf.

Yang, Rae, *Spider Eaters: A Memoir*. Berkeley: University of California Press, 1997.

Zhang, X. *Grass Soup*. Trans. Martha Avery. London: Secker & Warburg, 1994.

INDEX

239

177; indirect speech, 8, 18, 86–89, 91–94, 110–12, 176–77; interpreting defectors' oral accounts, 15–17, 176–79 (*see also* interviews); lack of information, 8, 11, 37, 38–39, 54, 193–94; language habits and collective understandings, 84–86; levels of communicative context, 90–91; between North Koreans and other nationalities, 170–72; performative speech, 88–89; politicization of speech, 173–74, 175; public executions as education, 114, 115–19, 120, 123–25 (*see also* executions); self-talk, 130 (*see also* *specific individuals*); in Soviet Georgia, 129–30; thought and speech regulated by government, 5–8, 17, 88–93, 101–2, 104–7, 121, 175–76, 185; use of euphemisms for famine, 106 (*see also* "March of Suffering" as term); use of "hunger" and "hungry" not permitted, 17, 104–5. *See also* language

communities: changing relationships due to famine, 76–82; helping one another, 45; Korean language and subjective relations, 52; life lived in relations with others, 50, 51; suspicion and distrust within, 90. *See also* social cohesion

compassion, breakdown in, 71

Confucian tradition, 58–59, 78, 174

consumer goods, foreign, 63

coping strategies: China connections as, 66; determination to survive, 104; humor as, 8, 18; market selling as, 12, 46, 50, 66 (*see also* markets); portrayed as act of national pres-

ervation, 47–48; regulation of, 131 (*see also* executions; punishment); swindling, 69; trading across the border river, 75–76; trusted relationships, 45; typical strategies illegal, 12; women more willing to employ, 74–76. *See also* alternate food sources; communication; defection; farms and gardens, private/secret; foraging; theft

corn (maize): growing secretly, 124; preparing rotten corn, 61–62; rationing and high prices, 187; as sole food, 25; thefts of, 70, 117; tobacco grown instead of, 29

Danchon (mining town), 31, 79–80

deaths from famine: attributed to other causes, 88, 90–91, 106; children's deaths, 9, 80, 139–40, 157–58, 163; collection and storage of bodies, 109–10, 159; death and the decision to defect, 126, 131–32, 147; entire families, 72; execution deaths as, 119–21 (*see also* executions); giving up, 19, 141, 142; hardheartedness toward, 71; inability to speak directly about, 76, 86–92, 109–10; increase in (late 1990s), 108–9, 141; intellectual class, 66; loyalty and, 43–44; mass graves, 198–99; numbers surmised from production cuts, 65–66; of people waiting for food distribution, 64–65; statistics, 183, 185–86; trauma of witnessing, 120–22, 172; ubiquity of corpses, 83, 109

deaths from trains, 72–74

on, 142; Mursi people on, 42–43; Sung-ho Lee on, 38. *See also* hope

energy crisis, 187–88

ersatz foods, 114, 189

Ethiopia, 42–43, 93, 184

executions: of coup leaders, 57; first-hand accounts of, 116–18; mouths gagged, 122, 123–24; public executions as education, 114, 115–19, 120, 123–25; for theft, 115–21, 123–24; trauma of witnessing, 120–22, 172; wrong thinking as cause of individual's crime, 7, 120

factory laborers, 26, 65–66, 75

families: children abandoned, 80–81, 159 (*see also* orphaned/abandoned children); death of whole families, 72; effects of hunger on, 78–81, 100, 144; families' decision to defect, 140–43; filial piety, 174; imprisonment/punishment of whole families, 7, 27, 142–43; marital separation and divorce, 70, 78; political classification by family, 142–43; separated by defection, 127, 161–68. *See also specific individuals*

famine (generally): ability to prevent, 183–84; in China, 14, 106, 180; cold and, 111, 200 (*see also* cold weather); in Ethiopia, 42–43, 93, 184; as the inability to access adequate food, 12–13; North Korean perceptions of, 20; "priority regime" famines, 11, 184; as process, 4; and revolt, 180; and ritual and tradition, 35; socialism's relationship to, 20; survivors rarely focused on, 4; typical coping mechanisms,

12 (*see also* coping strategies); way of life and authority strengthened by, 37

famine (North Korea, 1990s): areas worst hit, 26; blamed on foreign countries, 37, 39, 40–42, 62–64, 67, 111; contributing factors, 1–2, 10–11, 23–24, 53, 183–85, 189–90, 199–201; determining starting point of, 23; difficulty of communicating about (*see* communication); government explanations for, 24, 67, 200 (*see also* ideological messages); growing awareness of, 45, 49; international assessments of, 197–99; interpretations of, 36; leadership change seen as linked to famine onset, 53–54, 56–57, 63–64, 102–3; location and starting point of, 5, 21, 23; malnutrition among children, 22, 27, 195–96; malnutrition predating famine, 1, 21, 183, 200–201; onset gradual, 23, 34; paradigm shift in studying, 174–75; potential for social unrest, 11–12; regime's responsibility for, 3, 11, 65, 183–85; statistics, 4; term not used by survivors, 13–14, 20; and the "three shocks," 204n6. *See also* alternate food sources; coping strategies; food distribution

farmers: crop theft as state crime, 115, 119; defection by, 26; executed for theft, 116–18; farmers' markets and black markets, 46, 95–96 (*see also* markets); farming as family punishment, 142–43; grain procurement program, 189; more able to survive, 70; and the PDS, 21, 192;

security police. *See* police and guards

self-criticism: as cultural/nationalist ritual, 6, 35, 37, 131, 176, 178; in school, 49, 76–77

self-reliance: familiarity with shortages, 24; national self-sufficiency not geographically viable, 53, 199; stressed by government, 4, 10, 199; as way of life, 23. *See also* Juche ideology

sleep, 49, 96–97

Slim, Hugo, 194

Snyder, Scott, 196

social class, 23, 97–98. *See also* political rank/classification

social cohesion: fear of informers, 90, 101; hunger and suffering and, 51; increase in hardheartedness, 71; language and, 51–52; maintained through national identity narrative, 67; rise in crime connected with nutrition, 70–71 (*see also* theft); self-segregation of those with and without food, 76–77; strains on, due to famine, 77–83. *See also* communities

socialism: defectors critical of, 151–53; ersatz foods common in, 114; and evocative transcripts, 93–94; as "society without beggars," 53. *See also* government of North Korea; ideological messages; Juche ideology

social structure: changes in, due to famine, 4; increase in social/cultural rituals, 35–36; maintained through warlike rhetoric, 39–42; stratification and food distribution, 21–22, 23, 30–31, 77, 98–99, 190–92. *See also* political rank/classification

soldiers. *See* military, North Korean

son preference, 22–23

Sorokin, Pitirim A., 60, 208n12

South Hamgyong province, 26, 188

South Korea: food aid from, 139, 195; hopes for unification, 154; mining contrasted with North Korean mining, 31; North Koreans' beliefs about, 14, 20, 53, 136, 140–41; North Koreans in, ix, 15, 26, 126, 154, 156–57, 165–68, 172–74, 215n2, 217nn8,10–11, 218nn15, 18; relations with North Korea, 165–66; seen as enemy by North Korean leadership, 40, 42, 62–63

Soviet Union (USSR), 10, 21, 180, 187–88. *See also* Russia

speech and speaking. *See* communication; language

Suarez-Orozco, Marcelo M., 101, 104

substitute foods. *See* alternate food sources

suffering: and the attribution of meaning, 181; characteristics similar to Stockholm syndrome, 43; continuance of, 178; and the decision to defect, 127 (*see also* defection; defectors); deferring personal needs, 43; and the hope of reprieve, 42–43; and the likelihood of opposition, 180; loyalty and, 43–45. *See also* deaths from famine; defectors; endurance; hunger

swindling, 69

Terry, Fiona, 196

theft: crop theft as state crime, 115, 119, 124–25; food trucks attacked by beggars, 70; increase in, 70–71;

theft (*continued*)
  public execution for, 115–21,
  123–25, 185; as threat to North
  Korean way of life, 65
thinking, regulation of. *See*
  communication
Thought and Language (Vygotsky), 89
tobacco farms, 28–29
tofu, 68, 69, 70
trains and train stations, 72–74,
  157–58
trauma: articulation of, 172–73, 178;
  defectors haunted by memories,
  156–61, 163–64; of near-death and
  recovery, 43; peninsular division re-
  enacted on individual level, 19, 165,
  167–68; posttraumatic stress, 172;
  of witnessing executions, 120–22,
  172. *See also* suffering
travel permits, 72–73
trees. *See* deforestation
truth, Havel on, 82–83
Turton, David, 42–43
Two Meals a Day campaign, 186–87

United Nations (UN), 59, 60–61,
  196, 197–98, 217n7. *See also* food aid
United States: aid for North Korea,
  60–61, 139, 195 (*see also* food aid);
  blamed for famine, economy, 4, 24,
  40–41, 62–64, 111; North Korean
  view of hunger in, 20; seen as military enemy by ROK leadership, 40,
  41–42; "starving soldiers" study, 40
uprisings, 8, 57–58, 130, 180, 184

violence, culture and, 121–22. *See also*
  executions; punishment
voice, sound of, 15–16

Vollertson, Dr., 106
Vološinov, V. N., 89, 211n8
Vygotsky, Lev S., 89

wild plants, as famine foods, 34,
  47–48, 67–69, 144, 149
women: deaths from famine, 109–10;
  defection by, 167 (*see also specific
  individuals*); extra rice given to new
  mothers, 22; famine's effect on
  gender roles, 99–100; market
  selling and trading by, 74–76,
  100; more willing to take extreme
  measures, 74–75; prostitution, 70,
  78, 209–10n27; resiliency of, 23,
  210n27; train travel by, 73–74
Worker's Department Store, 95–96
World Food Program (WFP), 61,
  195, 196. *See also* food aid

Yanggang-do province, 26
Yoon, Jae-young: on avoiding the
  word "hungry," 86–87; on black
  markets, 45–46, 95–96; on decid-
  ing to leave, 139, 147; on defecting,
  126; on the difficulty of articulating what they experienced, 171–72,
  174; on famine foods, 96–97; on
  foraging lectures, 47–48; on getting along in life, 107; on government rhetoric, 40; on his son's
  death, 9, 139, 140; on learning of
  international aid, 138, 139; on migration in order to survive, 72; on
  propaganda during the famine, 93
Young People's League for Freedom,
  58

Zhang, X., 114

CPSIA information can be obtained
at www.ICGtesting.com
Printed in the USA
LVHW020141061118
596055LV00004B/4/P